George Allen's GUIDE TO SPECIAL TEAMS

George H. Allen, MA
Joseph G. Pacelli, BFA

Leisure Press
Champaign, IL

Library of Congress Cataloging-in-Publication Data

Allen, George Herbert, 1922-
  [Guide to special teams]
  George Allen's guide to special teams / by George H. Allen and
Joseph G. Pacelli
    p. cm.
  ISBN 0-88011-370-0
  1. Kicking (Football) 2. Football--Coaching. I. Pacelli, Joseph
G., 1934-   . II. Title. III. Title: Guide to special teams.
  GV951.7.A44 1990
  796.332'27--dc20

                                                        89-37574
                                                        CIP

ISBN: 0-88011-370-0

Developmental Editor: June I. Decker, PhD
Assistant Editor: Timothy Ryan
Copyeditor: Wendy Nelson
Proofreader: Phaedra Hise
Production Director: Ernie Noa
Typesetter: Brad Colson
Text Design: Keith Blomberg
Text Layout: Denise Lowry and Denise Peters
Cover Design: Tim Offenstein
Cover Photo: Nate Fine/NFL Photos
Illustrations: Gretchen Walters
Interior Photos: Bruce Allen, Nate Fine, Mike Kapusta, Rusty Tillman, Chicago Bears, Cleveland Browns, Detroit Lions, Green Bay Packers, Indianapolis Colts, Kansas City Chiefs, Los Angeles Raiders, Los Angeles Rams, Minnesota Vikings, New York Giants, New York Jets, Philadelphia Eagles, Phoenix Cardinals, Pittsburgh Steelers, San Diego Chargers, San Francisco Forty Niners, Washington Redskins
Printer: Versa Press

Printed in the United States of America

10 9 8 7 6 5 4 3 2 1

Leisure Press
A Division of Human Kinetics Publishers, Inc.
Box 5076, Champaign, IL 61825-5076
1-800-747-4457

CONTENTS

Foreword

It is with a great deal of pride I write this foreword to *George Allen's Guide to Special Teams*. You see, George Allen hired me as the first special teams coach in the NFL in 1969 while he was coaching the Los Angeles Rams.

I was coaching the quarterbacks at Stanford when George called to inquire whether I had an interest in this all-new position he was creating. To be honest, I really thought it was one of my friends pulling a joke on me, as they would often do that; one of them would call and say he was the head coach at some major university and ask whether I was interested in a coaching position on his staff. I remember saying, "All right, Homer, quit giving me this line of bull," thinking he would break down and start laughing. But the person on the other end of the line said, "No, this is no joke! I'm George Allen, and I would like to have you drop by my office in Long Beach when you are in the area to discuss the possibility of becoming our special teams coach."

You can guess what I said: I'd be in the area tomorrow and would definitely drop in and visit. I found out the next day that George was a friend of Payton Jordan, the Stanford track coach, and he had called Payton to ask whether he knew of a possible candidate. I will always be grateful to Payton for giving George my name.

George said he was going to interview a couple of other young college assistant coaches and would get back to me in a week. Within 2 weeks George called back with the job offer. You can't believe how excited I was. I wasn't really happy about leaving Stanford at that time, because Jim Plunkett was just starting to come on, but I couldn't turn down this opportunity.

It didn't take me long to realize I didn't really know that much about the details of the kicking game. Thank heaven for Howard Schnellenberger. Howard was the wide receiver coach of the University of Alabama coaching staff, and he had been doing most of the coaching of the special teams. Howard trained me!

George wanted someone who would not only detail the preparation from a technical standpoint, but also organize the motivation of the teams, as well as do a good job of evaluating performances throughout the year. George felt that what went on in the preparation of the special teams was always secondary to the coach's primary coaching responsibilities. Of course, he was right! He wanted all his teams to be given equal time in organization, preparation, motivation, and evaluation. This is why he talked the Rams management into letting him add an extra salary for a special teams coach.

What convinced George that this had to be done, if the Rams were going to continue to gain a winning edge, was a kickoff return for a touchdown against the Rams that ultimately thwarted a chance at the championship in 1968. That following off-season he found out there were two guys on the coverage team that had given up the long TD return who hadn't made a tackle all year. As it turned out, these two guys were at fault on the TD return. George was not going to allow this to happen again in 1969. He also surmised that this very same thing must be happening on the other NFL teams and that hiring a special teams coach might help him gain an edge until everyone else did the same.

I wasn't in my new office 10 minutes before George came in and outlined some studies he wanted me to do in preparation for the 1969 season. The first one was to grade each player on all the kicking teams in all 14 games and report to him the findings.

The study wasn't as revealing as you might think. For the most part everyone was doing a good job and appeared to be better prepared than their opponents. It was going to be my job to improve on a job already well done. What made this possible was George's attitude toward special teams. He never said no to any suggestion I made in regard to meeting time, practice time, and use of front line players on the teams.

I found that the hardest thing for me to do was to establish credibility with the players. Because I had never played or coached in the NFL before joining the staff, the players didn't automatically give me their respect; I had to earn it. Thanks to George's support and his deep belief he had found another way to gain an edge, the players really came around quickly.

Another study George had me do was evaluate the top-ranked special teams in each area and report to him *what* the teams were successful at and *why*—was it design, personnel, or good fortune? This was very time-consuming but also very educational. George was never too busy to drop into my office and inquire about the findings of these different studies.

If there was one thing that helped improve our special teams, I would have to say it was George allowing me to upgrade the coaching tempo for the kicking game. At first the players thought I was crazy. Who is this guy running up and down the practice field yelling "Faster! Quicker! Tougher! More intensity!"? To this day when I run into one of the original special teams members on my teams, they say, "Dick, let's have live field goal protection" and then laugh like hell. Like I said, they thought I was nuts. I will never forget the times I walked into the locker room following a practice session and found Dick Bass standing on a bench yelling, imitating me. It was good for more than just laughs; I think it helped us come together as something really special in special teams. The players gradually found out that an enthusiastic approach to preparation was fun and reflected as a real benefit on Sunday afternoon.

Guys like Pat Curran, Bob Klein, Jim Purnell, John Pergine, Willie Ellison, Alvin Haymond, and Larry Smith were real special special–teamers. In fact, George had traded for and kept some of them on the squad just because of their contributions to the kicking game. We weren't too far into the '69 season before the players really started to take pride in and identify with their respective units.

I used to try to stay away from George before the game—at the hotel, on the bus to the game, or on the field during warm-ups—because he would always ask a question about the preparation of the special teams that wasn't easy to answer. The one time I remember the best was in Chicago late in the '69 season. George and I were coming down in the hotel elevator to head over to Soldier Field when he asked, "Dick, did you check out the position of the sun at game time so you can instruct Alvin Haymond how to cope with any problems fielding punts?" At first I thought he was teasing a rookie coach, but he was serious. I had to say I hadn't as yet, but planned to check it out as soon as I got to the stadium.

He would do the same thing during the game. The punt team would run onto the field, and George would ask me some question I had never

thought of and doubt very much anyone else had. What he was doing was stimulating me to make sure every possible detail had been covered.

Another revealing thing I learned about George that year was that he is an end-result guy. Case in point: We were playing Philadelphia in Philly at Old Franklin Field, and we weren't playing well. We were undefeated at that time but not playing like an undefeated team. It was late in the game, and we were about to attempt a field goal with Eddie Meador doing the holding. Eddie came over to me and asked about the fake field goal that was in the game plan. I told him he would have to get permission from George Allen. We walked over to George, asked for permission to run the fake, and he said, "No, go ahead and kick it!" The next thing I see is Eddie coming up out of his holding stance, running the fake field goal. We needed about 2 yards for the first down. He rolled right looking for the designated receivers, but they were covered. I darn near died! Eddie, realizing the pressure was on, tucked the ball under his arm and ran like an all-pro fullback. You've never seen a more courageous effort for a measly 2 yards. He made the first down by a measurement!

When Eddie came off the field, he entered the bench area at the end opposite from where George was standing. George looked over at him, then walked to me and said, "That's what I like, a player with initiative." George was an end-result guy. No telling what he would have done to Eddie if he had failed to make the first down and we lost the game. Incidentally, the offense took the ball on in for the winning score.

By the end of 1968, the Rams special teams were being recognized as the best teams in the NFL. We never lost a game due to a breakdown in the kicking game, and special teams were given credit for a couple of big wins. Alvin Haymond was the number-one punt returner in the NFL, and our other units were ranked among the top. The other thing that became apparent was the positive contribution the improved special teams morale made on the rest of the squad. The great enthusiasm and intensity of the special teams was contagious. I really believe that the teams felt they were something special because they were the only teams at that time with their own coach; and because George was the guy who created the position, the players knew how important their contribution was to George.

Yes, George was an innovator. No detail was so small that it would be considered insignificant. Of course, this detailed preparation was how George had been coaching the offensive and defensive teams all along. He just happened to be the guy who felt that the kicking game should be coached the same way.

When you work for George Allen, if you aren't a guy who thinks he knows it all, you can learn so much. His continuous effort to improve detail preparation was the number one thing that impressed me. From him I learned what true detail preparation is all about. The projectors never quit running in the Rams coaches' offices during game week. Not only was George a great film study coach, but his entire staff followed his lead. Ted Marcibrada, Ray Prochaska, and Howard Schnellenberger taught me how to study films when putting together a game plan. When you stop and analyze, you recognize that the only thing you as a coach have total control of in a football game is your preparation for the game. In the 1960s, no one did it any better than George Allen and his staff.

I appreciate very much what George gave to me beyond the opportunity to coach in the NFL: an understanding of the importance of attention to detail, motivation, and experience, and the realization that the age of a player alone should not be an eliminating factor when it comes time to cut the squad. I also learned from George how to create a crisis for the squad to rally around. He was a master at it.

No book has all the answers, but I do think you will find it a good investment to read and study what George Allen and Joe Pacelli have to say in this book about the kicking game.

Dick Vermeil

Preface

It is rare, indeed, that two men previously unknown to one another except perhaps by reputation are given the opportunity to work closely on a project that they both strongly feel is significant to the development of true success in their own field. We have had just such an opportunity, working together on this book. From the beginning we agreed to make our best effort to create the most complete book ever written on the kicking game. We believe that we have accomplished our goal with *George Allen's Guide to Special Teams*.

Another fortunate benefit derived from this collaboration is the broad spectrum of coaches who can use this text to aid their programs. Drawing on our different recent coaching backgrounds, one on the professional and 4-year college level and one on the high school and junior college level, we have taken specific care to make this a practical guide that can be used by coaches at any level of football. The material is taken from professional football playbooks (Los Angeles Rams, Washington Redskins, and Philadelphia Eagles) and details the optimum requirements needed for development of an outstanding kicking game at that level; but it is meticulously outlined and organized in a way that allows a head coach, say at the small high school level, to select what will work best for his program in terms of available practice time, personnel, and staff and to use only those areas that he feels his team can properly execute.

We mention consistency quite often in this book because we both believe that consistency is the truest measure of performance. You will find that we stress consistency in many ways—emphasizing specific coaching points, techniques of proper execution, kicking game drills, and exercises geared to each phase of special teams play. This will guide you in the development of your own special teams philosophy, including the commitment required by the head coach, the selection of personnel (both players and coaches), and the proper approach to motivate your special teams players.

The rules of the kicking game are outlined, and certain important areas are emphasized. Basic coaching requirements and kicking game goals are discussed in depth. We believe in paying infinite attention to infinitesimal detail, the measure of consistent champions, and this book will show you how to do that with your special teams. This is not simply a manual of special teams plays and diagrams. This is *the book* on the kicking game—concepts, philosophy, rules, motivation, fundamentals, timing, grading, special situations, techniques, the whole 9 yards—the *entire* kicking game!

In addition to all the information you need on playing and coaching special teams, each chapter contains personal comments on that phase of the kicking game, citing examples and personal experiences illustrating the potential effect each phase can have on the outcome of a game. Each chapter dealing with a particular phase of special teams contains a selection of "the best players I've ever seen" play on that unit. From those players, we have selected a special teams hall of fame, which is our personal recognition of the most dedicated, toughest, smartest, and most disciplined athletes, who have earned a place in history despite spending most of their playing career in relative obscurity.

To our knowledge, the only books available on the kicking game are, understandably, subjective writings by coaches (generally quite successful ones) devoting few, if any, words to the fundamentals, critical importance, and sound development of a special teams *program*. We were unable to locate a single source on the kicking game with the scope of this book.

George Allen's Guide to Special Teams insists that the kicking game be given its proper place in your program. The reason is simple: the success of four professional football team programs in which George Allen gave special teams an equal standing with offense and defense.

program. The reason is simple: the success of four professional football team programs in which George Allen gave special teams an equal standing with offense and defense.

We promise you that this text, like no other you have ever read about special teams, will stand proudly in your library between the best books you have ever found on offense and defense. We have challenged ourselves to deliver this result and have both enjoyed that challenge. We believe that this book is an historic first in football coaching books, and we sincerely hope the benefits you will derive from our efforts will help you achieve some of your most sought after, but as yet unattainable, goals.

George H. Allen
Joe Pacelli

Acknowledgments

Webster defines ''special'' as follows: (a) distinguished by some unusual quality; or being in some way *superior*; (b) *held in particular esteem*; and (c) readily distinguishable from others in the same category, or *unique*.

In 1955, my Whittier College football team blocked *eight* kicks (we led the nation for small colleges). The team was outweighed in every game we played, sometimes as much as 24 pounds per man, and still we won eight games and lost only two that season. We upset San Diego State—and Chico State, which was undefeated at the time. I have always held that 1955 team *in particular esteem*, and I have always considered my special teams as *superior* and *unique*—I agree with Mr. Webster.

This book is dedicated to that 1955 Whittier College team and to all the dedicated and hardworking players and coaches who helped to make my special teams ''special'' throughout my head coaching career.

This book is also dedicated to all the special team players of America and their special team coaches, with the hope that the instruction, knowledge, and training methods in this book will further their progress.

I have had several outstanding special teams coaches over the years—Dick Vermeil, Marv Levy, Paul Lanham, and Bob Lord—as well as Lester Josephson, Tony Guillory, Alvin Haymond, Rusty Tillman, Ted Vactor, and Bob Brunet as special teams captains. In addition, my centers were Ken Iman, George Burman, Len Hauss, Ted Frtisch, Jerry Sullivan, and David Ohton in USFL.

These active special teams coaches have been most helpful: Lynn Stiles (San Francisco 49ers), Artie Gigantino (Los Angeles Rams), Frank Gansz (Detroit Lions), Paul Lanham (Cleveland Browns), and Rusty Tillman (Seattle Seahawks).

I've been very fortunate to always have the support of my wife, Etty Allen, in everything I have attempted. My son Bruce gave me the idea to design the principle of a special team player for this book. My sons George and Gregory have given their father advice from time to time. My daughter, Jennifer, an author, has been most helpful. I'm proud of my children—they all have made successes of themselves, in spite of their father!

CHAPTER 1

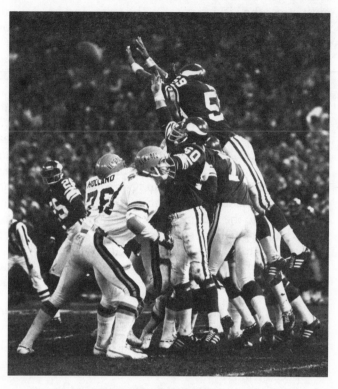

One Third of Your Season

There are three equally important departments of play in football: defense, offense, and kicking. Most teams give sufficient attention to defense and offense but tend to neglect the kicking department. When teams neglect any one of these three departments, they operate at only 66-percent efficiency. Performing at 66-percent efficiency in any area of life is barely average; in competitive sports, especially football, it is an absolute guarantee of failure.

One out of every five plays in a football game is a special teams play. Unlike plays on offense and defense, something very unusual occurs on every kicking play. Either there is a change of ball possession, or a sizeable amount of yardage is involved, or there is a specific attempt to score points. Sometimes two, or even all three, of these things happen on the same play. It is easy to see that special teams can, and most often do, affect the tide and outcome of any game. A head coach should constantly be aware that the opportunity for the big play—the

momentum changer—is most prevalent in the kicking game.

IMPORTANCE OF THE KICKING GAME

These big plays or "breaks" usually happen when a team or player is unprepared for a situation. When a team has been properly prepared, it has the chance to capitalize on the break. The ability to take advantage of kicking game breaks marks the difference between winning and losing many games. When a team takes too little pride in and neglects the attention required to develop a proper kicking game, they become the victims of these bad breaks. You can be truly successful in this area only if you consider the kicking game to be an exact equal of the other two departments, defense and offense.

Only the head coach can create the right attitude for this to happen. He must truly believe that the kicking game is a major priority! The head coach must stress the kicking game to the team, and he must back up his words by scheduling sufficient, well-organized, quality practice time for special teams. The head coach must sell the importance of the kicking game to his team and his coaching staff. And it is most important that he not just pay lip service to this effort; he must get personally involved by attending and participating in special teams meetings and practices. As a matter of fact, the very first game film I looked at after a game was the special teams film. It took a lot of time and scrutiny, but it paid off in the end, and there was never a doubt in the minds of any of my players about *my* commitment to the kicking game. In fact, I thought the kicking game was so important that I fined players $500 for losing their kicking playbook!

Just how important is it to concentrate on the kicking game? Here are the important facts:

- Special teams start every game and often, in the closing seconds, end the game—determining the winner.
- One fifth of every game is played by the special teams.
- Statistically, approximately 40 percent of the football games played in high school and college, and almost 30 percent of professional football games, are won or lost by the kicking game—by a big play or mistake on the part of the special teams.

The answer to the question is obvious. Improve your overall special teams play, and you will improve your chances of winning.

SCOPE OF THE KICKING GAME

When most people think of the kicking game, they think only of the person doing the punting or the placekicking. As important as good, sound kickers are, they are only part of what we refer to as the "kicking game."

The kicking game that we will be discussing has six primary phases: (a) punting, (b) punt defense, (c) kickoff, (d) kickoff return, (e) point-after-touchdown (P-A-T) and field goal, and (f) P-A-T and field goal defense. Each of these phases, in turn, is split into smaller subdivisions to allow for greater concentration on fundamentals and details within each phase.

Punt protection and coverage, fielding kicks, punt returns, punt blocks, field position considerations, P-A-T and field goal protection, defending P-A-Ts and field goals, field goal coverage and returns, fake kicks and fake-kick defense, kickoff coverage, squib kickoffs, onside kickoffs, defense of the onside kickoff, kicking tactics, strategy, fundamentals, kicking game rules—all of these are comprised in the scope of the kicking game. To have a good kicking game, you must be proficient in all these areas.

After many years of coaching this game, I have come to the firm conclusion that the *punt is the most important play in football*. Certainly, all six phases of the kicking game are important; however, I feel that you must concentrate on and develop your punt team first. This should take a great deal of your special teams practice, particularly in the pre-season.

Beginning with the punt, I will briefly describe the importance and main areas of concentration of each phase of the kicking game.

Punt security: A blocked punt against you is devastating; your protection technique must be perfect to secure the punt.

Punt coverage: Keeping your opponent to a minimum return is your main goal; your punter's hang time and covering punts with all-out speed are the essential ingredients for success.

Punting out of your end zone: This is a critical situation that could turn into disaster if execution is not perfect; constant practice to develop the punter's confidence in your scheme is needed.

Punting going inside the 10-yard line: Eliminate the touchbacks; determine what your punter can do best in this situation, and use it. Control your 10 coverage men rather than trying to change the punter.

Net punt: This is a valuable team statistic, a good element to use for unit pride. It combines distance, hang time, and coverage—requiring success by all 11 men.

Punt return: This element presents an opportunity like no other to influence the outcome of a game. The punt returner is critical to success—he must have sure hands, good judgment, toughness, quickness, and speed (in that order).

Punt holdups: Delaying the coverage releases, holding up the ends, and forcing the punter to kick on time creates the opportunity for a big punt return.

Punt blocks: The punt block is a game-breaking play; timing and exact execution require constant practice to eliminate errors.

Punt defense (general): Penalties are extremely costly; they could mean loss of possession. Work on consciously avoiding penalties.

Organization after a safety (safety kick): It is most urgent that this be executed to perfection to negate any change of momentum provided by the safety; a deep, high punt with all-out coverage is a must.

Kickoff coverage: This can establish the tempo of the game. Deep, high kicks and coverage men who stay in their lanes and go all out will make for minimum returns.

Squib kickoff coverage: Good coverage will keep the great return man in a hole; the kicker must keep the ball down on the ground.

Onside kickoff coverage: This should be used in desperate or high-advantage situations; recovery men must keep the ball in front of them and see that it does not go out of bounds.

Kickoff return: The kickoff return is your best opportunity to establish good field position and control the game; hard, all-out play makes it happen.

Kickoff onside defense: You must recover an onside kick, or the momentum of the game may change; use special personnel with quickness and good hands.

Squib kickoff defense: A modest return is acceptable; loosen men in a wedge to cover the field; the return man should cover the ball with both arms.

Kickoff defense (general): Penalties on a kickoff can put you in a deep hole; work on avoiding penalties, especially clipping and illegal blocks.

Free kick: This is a rare uncontested opportunity to score following a fair catch; you must cover after the kick.

P-A-T and field goal security: A block of your field goal usually results in points for your opponent; a good blocking scheme and proper timing will score points for your team.

P-A-T and field goal execution: This begins with a perfect snap and a good hold; precise depth of the holder and consistently good snaps make the blockers' job easier.

Field goal coverage: It is essential to cover field goals after the ball has been kicked; cheap scores by your opponent due to lack of attention in this area can destroy an otherwise great effort.

P-A-T defense: Success in blocking P-A-Ts can provide the margin for winning close games; use an all-out 11-man rush.

Basic field goal block: This has built-in elements of rush, possible-fake precaution, and return provisions; use it when a fake is possible but not probable.

All-out field goal block: Use this in a positive kicking situation; commit all resources to the rush with no concern for the fake or the return.

Field goal rush with added precaution against a fake: Use this when a fake is probable; it is similar to the basic field goal block—take the middle backer off the rush to key the holder for the fake.

Field goal prevent: Use this when you want your opponent to kick. Your main concern is to guard against a fake. This is a good alignment for returning a short kick.

ELEMENTS OF A SUCCESSFUL KICKING GAME

There are four elements, above and beyond the plays and personnel, that are essential to a successful kicking game: (a) elimination of mistakes, (b) intensity, (c) fundamentals, and (d) practice time. Without these elements present you might as well not even issue uniforms, because one third of your game will be useless, one third of your practice time will be wasted, and no matter how good your offense and defense are, you will probably lose 30 to 40 percent of your games due to poor special teams play.

Elimination of Mistakes

Elimination of mistakes, particularly in the kicking game, is paramount. Mistakes in the kicking game usually cause a loss of possession, negate field position advantage, eliminate scoring possibilities, or give your opponent an opportunity to score that they might not otherwise have. None of the above are very positive!

Most mistakes made in the kicking game are caused by lack of belief in its importance. Lack of belief leads to lack of concentration, and from that follows poor protection, poor coverage, and slipshod application of the kicking game rules. Belief in the importance of the kicking game is the key to elimination of mistakes.

Intensity

It is doubtful that anyone can be truly successful in any area of life, whether it be business, medicine, art, or sports, without intensity. The relationship between intensity and success, however, is most immediately apparent in sports, particularly in football and most specifically in the play of special teams. Although intensity is essential in all areas of the kicking game, it is best observed in how one covers punts, kickoffs, and field goals. Football's true test of courage is covering kicks. No opponent will ever return a kick for a touchdown against you unless one man on your team fails to go all out.

Fundamentals

As the word implies, fundamentals are the basic skills required to succeed in sports or in life. The kicking game involves many precise skills. Punters, snappers, holders, and placekickers must work many extra hours at perfecting their individual skills. These types of precise skills require intense concentration while practicing. Distances at which punters, kickers, and holders must locate themselves, timing on snaps, and getting kicks away are all details that must be worked out earnestly and tirelessly. These time and distance requirements must be exact and consistent, and they require constant attention. Attention to the fundamentals of punt and placekick security is also required; learning all the details of how and whom to block, under a variety of circumstances, takes a great deal of time and concentration.

Practice Time

If you believe, as we do, that special teams are an equal partner with offense and defense, then you also must agree that the kicking game requires at least as much regular practice time as the other two departments. There is no question that the specialists require extra practice time in the pre- and postpractice periods. Although all special teams practices will be supervised by your special teams coordinator, the head coach must also be at all practices to be sure that they are well organized and efficient. Due to all of the details that must be thoroughly covered in each practice, it is mandatory that every minute count—you cannot afford to waste time.

SPECIAL TEAMS COORDINATOR

As a general rule, the head coach cannot coach the special teams. That job would be too demanding of his time, and other departments would be negatively affected by this time commitment. For many years, special teams coaching was divided up among the entire coaching staff without a specific coordinator. The problem I discovered with that approach was that everyone wound up coaching the kickers, even though each coach had been given a specific area of responsibility. Because there was no coach to coordinate the activities, each of the coaches felt that he could and should contribute to the kicking instruction, so they all became kicking coaches. Now you must understand that at the professional football level most of the assistant coaches had been outstanding athletes and at one time or another in their playing careers had done some punting or placekicking. There was valid reason for their feeling qualified to coach kickers—it was not simply an ego or power trip. However, proper motives aside, a punter or placekicker could not possibly benefit from uncoordinated instruction from five or six different coaches. The effort became counterproductive, and the entire kicking game suffered as a result.

The common consensus at the time was that when covering kickoffs the most essential element was speed. Ray Prohaska, one of my assistant coaches with the Los Angeles Rams, felt that a rookie we had drafted out of Whitewater State Teachers College, Vilynis Ezerins, was the perfect player for the kickoff team. Ezerins weighed 220 pounds and ran a 4.5 forty, which at the time was extremely fast, particularly for a man of that size. I went along with Coach Prohaska's recommendation, and as a result we lost a game to the Chicago Bears by one point, only our third loss of the 1968 season, which cost us an opportunity to play for the conference championship. Clarence Childs returned a kickoff 90 yards for a touchdown, as the result of a missed tackle by Vilynis Ezerins.

I realized, after analyzing that play and our overall special teams play for that entire season, that the fault for the loss, and the abrupt end to an otherwise fine season, was as much in our approach to coaching special teams as it was in Ezerins' missed tackle. Because of Ezerins' lack of tackling fundamentals, we never should have placed him in that position; he was not the right man for the job. It was then that I decided a special teams coordinator was needed!

I convinced Dan Reeves, then the owner of the Los Angeles Rams, that a special teams coach was a necessity and would pay dividends in victories. Mr. Reeves asked how I was going to keep this new coach busy, and I told him that the special teams coordinator will be the busiest coach on the staff—and I was right.

We held a series of interviews with several college and pro coaches; among them was Dick Vermeil, whom I finally selected for the job. Before I made my final decision, however, we brought Dick back for a second interview to be sure he really wanted the job. At that time a special teams coach was considered low man on the totem pole, not highly regarded. After making the status of this new position quite clear to him, we hired Dick Vermeil as the very first special teams coordinator in the National Football League (or anywhere else, as far as I know). If it had not been for Vilynis Ezerins' missed tackle, the position of special teams coordinator might never have been created.

Experience

We believe that, other than the head coach, the special teams coordinator is the most important coach on the staff. When you search for a special teams coordinator for your staff, there are certain criteria you should use. First, each candidate should be a former head coach, offensive coordinator, or defensive coordinator. Your special teams coordinator must have the experience of dealing with an entire team or unit, so that he understands the role of a coordinator with all that it involves in the areas of responsibility, authority, motivation, discipline, and organization.

Knowledge

Second, he must know the kicking game completely. Your special teams coordinator must know more than just when to punt and when to fair-catch a punt. It is extremely important to have a working knowledge of all the subtleties and nuances of each phase of the kicking game. We believe that the head coach must always decide which special team is to be called at any given time during the game; however, the special teams coordinator must know when and how to use the kicking game as an aggressive offensive tool, as well as when and how to make the most of a purely defensive situation. With a sound knowledge and understanding of special teams will come innovative ideas and suggestions that may often spell the difference between winning and losing.

Organization

A third essential criterion for selecting a special teams coordinator is his penchant for organization—he must be very well organized. The person you select to supervise your team's kicking game cannot afford to waste 1 minute of time. He must create ways to combine special teams drills with conditioning; incorporate many of his kicking game techniques and fundamentals into general preseason instruction to save time during regular season practices; observe both offensive and defensive practices, as well as work both sides of the ball during his own special teams practices, to better evaluate more people in his allotted time; and organize many of his practices in small groups to teach concepts and schemes as "part of the whole," just as one would do on offense or defense.

Commitment

Although the next element for judging this coach may seem obvious, it is, amazingly, often overlooked for that very reason. All your candidates must be committed to the value and importance of the kicking game. The man that you select to head your special teams must share your view on how critically important this facet of the game is to the success of your team. He should believe that improvement in your kicking game will ensure the team of winning at least two more games each year and keep you in the close games so that you may have the opportunity to win some other games you might otherwise lose.

Analytical Ability

Finally, your special teams coordinator must be an excellent film-study man with exceptional ability to spot and analyze the most minute details, ones that others often overlook. Besides the attention he must pay to detail when teaching and coaching kicking-game fundamentals to his own players, the coach must be able to perceive weaknesses in those fundamentals in all of your team's opponents, in order to make them work to your advantage. He should have the ability and patience to evaluate the snap time of every center you face, to determine where the laces are when each of your opposing punters and holders receive their snaps, to define the characteristics of each blocker and coverage man in your league, and so on. It is not possible for anyone to be successful at this position unless he possesses these particular qualities and the basic background already outlined.

Many high school head coaches may feel that it would be extremely difficult, if not impossible, to find such a qualified person to coordinate special teams at their level. However, before you burden yourself with this formidable task, we suggest that you first read Joseph G. Pacelli's *Building Your High School Football Program: In Pursuit of Excellence* (Champaign, IL: Leisure Press, 1987). In the two chapters dealing with recruiting coaches, organizing, and selecting a staff, you will find information that can be quite beneficial to head football coaches in small high schools or those with limited-budgets.

The position of special teams coordinator can be a great job if the coordinator is required to report only to the head coach and does not need to worry about interference from others. The special teams coordinator is like a head coach in that he has the whole roster to pick from to develop his special units. He will be the busiest coach on your staff, and he must be dedicated, creative, and hardworking to succeed.

SPECIAL TEAMS PLAYERS

When you begin your search for kicking team personnel, it is important to start from the beginning—with the center (long-snapper). Unless the snap is exactly right, the punter's rhythm will be off, the holder's placement will be inaccurate, and the kick will be off line. What is important is not the size of your center but only his ability to snap the ball. When I went to the USFL, we got a young man from Arizona State, David Ohton, who was only 5-foot-9, about 175 pounds, but a great snapper, who helped us to win the Western Conference Championship. So my advice is to start your player selection with a search for a center.

The selection of player personnel for each team or unit in your kicking game should be the combined effort of the head coach and the special teams coordinator. The special teams coordinator should prepare a list of players for each unit, in depth-chart form. These lists should be reviewed by the head coach, with input from his offensive and defensive coordinators (when any of their starters or key players appear on a particular list). Then, in a meeting with his special teams coordinator, the head coach should review the lists on a player-by-player basis to correct, adjust, revise, and finalize the personnel (in depth) for each special unit.

The following general guidelines may help you in the selection of personnel for your special teams:

- Attempt to select a group of 7 or 8 backup players to form the nucleus of your special teams. Surround this nucleus with the best players (starters or backups) for the balance of the positions on each unit.
- The major factors to look for in a special teams player are toughness, intensity, quickness, speed, and basic football intelligence. Size is *not* a major factor.
- Each player you select must be self-disciplined, dedicated, and a team player, and must have pride in accomplishment.
- A special teams player must be the type of athlete who can and will play with bumps and bruises (not serious injury, of course).
- Special teams players must be able to grasp concepts quickly, adjust to unforeseen situations, and recognize details.

RECOGNITION OF SPECIAL TEAMS

The true special teams player is an unusual and special "breed of cat." He must be tough, self-disciplined, and self-motivated. He lives in anonymity, yet he loves the game of football and is grateful for any opportunity to play. The special teams athlete lives in the shadow of the star athlete, giving as much to the team effort but without the praise and adulation. I have believed, for many years, that special teams players are indeed *special* and deserve to be treated and recognized as such.

In 1976, I received a letter from NFL Commissioner Pete Rozelle asking me to refrain from introducing my special teams players on network TV prior to the Monday Night Football games. At that time the Washington Redskins were a big attraction on the Monday night games—we were the first team to win 10 games in that time slot. The Commissioner felt that the fans and the network were more interested in the more famous names like Sonny Jurgenson, Billy Kilmer, Larry Brown, Roy Jefferson, and Charlie Taylor—not Mike Fanucci, Pete Wysocki, Mike Hull, Jeff Severson, Bob Brunet, Rusty Tillman, Eddie Brown, Bill Malinchak, and Ted Fritsch.

In my return letter, I explained that I understood his position and the feeling of the network, and that our introduction of these players was an important part of our program, not a slap at the league or the network. I told the Commissioner that we were not as talented as the Dallas Cowboys or many of the other teams we played, and that the only edge we had, particularly in the Eastern Division, was the excellent play of our special

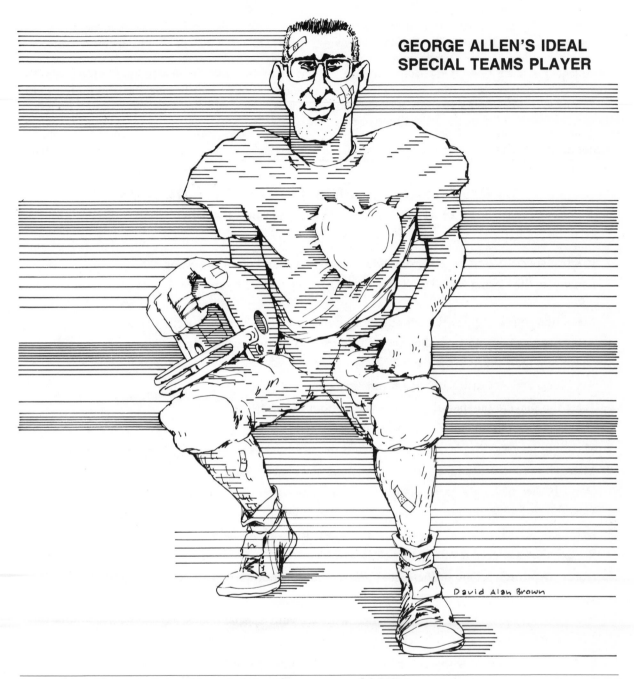

GEORGE ALLEN'S IDEAL
SPECIAL TEAMS PLAYER

David Alan Brown

Lots of intelligence, lots of heart, lots of scrapes and bruises.

teams; I explained our strong belief that the special teams players deserved recognition for the outstanding job they did, and that we felt these introductions were essential to the continued success of our program. Commissioner Rozelle and ABC accepted my explanation, however reluctantly, and at that point the kicking game began to rise in importance. Today, good special teams play is regularly discussed on network broadcasts, and special teams players are often introduced before games.

The point here is that even though your special teams players function well without public recognition, as head coach you owe them recognition commensurate with their contribution to the success of the team. It is also fitting that you develop a series of awards, over and above basic weekly team awards, exclusively for your special teams. In professional football it is possible to give awards such as clock radios or color TV sets. In high school and college, however, the awards have a symbolic, rather than monetary, value. But, besides the normal trophies, certificates, and helmet stickers, you can use promotional items from local merchants, like certificates for free ice cream or pizza, free passes to a movie theater or local amusement area, and so forth. These unique awards should be given only to the special teams and not to the rest of the team—in other words, *special awards* for the *special teams*.

George Allen's Tips for Head Coaches
25 Ways to Lose While Trying to Win

1. Practice special teams on Saturday only, or just the day before the game.
2. Remember the kicking game is just a necessary evil that takes time away from your offense and defense work.
3. Make out your daily practice schedule; if any time is left, include special teams.
4. After practice, devote your time to the offense and ignore special teams.
5. Don't lengthen practice for special teams.
6. Act bored and get distracted when practicing special teams.
7. Treat the players on special teams as the bottom of the barrel.
8. Place your worst athletes on the special teams.
9. Make the players on special teams feel as if they are necessary only to get the ball for the offense.
10. Make all your coaches take a part in coaching the special teams.
11. Don't bother making a game plan for special teams—you don't need one.
12. Talk about the importance of special teams, but don't practice what you preach.
13. Don't bother with special teams meetings—just do it on the field.
14. Realize that a special teams notebook is worthless.
15. Don't spend much time on field goal protection—touchdowns are what win games.
16. Don't emphasize punt protection.
17. Don't worry about the depth chart when working your special teams.
18. Remember that anyone can block a punt.
19. Build your offense first, defense second, and special teams last.
20. Consider speed the most important factor on special teams.
21. After any loss, proclaim, ''We have to improve our kicking game.''
22. Blame the special teams when you lose.
23. When something goes wrong during the game, scream at the special teams.
24. Avoid talking about special teams; stick to offense and defense.
25. Keep changing and blaming the special teams coach when you lose.

CHAPTER 2

Inside the Kicking Game

When I was head coach of the Los Angeles Rams (before I hired a special teams coordinator), we would occasionally play the Detroit Lions, who had an excellent kick returner by the name of Lem Barney. The week before one of our games against Detroit I decided that we would squib kick to him, and I announced it to the team on Tuesday. The kickoff unit hated the idea of squib kicking—it was like a slap in the face to them. They wanted to go downfield, cover a long kick, and tackle the returner deep in his own territory. Nevertheless, we practiced the squib kick all week because I knew it was the proper strategy to use on a kick returner this good.

Just before the game, the captains came up to me and said, "Coach, we have been talking, and we would like to kick deep to Barney. We want to go down and get him inside the 20." I told them that because we had practiced the squib kick all week, it was really against my better judgment. Then one of the coaches approached me enthusiastically and told me, "You know, Coach, these guys are really

gung ho and ready to go. They can't wait to hit someone!" That started me thinking that maybe a deep kick might work; it might give the Lions poor field position and at the same time give us a positive lift to begin the game against a good team, which Detroit was at that time.

In the locker room, as we were about to go onto the field to start the game, I brought the team together and told them that I had changed my mind—the hell with the squib kick, we were going to kick deep! Well, you have never heard such a sound in your life. It was like the roof was blown off of the locker room with yells and screaming. We went onto the field all pumped up and ready, Detroit won the coin flip, and we sent out the kickoff unit. Everything was set up just right for us, I thought.

We kicked the ball deep to Lem Barney, who returned it 92 yards for a touchdown. The bottom fell out of our sideline. The depression was so thick you could cut it with a knife.

The rest of the ball game we squib kicked. That

was the only touchdown we allowed all day, and we did win the game. However, this incident illustrates an important point that highlights this chapter: How and what you prepare, the "inside" of your kicking game, is what will determine your degree of success; all other factors are extraneous and misleading.

KICKING GAME GOALS

Each game requires a set of goals for your kicking game that takes the form of a game plan. In much the same way that you put together an offensive or defensive game plan, you should develop your kicking game plan for each of your opponents. And as the opening story of this chapter clearly suggests, once you have spent the time studying, planning, and practicing to devise and execute a sound game plan, you should stick to it, unless unexpected disastrous events force you to make adjustments.

However, we are going to leave to you the kicking-game goal planning for individual opponents. We would like you to use the following overall kicking game goals as guidelines when drawing up your individual game plans. In each case, consider the personnel, talent, and ability of your own players and those of your opponent, and determine how you can best accomplish these goals within the scope of your kicking game.

Averages

Establish realistic season averages for your team, adjusted yearly. (The following averages are for all levels of football—high school, college, and pro—except as noted with •• for adjustment due to the ability of the kicker.)

- Have a kickoff return average of 25.5 yards or better.
- Have a kickoff coverage average of 19.5 yards or less.
- Have your average starting point after a kickoff return be the 32-yard line or better.
- •• Your opponent's average starting point after returning a kickoff should be the 23-yard line or less.
- Allow an average punt return of 7.5 yards or less.
- •• Allow punt return yardage of 3.5 yards or less every time you punt.
- Have a season total of 550 yards on punt returns.
- Have a punt return average of 10.0 yards.

- •• Allow the opponent a punt net of 32 yards or less for each punt.
- •• Have a net punt average of 36 yards or better.
- Force 5 turnovers in the kicking game each season.
- Place the opponent inside the 10-yard line on 6 occasions during each season.
- Block 4 punts each season.
- Block 5 place kicks each season.

Game Breakers

Using your best talent to create mismatches and exploiting your opponent's special teams weaknesses, you should work to achieve at least two of the following game breakers each game:

- Return a kickoff for a touchdown.
- Return a punt for a touchdown.
- Return a missed field goal attempt for a touchdown.
- Force and recover a kicking game fumble.
- Block a punt.
- Block a field goal.
- Block a P-A-T if they have scored.
- Force a bad snap.
- Recover onside kickoffs (if any are attempted).

Field Position

Don't just kick and pray. Use your kicking game as an offensive tool to gain valuable yardage advantages over your opponent. Regularly practice and employ the following strategies in kickoffs and punts:

- Squib kickoffs to minimize the threat of a good return man.
- Hashmark kickoffs to force the return man into the sideline, limiting his return possibilities.
- Deep kickoffs into the end zone (if you have a strong kicker).
- On side kickoff after a major penalty against your opponent on your P-A-T attempt.
- Out-of-bounds punts to minimize the threat of a good return man.
- "Coffin corner" punts to back up your opponent to their own goal line.
- High, short punts in the opponent's territory to down the ball inside the 10-yard line.
- Quick kicks (low, angle kicks with a long roll) to eliminate possible returns and specifically control field position advantage.

Goal planning is not wishing—it is study, planning, and hard work. To accomplish the goals outlined in these three areas of concentration, the techniques and fundamentals required to execute them must be practiced, reviewed, discussed, and practiced again and again to perfection. Players and coaches must be confident that when the team attempts to reach a particular goal they will be successful.

KICKING TEAM MUSTS

When I was attending Lake Shore High School in St. Clair, Michigan, I played football for a coach named Carlton Worden. I got my training early on the importance of special teams, because Coach Worden worked on them all the time. We won games with kick returns, punt returns, field goals, and blocked punts—I was fortunate enough to make a punt block that resulted in a winning touchdown. We were prepared for whatever happened with the kicking game. Together with a great defense, we had excellent special teams and a good offense, which led to an undefeated championship season in which we scored 398 points while only allowing 27 points. The key factor leading to that kind of success was the play of the special teams in constantly and consistently maintaining good field position, turning games around by blocking kicks, shifting game momentum by scoring points on returns and blocked kicks, and always winning the kicking game battle.

In order for you to mount a championship season, your kicking game *must* win its battles. For this to happen, there are certain *imperatives*.

Practice

Let us start from the beginning—with practice time. You must allow sufficient practice time each day to thoroughly cover all the plays that *may* be required of your special teams in a given week so that you will be prepared for any eventuality. Next, these practices must be well organized and efficient, keeping in mind both short- and long-term goals and always working to achieve those goals. It is equally important for both players and coaches to be aware of your goals and the methods you employ to reach them (drills, exercises, film study, meetings, etc.). This is a team effort, and each person must fully understand his own responsibility.

Personnel

Although we have already discussed the criteria to be used in selection of special teams players, let us add some *musts* with regard to specific positions in the kicking game.

Center

First, it is essential that you find at least two long-snap centers. Every play in the kicking game (except a kickoff) starts with the center. A good long-snap means a good beginning to each play, and a poor long-snap can result in anything from bad timing to disaster; rarely does anything good happen after a poor snap. You cannot afford to be without a good long-snap center, so the more backups you can train, the more confident you can be that each play will begin well.

Punter

Because the punt is the most important play in football, the punter is a key player. Ideally, the punter should be a good all-around athlete with good hands, good quickness, and, of course, strong legs. The three qualities to look for in his punting are these: (a) height—good hang-time is extremely important to good coverage; (b) accuracy—in order to cover the punt effectively, it is necessary to know where the punt is headed; and (c) distance—an important feature in a good punter, but difficult to use effectively without good hang-time and accuracy.

Your punter can be your single most effective tool for keeping your opponent in poor field position. If you work hard on protection and coverage to maximize the effect of your punter's skills, your punting game can be devastating to your opponents.

Holder

At the heart of your place kicking unit are the three men directly in line with the football—the center, holder, and kicker. We have already discussed the importance of the center: He and the other two men must form a precise, unbroken chain of action to score under heavy pressure. The holder *must* be an intelligent athlete with soft, quick hands, excellent overall quickness, and extremely good hand-eye coordination. He should be calm under pressure and able to exercise good judgment in a crisis.

Placekicker

The physical ability of the placekicker must start with consistent accuracy, followed by a sound technique for getting the ball up quickly and the ability to get good distance on his kicks. Place kicking must always be practiced with a holder (except for kickoffs) and, as often as possible, should also include the center. If this trio works in total unison all the time, and you teach sound protection and coverage fundamentals to the balance of the place kicking unit, you will be able to develop a valuable scoring dimension to your game.

Team Achievement

In order for your special teams to be a major factor in winning games, there are certain dos and don'ts that the entire team *must* observe:

- Avoid costly errors and penalties.
- Average better yardage per punt return than the opponent.
- Average better net yardage (punt minus return) than the opponent.
- Kick opponents into trouble (inside their own 10-yard line) at least once per game.
- Score at least once, or set up at least one score per game, on a kicking play.
- Get at least one game-breaker advantage.
- Never commit a game-breaker error.
- Never make decision mistakes in fielding and returning kicks.
- Never allow any field goals you've missed to be returned past the 20-yard line.
- Never allow an opponent to score, or set up a score, on a kicking play.

If you practice your kicking game properly and sufficiently, using this *must* list as a constant point of reference in your preparation, you will be successful.

Successfully accomplishing these *musts* will contribute to winning which in turn will support the team's ability to achieve its goals. Success in any field depends directly on one's ability to do what *must* be done.

BASIC COACHING REQUIREMENTS

The intricacy and sophistication of special teams is directly related to the time, effort, and imagination devoted to them. Many coaches place great emphasis on them; unfortunately, many more do not. Even among those coaches who spend sufficient time on the kicking game, many fail to accomplish their objectives. There are certain basic coaching elements that are absolute requirements to develop an effective kicking game. These elements include: detailed scouting reports and film study, a proper approach to practice, precise timing, grading of players, knowledge of important rules, and practicing of special situations.

Scouting

As head coach of both the Los Angeles Rams and the Washington Redskins in the NFL and of the Chicago Blitz and Arizona Wranglers in the USFL, I spent a lot of time with my special teams coordinator breaking down special teams film of our opponents. It is important that you, as the head coach, be closely involved with the analysis and preparation of the special teams scouting reports. This will require a great deal of your time. Even though the extensive detail work can and should be done by your special teams coordinator, you must have firsthand knowledge of the information he will present when he suggests a kicking game plan.

Scouting Information

To expedite the collection of information, make your own checklist, including all of the detail information you require on each opponent's special teams play, and present this to your special teams coach during the film-breakdown period. This list must always include the following items:

- complete charting of distances and directions of punts and placekicks, to allow proper placement of your return personnel to have the best chance for a successful return;
- a chart showing the time it takes for each snap to reach the holder and the punter, where the laces are when the ball is caught, the time it takes to adjust the location of the laces, and the time it takes for the kick or punt to get off, so you can determine whether there is sufficient time to block a kick or a punt;
- a breakdown of the blocking schemes for punting and placekicking, and the weaknesses or "soft spots" in those schemes, to suggest the path or paths that may best be used for a successful block attempt;
- complete analysis of the punter (two step or three step, ball drop, ball trajectory, etc.) and the placekicker (soccer style or straight ahead, location of plant foot, leg quickness, ball trajectory, etc.), to plan the exact spot for blockers to impact the ball without committing a roughing penalty or to determine the best methods for returning a kick;
- analysis of the performances of each blocker and coverage man to enable you to preplan mismatches and attack the weakest link; and
- a chart of the decisions of the coaching staff showing the types of kicks attempted, the

type and number of fakes used, and how these relate to down, distance, field location, or time, to afford you the opportunity to prepare and anticipate a proper defense in any given situation.

In addition to these items, there are two other areas that must be fully charted and diagramed. For both punt returns and kickoff returns, you need complete charts of the types and frequency of each return used, the specifics of each returner (quickness, speed, hands, method of carrying the football, and toughness), and a full analysis of each blocker. Obviously, this information is required to prepare the coverage best suited to minimize their returns. On each opponent you will require additional information about their approach to special teams play, which can be determined after your initial film study session with your special teams coordinator.

For your use when structuring a workable system for collecting the scouting information you require, we have included a set of forms I used with the Redskins (Appendix C). These forms may be used during film study, and live game scouting. The information collected on each opponent can be either hand-sorted or, if you have the assistance of a properly programmed computer, quickly and more efficiently broken down electronically. Regardless of the means used to collate the information, the analysis, conclusions, and proper strategic use of the information must be done by the head coach with the assistance of his special teams coordinator.

Practice Process

The key to proper special teams practice is a three-part process that is relatively simple in concept but must be approached with patience and consistency or time will be wasted.

Emphasize the Little Things

The first part of the process is to place emphasis on the little things so that they become an instinctive part of each player's approach to his position. The following list of emphasis-points for each position illustrates the little things that must be worked on regularly.

I. Punter
    A. Be sure to call the direction of the punt ("Left," "Right," "Middle," "Short").
    B. Get in front of the bad snap.
    C. Work on kicking when the bad snap occurs. When you get a bad snap in practice, use this as practical experience.
    D. When punting from in or near your own end zone, know the situation so that you can decide correctly whether to take an intentional safety if a bad snap occurs.
    E. Your most effective punts kill the ball inside the opponent's 10-yard line.
    F. The punter with the best punt-yardage average is hardly ever the league's best punter. Punting short in the opponent's territory and punting for height rather than for raw distance are not reflected in the statistics, but they are very effective punting weapons.

II. Snapper
    A. Vary your snapping rhythm so that opponents will not know exactly when to take off in rushing kicks.
    B. Approach the ball differently each time you snap in practice situations. Do not stay in one spot and merely get in a groove—this does not provide a game-like situation.

III. Protecting on Punts
    A. Get part of your helmet (not just a "wing") on anyone you are assigned to block.
    B. Fullback—anticipate blocking where you see an overload. *Do not back up* to block.
    C. The center has only one responsibility before leaving on coverage—making a perfect snap.
    D. Talk to each other and call out the number of the man you are blocking. Proper communication is essential to good protection.

IV. Blocking Punts
    A. We scout and key opposing snappers to see if they
        1. rock or wind up, and
        2. snap on rhythm.
    B. We scout the opposing punter to see where his foot meets the ball. Rushers then have a landmark to cross that is about 18 inches in front of where the punter's foot meets the ball.
        1. Do not go through this landmark *toward* the punter.
        2. Do go across this landmark *in front of* the punter. *Lay out* across this landmark.

V. Blocking P-A-Ts and Field Goals
  A. We scout and key opposing centers to see if they
    1. rock or wind up, and
    2. snap on rhythm.
  B. Interior rushmen should use strength and takeoff to drive as deeply and quickly into the backfield as they can. Get your hands high as the kicker's leg swings forward.
  C. Outside rushers:
    1. The man lined up inside the halfback should seek to drive through the natural gap between the halfback and the end. Try to get on a course almost parallel to the line of scrimmage.
    2. The widest rusher should drive as close outside the hip of the offensive halfback as he can. As soon as he clears he should try to get in the ball's line of flight. This means adjusting *immediately* to a course almost parallel to the line of scrimmage.
      a. Do not go at the kicker and holder.
      b. *Lay out* along the line of flight for the ball.

VI. Punt Return Safeties
  A. Calls:
    1. One safety is designated to call "Me" or "You" on all punts.
    2. The safety not fielding the punt calls "Fair catch" or "Go" so that the man fielding it will know whether to fair-catch the punt. Also, we attempt to help locate the most dangerous cover's position for the return man.
  B. Safetymen should never line up deeper than their own 10-yard line. They should not handle a punt for which they have to retreat inside the 10.
  C. Do not signal for a fair catch unless you actually plan to catch the ball.
  D. Generally, your first moves should take you upfield rather than wide. Start forward and *then* break to the sideline.
  E. Always think in terms of breaking that first tackle. This is how most long returns develop.
  F. It is bad procedure to double back in trying to evade coverers. Do not develop this habit.
  G. Body position in fielding the ball is very important. Try to be nose-up and moving into the ball instead of going laterally or

backward. Good position can add several yards to each return.

VII. Kickoff Return Safetymen
  A. Calls:
    1. The middle safety is designated to call "Me" or "You" or "Short" on all kick-off receptions.
    2. The left safety calls "Stay" when a ball is kicked so deeply into the end zone that an attempted return is unwise.
    3. The right safety calls "Go" to the wedge at the appropriate time.
  B. The safety returning the kickoff should carry the ball out using a technique that is essentially *straight, hard,* and *fast:*
    1. It is important to be moving into the ball as you catch it instead of standing still. It gives us that extra 1/2 second vital for a successful return.
    2. Think in terms of trying to blast it straight out to the 35-yard line.
    3. *Do not* come under control waiting for an opening to develop.

VIII. Miscellaneous
  A. The call of "Peter" means get away from a kicked ball downfield. We use it when we do not want to touch or handle a ball that has been kicked to us.
  B. Men responsible for containing the kicker (on a punt or field goal) when a fake kick is feared, or when we are in a prevent return, should not attempt to block the kick. Your responsibility is to force the kicker to kick on rhythm and to contain all fakes.
  C. Coverers on a punt close to an opponent's goal line should not slow down if the opponent's safety signals for a fair catch. Go past him to the goal line and attempt to down the ball before it goes into the end zone.
  D. The best way to avoid crossing blockers when we are on kickoff coverage is by utilizing maximum speed, not by slowing down to dodge.

Practice Every Day

The second part of this process is to practice a portion of your kicking game each day. Do not miss a day during the week of practicing some phase of your special teams in detail; this will ensure that everyone understands their assignments fully. Plan your week of special teams practices to include all you need to work on in precise detail, allowing time for a brief review during the last day of practice. Work on the more routine aspects early in the week and the new or more difficult aspects toward the end of the week, allowing your players the benefit of having the newly learned information fresh in their minds at game time.

Practice time for special teams will vary with each school's circumstances. Most colleges have sufficient practice time, resources, and personnel to schedule kicking game practices like those of a professional team. High schools, on the other hand, have more limitations in time, team size, ability to isolate player specialists, and depth of coaching help. The practice schedules in Figures 2.1, 2.2, and 2.3 are drawn on the basis of professional and college football team needs. The elements most essential for a quality special teams program, even at the small high school level, are shown in bold print. To be successful in the kicking game, you should practice these elements!

Repetition

The final part of the process is the one that demands the most patience—repetition. This is the key to proper long-term comprehension! You must work in practice on what you will actually see on game day, so that when it happens everyone will be prepared to cope with it promptly and effectively. And this practice must be repeated as often as time permits.

Timing of Kicks

Precise timing of punts and placekicks takes a great deal of extra practice time, and your punters, placekickers, long-snappers, and holders must expect to spend at least 15 to 20 minutes after practice to work on this element of the kicking game. Your commitment to success in this area requires that you be at all of these postpractice sessions, unless you have urgent business elsewhere.

For best results and for reasons of safety, there are certain time requirements that serve as performance guides for the three basic types of kicks in the game. The following are optimum times to work toward:

For Punts

Snap (15 yards)	0.9 seconds
Punter	1.3 seconds
Total getaway time	2.2 seconds
Minimum hang time (40-yard punt)	4.3 seconds

For P-A-T and Field Goal

Total getaway time	1.3 seconds

For Kickoff

Minimum hang time (55-yard kickoff)	4.0 seconds

Achieving these optimum times takes a great deal of practice, even at the professional level. As the level of play descends from major college down to high school, these times naturally will increase. However, it is important to concentrate on the times indicated here as goals of excellence to work toward, for without such goals you will never improve.

Grading of Players

I have always believed it important to use a point system that serves as one indication of the type of contribution each player is making to the special teams. However, some players are at positions where points are not easy to accumulate. Any form of grading players is just *one* measure of the player's special teams performance and is not intended to serve as a total evaluation of the contribution a player is making. In this system of grading, points are awarded as follows:

Unassisted tackle	3 points
First hit on tackle	2 points
Assist on tackle	1 point
Block	2 points
Second-effort play	3 points
Big play	5 points
Hit of the game	5 points
Game breakers	10 points

Combine this grading system with other criteria of your own to make a total evaluation of each player's contribution to the success of your special teams.

Knowledge of Rules

It is my feeling that all players should have a functioning knowledge of all the rules of football. Beyond that, there are specific rules applying to the kicking game that special teams players must know to avoid mental errors and costly penalty mistakes. The important general kicking game rules must be memorized and understood by *every* member of *every* special teams unit. If there are players who cannot or will not memorize the rules, they should not play in the kicking game—they will hurt you more often than they will help you.

Figure 2.1
Morning Practice Schedule

Date: _____/_____/#_____

_____/_____   **Specialist period (   )**

_____/_____   Stride/stretch period (   )

_____/_____   Agility period/defense walk-through
(   )

_____/_____   Cadence/defense get off-period
(   )

_____/_____   Individual fundamental period
(   )

QBs: _____	DBs: _____
RBs: _____	
WRs: _____	LBrs: _____
TEs: _____	
OL: _____	DL: _____

_____/_____   Group fundamental period (   )

QBs: _____	DBs: _____
RBs: _____	
WRs: _____	LBrs: _____
TEs: _____	
OL: _____	DL: _____

_____/_____   Play action 7-on-7 period (   )

QBs/RBs/RECs: _____	DBs/LBrs: _____
OL: _____	DL: _____

_____/_____   Outside perimeter period (   )

OFF: _____	DEF: _____
OT/TE: _____	DL: _____

_____/_____   9-on-7 period (   )

	W—M—S
OFF: _____	DEF: _____
QB/WRs: _____	DBs: _____

_____/_____   Team period (   ) Inside/outside
runs/play action passes

OFF: _____	DEF: _____

(Announcements)

_____/_____   **Special teams period (*)**
Team: _____

*Denotes to be filmed

Figure 2.2
Afternoon Practice
Date: _____/_____/#_____

_____/_____   **Specialist period (   )**
_____/_____   Stride/stretch period (   )
_____/_____   Agility period (   )
_____/_____   Cadence/defense get off-period
                   (   )
_____/_____   Individual fundamental period
                   (   )
                   QBs: _____   DBs: _____
                   WRs: _____   LBrs: _____
                   TEs: _____
                   RBs: _____
                   OL: _____   DL: _____

_____/_____   Group fundamental period (   )
                   QBs: _____   DBs: _____
                   WRs: _____
                   TEs: _____   LBrs: _____
                   RBs: _____
                   OL: _____   DL: _____

_____/_____   Combo period (   )
                   QB/RECs: _____   DBs: _____
                   RBs: _____   LBrs: _____
                   OL: _____   DL: _____

_____/_____   Situation period (   )
                   Nickel/ + 20/ + 10/2 min.
                   QB/RBs/RECs: _____   LBs/LBrs: _____
                   OL: _____   DL: _____

_____/_____   Combo #2 period (   )
                   Stunt/dog/screen/draw/big play
                   QB/RBs: _____   DL/LBrs: _____
                   QB/RECs: _____   DBs: _____
                   OL: _____   DL: _____

_____/_____   7-on-7 period (   )
                   QBs/RBs/RECs: _____   DBs/LBrs: _____
                   OL: _____   DL: _____

_____/_____   **Special teams period (*) Walk-**
                   through
                   Team: _____   OFF: _____ DEF: _____

_____/_____   Team Period (   )
                   OFF: _____   DEF: _____

Announcements: Striders _____ × _____

*Denotes to be filmed

Figure 2.3
Double Day Routine

7:00 TO 7:30 a.m.	Breakfast or snacks served (mandatory)
7:30 a.m.	Training room opens (rookies report early)
8:45 a.m.	**Specialist period (15 minutes)**
9:00 a.m.	Practice begins
11:00 a.m.	Practice ends (flexible)
12:00 TO 12:30 p.m.	Lunch served (mandatory)
12:45 TO 1:15 p.m.	Individual/group meetings (if scheduled)
3:00 p.m.	**Specialist period (20 minutes)**
3:20 p.m.	Practice begins
5:30 p.m.	Practice ends (flexible)
6:00 TO 6:30 p.m.	Dinner served (mandatory)
7:15-8:00 p.m.	**Special teams meetings**
8:00-10:30 p.m.	Team/group meetings

Following meetings—night treatment in dorms

10:30 p.m.	Snacks served
11:00 p.m.	Bed check!

Rain-Out/Very Hot Day Routine

(Morning schedule same as basic routine)

7:00 TO 7:30 a.m. (Wake Up Alarm)	Breakfast or snacks served (mandatory)
7:30 a.m.	Training room opens (rookies report early)
8:45 a.m.	**Specialist period (15 minutes)**
9:00 a.m.	Practice begins
11:00 a.m.	Practice ends (flexible)
12:00 TO 12:30 p.m.	Lunch served (mandatory)
12:45 TO 1:15 p.m.	Individual/group meetings (if scheduled)
3:00 p.m.	Group meetings
4:30 p.m.	Dinner served
6:40 p.m.	**Specialist period**
7:00 p.m.	Practice begins
9:30 p.m.	Practice ends (flexible)
10:30 p.m.	Snacks served
	Night treatment in dorms
11:30 p.m.	Bed check!

Special Situations

Over and above the normal kicking game situations and the anticipated situations relating to a specific opponent, there are special situations that must be practiced as a matter of course. These are relatively easy to understand, so I will simply list these situations, and you can refer to later sections of this text for the specific techniques of each. These special situations are the following:

Punting from hashmarks
Punting from your own end zone
Punting from the 45- or 50-yard line
Punting from bad-snap situations
Covering the fair catch
Reaction to a blocked kick
Reaction to a partially blocked kick
Receiving a punt deep in your own territory
Rushing a punt when the opponent is backed
    up to his goal line
Prevent on punt defense
Reacting to a fake punt
Onside kickoff
Onside kickoff defense
Surprise onside kickoff defense
Squib kickoff
Returning squib and short kickoffs
Bad snap on P-A-T and field goal attempt
Field goal prevent
Defensing a fake field goal
Field goal return
Unbalanced-line field goal
Defending an unbalanced-line field goal
Field goal attempt after a fair catch (free kick)
Taking an intentional safety
Kicking off after a safety
Receiving a kickoff after a safety

MOTIVATING THE SPECIAL TEAMS PLAYER

When we built Redskin Park in 1971, I designed into the plan one very important room I wanted, a special teams meeting room. John Madden, then head coach of the Oakland Raiders, came to Washington and asked to have a tour of Redskin Park. When he saw the room he said, incredulously, "Do you mean that you have a room for *only* the special teams?" I told him yes and that no one else used it. I wanted them to have a room that they could say was their own, something that no other segment of the team could do. The Redskins special teams players took great

pride in that room and enjoyed kidding the big name players by saying things like, "Billy Kilmer and Larry Brown, you don't belong in this room—it's for special teams players only."

My interest in special teams and in the personality of special teams players goes way back to when I was head coach at Whittier College in the early 1950s. I began to understand then that the true special teams personality took more pride and satisfaction in the recognition of his accomplishments by his coaches and teammates than in recognition from any outside entity. He is most often a self-motivated individual who is triggered to a height of enthusiasm by the excitement of those he respects and whom he feels identify with him and genuinely care for his success and well-being. Therein lies the key to motivating your special teams players, and it is up to the head coach to do it.

To build the right rapport with special teams players, the head coach must develop a true empathy for and identity with these players. He must care about them and show his appreciation for their efforts more than he does for the more publicly recognized players on his team. Of course, the head coach must recognize and acknowledge the efforts of all his players, but his reactions should be a bit more enthusiastic and demonstrative with his special teams players.

To illustrate this point I would like to tell you what we did in Washington, where, I believe, we had the most successful special teams program of my entire career as a head coach. After every game, when the team came into the main locker room at RFK Stadium, I would talk with the entire team, make some brief statements about the game, and set the tone for the following week. Then I would take all the regular special teams players into an adjacent, smaller locker room for their own meeting. After I talked to them about the game, I would get up on top of a large table and start setting the special teams tone for the following week, telling them what we could do to the other team, getting them excited about their potential, and stimulating their enthusiasm to work hard during next week's practice. Often the meeting would get quite emotional, and a player would hand me a wooden folding chair that I would throw against a wall; sometimes they would hand me two or three chairs, and they loved it!

The next day when the other players would ask what all the racket and broken chairs were all about, the special teams players would smile with pride and say, ''It was just our regular after-game meeting.'' My special teams in Washington used to really look forward to those meetings after our games at RFK Stadium; the meetings made them feel really *special*, and triggered their self-motivation to work hard all week!

You have to find an approach to motivating your special teams that is unique to your personality and apropos to your coaching circumstance. But before any motivating tool or exercise can be effective, you must develop that personal rapport we mentioned earlier. Without that, no amount of yelling, screaming, or breaking of chairs can motivate anyone.

STATISTICS

Sometimes statistics can be misleading, but in the case of the kicking game, statistics are a true measure of one thing—the head coach's commitment. By reviewing most special teams statistics, it is not very difficult to recognize a head coach who is giving the kicking game more lip service than concentrated thought and respect.

The following statistics were researched and developed by Dick Vermeil specifically for this book. They present a breakdown of the kicking game over the past five seasons in the NFL. The first group of charts (Tables 2.1 through 2.5) present per-yard, per-team, and per-game averages for each phase of the kicking game.

Table 2.1   Punts

Total per year	Per team	Per game	Ratio
2,248 punts	80.00	5.00	—
21 punts blocked	0.75 (.009%)	0.05	1 in 107 punts blocked
1,162 punts returned	41.5 (52%)	2.50	1 in 2 returned
10.6 returned for touchdown	0.38 (.009%)	0.024	1 in 110 returned for touchdown

Note. One in every 212 balls punted returned for a touchdown.

Table 2.2   Kickoffs

Total per year	Per team	Per game	Ratio
2,124 kickoffs	76.00	4.7	—
1,762 kickoff returns	63.00 (83%)	3.9	1 in 1.21 returned
5.8 returned for touchdown	0.21 (.003%)	0.013	1 in 303 returned for touchdown

Table 2.3   Points-After-Touchdown (P-A-T)

Total per year	Per team	Per game	Ratio
1,105 P-A-T attempts	39.5	2.500	—
1,058 P-A-Ts made	37.8 (95.7%)	2.400	1 in 1.04 made
47 P-A-Ts missed	1.7 (.043%)	0.105	1 in 164 missed

Table 2.4 Field Goals

Total per year	Per team	Per game	Ratio
796 field goal attempts	28.5	1.80	—
564 field goals made	20.1 (70.8%)	1.30	1 in 1.4 made
232 field goals missed	8.2 (29.1%)	0.52	1 in 3.4 missed

Table 2.5 Safeties

Total per year	Per team	Per game
17 safeties	0.61	0.038

By studying these types of statistics and numbers, you can do more than a good job of assigning practice times; you can also compare your individual numbers and performance. For example, if your ratio of punts blocked to total punts is greater than 1 in 107, you are below average. You may also find out, if your ratio in returning punts for touchdowns is better than 1 in 110, that you are doing a better job than most.

One way to evaluate the total contribution of the kicking game is to compare the winners with the losers. With 28 NFL teams playing 16 games per

Table 2.6 Differences Between Winners' and Losers' Kicking Games

Special Team	Winners	Losers	Difference
1. P-A-Ts scored	2.90	1.70	+1.20
2. Field goals attempted	2.10	1.50	+0.60
3. Field goals made	1.60	0.92	+0.68
4. Total punts	4.90	5.50	−0.60
5. Average yards per punt	40.10 (33.30)*	40.90 (32.40)*	−0.80 (+0.90)
6. Punts returned	2.80	2.30	+0.50
7. Opponent punts returned	2.20	2.95	−0.75
8. Yards per punt returned	8.40	6.97	+1.43
9. Opponent yards per punt returned	6.80	8.50	−1.70
10. Punt returns for touchdown	0.05	.01	+0.04
11. Kickoffs returned	2.90	4.60	−1.70
12. Opponent kickoffs returned	4.50	3.00	+1.50
13. Kickoffs returned for touchdown	0.02	0.01	+0.01
14. Yards per kickoff return	19.40	19.80	−0.40
15. Opponent yards per kickoff return	19.60	19.50	+0.10

Note. This information was gathered by Bud Goode, an independent professional football statistician, and computed over the 1986 season.

*Indicates net yardage.

year, you have a total of 224 games being played, meaning you have 224 games won and 224 games lost. The results listed in Table 2.6 compare the winners' kicking games with the losers' and show the difference between the two.

As you study these numbers you can easily see that the winners each weekend do average out to have better kicking games on those days than the losers. It also shows that certain statistics are more important to winning than others; for instance, it is important to average more yards per punt return that your opponent. These numbers are another way of verifying how important the kicking game is, and they can also be used to formulate seasonal goals.

Tables 2.7 and 2.8 provide detailed comparisons of the NFL teams' kicking games, based upon the teams' performances since 1978. The 1987 season statistics were not included due to the strike games. The tables allow a football coach to grade the performances of the special teams and rank them over the year, letting the numbers tell him whether he is investing enough time in certain areas of the kicking game.

What has become more apparent since 1969 when I initiated the position of a special teams coach is that it is tough to be a consistent winner with a poor or inefficient kicking game. Coach Vermeil's tables are vivid pictures of the impact special teams make in football today.

For comparison with these statistics, let's look at some of the statistics compiled during my last year or so as head coach of the Washington Redskins.

Table 2.7 Special Teams Plays Per Game and Per Year

Type of play	# per game	# per year
Punts	5	8
Punt returns	2.6	42
Kickoffs	4.7	62
Kickoff returns	3.9	62
P-A-T attempts	2.5	40
P-A-Ts made	2.3	37
P-A-T defense on field	2.5	40
Field goal attempts	1.8	29
Field goals made	1.3	21
Safeties	0.04	0.64
Safety returns	0.04	0.64
Total special team plays	28	448

Between 1971 and 1976, the Washington Redskins built a well-earned reputation as an outstanding kicking game team. Among the NFL teams, in cumulative kicking game statistics we ranked first in 1971, sixth in 1972, tied for first in 1973, second in 1974, and first in 1975 and 1976. No other NFL team has ever matched this consistency. This reputation was maintained only through all of the players wholeheartedly believing in the importance of kicking.

Table 2.8 Kick Games and Teams' Performance

Statistical category	NFL average	Non-playoff teams	Playoff teams	Super Bowl average conference champions	Super Bowl losers	Super Bowl winners	Differential: nonplayoff teams versus champions
Total number of punts	5.10	5.16	5.07	4.72	4.86	4.58	0.58 punts
First downs per punt	3.82	3.69	3.92	4.54	4.53	4.56	0.87 first downs per punt
Average yards per punt	40.35	40.45	39.85	41.50	41.08	41.93	1.48 yards per punt
Punt efficiency net	31.97	31.76	32.23	32.91	32.48	33.34	1.58 yards per punt net
Punt returns per game	2.71	2.57	2.91	3.15	3.05	3.25	0.68 punt returns
Opponent punt returns	2.71	2.82	2.54	2.42	2.58	2.26	0.56 punt returns
Average yards per punt return	8.42	8.18	8.86	8.90	8.89	8.91	0.73 yards per return
Average yards per opponent punt return	8.38	8.69	7.62	8.59	8.60	8.59	0.10 yards per return
Punt returns for touchdowns	0.02	0.02	0.02	0.02	0.03	0.02	No difference
P-A-Ts scored	2.30	2.13	2.51	3.00	3.05	2.94	0.81 P-A-Ts
Kickoffs returned per game	3.86	4.09	3.48	3.26	3.38	3.15	0.94 kickoff returns
Opponent kickoff returns	3.86	3.70	4.07	4.48	4.52	4.44	0.74 kickoff returns
Average yards per kickoff return	20.24	20.28	20.17	20.24	19.67	20.80	0.52 yards per return
Average yards per opponent kickoff return	20.31	20.34	20.20	20.47	20.49	20.45	0.11 yards per return
Kickoffs returned for touchdowns	0.03	0.03	0.02	0.02	0.00	0.05	0.02 returns for touchdown
Field goal attempts	1.71	1.67	1.75	1.94	1.86	2.02	0.65 field goal attempts
Field goals made	1.16	1.12	1.22	1.27	1.20	1.34	0.24 field goals made

CHAPTER 3

Punting

Field position is in my opinion the most important factor in the game of football—it literally dictates the type of offense and defense a team must use to aggressively take advantage of good field position or carefully protect against poor field position. Field position is most often created by the punting and punt return teams, which is why I emphatically believe that *the punt is the most important play in football!*

THE REALLY GOOD PUNTER

My son Bruce started his high school football career as a quarterback; after a serious shoulder separation, he became a receiver. He was doing quite well as a receiver until he was injured again. He still wanted to play football, but he was told by the doctors that all he could do was kick. So he decided to become a punter. I wanted him to learn how to punt from the best, so I sent him to spend a week with Ray Guy at his home in Mississippi, and when Bruce came back he was well on his way to being an excellent kicker. As a matter of fact, as a punter at University of Richmond, in Virginia, Bruce averaged 42.9 yards, was ranked 6th in the nation, and broke all of Mike Bragg's records (Mike was my punter with the Redskins at that time). Even though Richmond was almost always outmanned, they won their conference championship in Bruce's last season, and they did it on the strength of their good kicking game—proof positive that the really good punter can keep even an outmanned team in position to win games by getting his team out of bad field position and constantly putting the opponent in a hole.

It is also important to understand that, unlike Bruce, a really good punter might *not* lead his conference or league in punting averages. First, all good punters kick for height, to maintain a consistent hang-time of 4.5 seconds or better. Second, the really good punters are accurate—kicking out of bounds, dropping the ball inside the opponent's 10-yard line, and pinning a good return man along the sideline are some of the best ways to control returns and minimize the opponent's big plays. The only time a good punter thinks of raw distance as a first priority is when he is backed up deep in his own territory. Otherwise, his first consideration must be to punt the football in the manner that most benefits the team.

Developing the agility and mental toughness required to be a really good punter takes repetitive, organized, well-directed practices. Self-discipline and focused concentration are the major tools the kicker needs to learn how to do the following instinctively:

- Develop a totally consistent drop.
- Field and kick almost any bad snap.
- Stay relaxed under the pressure of a rush.
- Develop an awareness of the rush (to know when to speed up the kicking rhythm or move to avoid kicking into the strength of the rush).
- Properly alert coverage to the direction of the punt.

The ability to routinely and effectively perform these five tasks spells the difference between the average or fairly good punter and the really good or great punter.

IMPORTANT PUNT TEAM RULES

There are a dozen important rules that apply specifically to the punt team. *All* players and their backups *must* know these rules thoroughly:

- On punts, only the end man can leave before ball is punted.
- A blocked punt can be advanced by either team.
- A partially blocked punt that crosses the line of scrimmage is treated like a regular punt.
- A fair catch cannot be advanced by either team, nor may the fair catcher be bumped or tackled.
- A muffed fair catch that hits the ground is a free ball and belongs to the team that recovers it.
- A muffed punt cannot be advanced.
- Coverers on a punt cannot interfere with the free movement of a receiver in his effort to catch any punt.
- To down a punt, the covering man must stay with the ball until the whistle.
- If the covering team on a punt touches the ball but fails to officially down it, the receiving team can try to advance it at no risk to themselves. If they gain, they can take the gain. If they fumble or lose yardage, they can elect to take the ball where it was touched by the covering team.
- To down a ball around the goal line, coverers must not let any part of their body get into the end zone. This means carrying the ball in or sliding into the end zone with it.
- When we punt, we go from offense to defense at the line of scrimmage.
- Past the line of scrimmage the opposing team cannot block below the waist.
- Only the kicking team can be penalized for not having enough people in the game. Make sure our punt team has 11 people on the field.

PUNT FORMATIONS

The spread punt is the basic punting formation used, normally on fourth down, in situations when one is not kicking from one's own 10-yard line or deeper. All other formations are adjustments to the spread punt. The following diagrams and itemized instructions were developed and refined by my staffs and myself during my tenure as head coach of the Los Angeles Rams and the Washington Redskins, as was all such information in the next five chapters. (The numbering system is from our playbook. I suggest that you transpose this to your own numbering system for consistency and ease of learning.)

Spread Punt

Time Elements

Center's snap: Strive to get the ball back in 7 to 9 tenths of a second. The risk of getting a punt blocked goes up with each tenth of a second beyond 9 tenths!

Punter's kick: The punter should be able to get the ball off within 1.1 to 1.3 seconds. Any time taken beyond this margin is not sound. With the coverage personnel waiting to release with the punt, time is extremely important.

Elapsed Time (combined snap and punting time): With the center getting the ball back in 8 tenths of a second, and the punter getting it off in 1.2 seconds, the elapsed time will be 2.0 seconds. This leaves a margin of error of 2 tenths of a second, figuring we are still sound when punting the ball in 2.2 seconds!

Hang time (the time the ball is in the air): Strive to keep the ball in the air 4.5 seconds. A punt hanging 4.5 seconds can be covered and the return held to a minimum!

Coverage time: Because the line cannot release prior to the punt, and the punt takes approximately 2.2 seconds to get off, you have approximately 7.2 seconds to cover the ball, from the time of the snap. This is assuming that the players releasing can cover 40 yards in 50 seconds.

Kicking against 10-man rush: The punter must now be able to get the ball off in 1.8 seconds. He may have to use a 2-step approach.

Example:

Snap – 0.7 seconds
Kick – 1.3 seconds
Hang – 4.5 seconds (40 yards)

Total – 6.5 seconds

Note: For each yard the punt goes while maintaining the same or less hang time, it creates that much more cushion for possible successful return yardage.

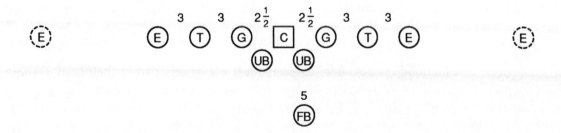

Personnel

The placement of personnel is based on the athlete's ability to carry out his responsibilities. The upback, guard, and tackle positions should be interchangeable with minimum adjustments.

Coaching Factors

Alert: If you are injured and cannot go, it's *your* responsibility to notify the coach.

Huddle: Our huddle will be formed in a circle with each player forming on the center relative to his position and the center aligned approximately 7 yards from the ball with his back to the ball. Most of the time we will huddle on the sideline.

Alert: Stay in the game and know the down and distance. We will assemble on third down.

Alignments: Line up off the line of scrimmage as deep as possible while maintaining a legal formation. G's head on the Center's numbers. Ts align on Gs. Es align on Ts. UB's head and shoulders on the hip of the guard. FB aligns 5 yards deep behind the UB. Punter aligns 15 yards behind the Center and adjusts according to the call.

Splits base: G/C split is approximately 2-1/2 feet. G/T split is approximately 3 feet. T/E split is approximately 3 feet. UBs shoe to shoe with C/G.

Alert: Use smart splits relative to responsibility (4 to 5 feet). Es split according to call or game plan.

Tight punt: Splits reduced to 2 feet with ends tight.

Stance: Assume a two-point stance with hands on knees and knees and elbows flexed so that you can uncoil.

Technique: Utilize a pass protection technique—head butts chest between numbers, hands strike chest, and arms extend. Bring the rusher to a halt and force him to the outside. Don't get tied up. Es run through the outside number of your block responsibility. Hinge technique is used by the Es on the backside of the call and necessitates blocking two people. On the snap, drive off outside foot backward as deep as possible and slightly to the inside, stay square, jam the inside rusher with both hands in order to stop penetration and flatten his charge. Catapult off the inside rushers back outside to block the outside rusher. Stop inside penetration *first*.

Alert: Don't allow inside penetration, and don't get overextended.

Responsibility: Utilize a man blocking scheme (illustrations to follow). Punt protection is the most time-consuming and challenging of all the special team responsibilities. *Remember, a blocked punt may cost you your job.*

Coverage: Except for the ends, everyone must wait until the ball is punted before covering. We would like to develop a rhythm for our release and coverage—approximately 2.0 seconds. We will execute our normal spread punt coverage responsibility unless otherwise indicated. Basic principles of coverage include release, spacing, contain, breakdown, and the hit—strip the ball (to be described in detail).

Cadence: To avoid establishing a rhythm, we will utilize three variations in our snap count. *One* is the quick count, in which case the FB calls "Ready-Set" as soon as we get aligned, and the snap occurs immediately following. *Two* is the normal call (first count), in which case we align, make calls and adjustments, and await the snap count "Ready—Set." *Three* is the delayed call (second count), in which case we make an early "Ready—Set" that will be ignored while calls and adjustments are made. Upon the second call of "Ready—Set" prepare for the snap. This call is usually made against shifting fronts.

Fake: There are two variations in our mechanics to call a fake punt. One is by making a predetermined call in the huddle (sideline), and the other is by making an audible call.

Huddle call: As soon as we are aligned, the FB diagnoses the defense in order to determine the direction of the fake. He then indicates the direction with a call (ITF) or "Omaha" if the fake is not there. If the fake is on, the ball is snapped on "Set" utilizing our normal cadence (first count). If the fake is off, then "Omaha" is called, and we proceed to utilize our normal punt mechanics.

Audible: The fake is automatically on when the FB calls "Red" (run) or "Blue" (pass) followed by the normal huddle mechanics for a fake as already described.

Example:

"Red—Loaded Right" (or "In" followed by a name)

"Red—Loaded Right"

"Ready—Set"—The ball is snapped on "Set," and we run right.

Alert: When a fake pass is on ("Blue"), the interior line cannot go downfield. We must get the first down.

Shifts: We have the mechanics to shift to different alignments according to game plans. The formation will be called in the huddle (sideline), and our delayed cadence (second count) will be used with the shift occurring on the first count. Fakes can also be incorporated into these mechanics.

Numbers: The corresponding legal receiver's numbers must be worn when you are playing a potential receiver's position, or you *must* report to the official.

Time-outs: Our FB will be alert to make a time-out call only when absolutely necessary. This decision depends upon what is best for the team—a penalty or time-out—under the circumstances.

The Tight Punt

Punting from deep in your own territory, or out of your own end zone, is one of the most critical situations you will ever face in a game. If the punt is not executed perfectly, disaster may strike in the form of a blocked punt for a touchdown or safety, a recovered fumble for a touchdown, a bad snap leading to a safety, and many more ugly things, all bad for your team. I urge you to devote constant, regular practice time to the execution of the tight punt.

Protection for the tight punt is similar to that for the spread punt, with the following exceptions.

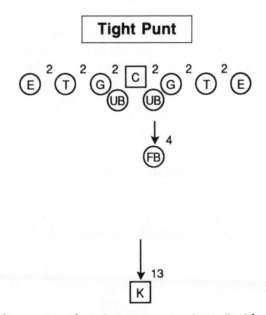

The tight punt is used when we are deep in our own territory (inside the 4-yard line). Maintain 2-foot splits with ends tight. *Hold* your block until you're sure of the punt. The punter aligns at 13 yards and the FB at 4.

Note: When the ball is placed at the 1-yard line (Red Zone), the punter must find the end-zone line and align one foot inside—never step back.

If at this point the ball is muffed, knock the ball out of the end zone or run it out. Don't be a hero! (A safety is better than a touchdown.)

Safety punt: We will execute this from a tight punt. It is vital that we do an outstanding job of protection. Our ends will not cover, to provide maximum protection. The punter will field the ball and run it out of the end zone. *Do not fumble!*

PUNT ADJUSTMENTS

On occasion, the game situation or an opponent's tendencies require variations in the type of punt or punt formation you might use. Following are a few examples of these variations for your consideration.

Wing Punt

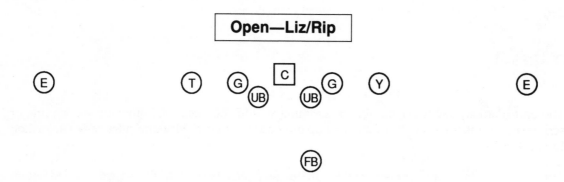

The wing punt can be used on the backside of a 10-man front to help stretch that side of the line and put the end in a better position to execute his hinge technique. The tackle can now cover on the snap. The disadvantage to the wing alignment is that the upback is not in as good a position to execute his block.

Open—Liz/Rip

Open—liz (left)/rip (right): The end may split according to his rule to get into a more advantageous position to release and cover. Normally, we can split both ends against an 8- or 9- (open) man front. Against a 10-man front, split as your rule dictates (''Liz'' or ''Rip'').

Freeze point: When we want to run the time out and we're not concerned with field position, we will call "Freeze punt." We will assume our alignments and then set there until the whistle blows. We will then take a 5-yard penalty and proceed to execute our normal spread punt.

Note: When we're ahead and it's late in the half or the game is won, we will always be conscious of running the clock down before punting.

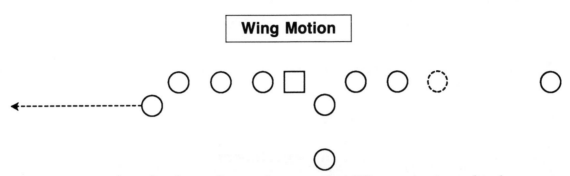

Wing motion can be utilized according to the game plan. Wing motion is used to free up our ends (sprinters). The UP goes into the line of scrimmage and the end aligns as a wing. Blocking rules adjust according to game plan.

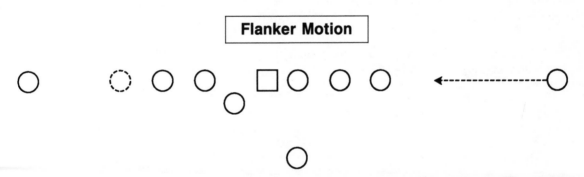

The end (flanker) aligns off the line of scrimmage, and the onside UP lines up on the line of scrimmage. Flanker motion is used to free up our ends (sprinters). Blocking rules adjust according to game plan.

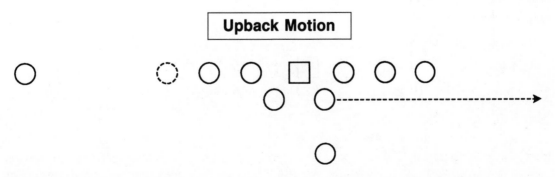

The onside UB goes in motion. UB motion is used to free up our sprinters. Blocking rules adjust according to game plan.

FB Motion

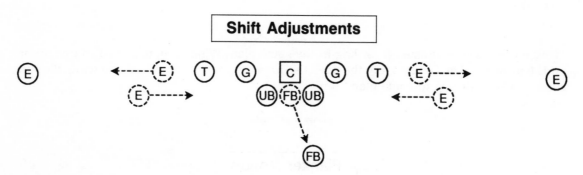

The FB goes in motion according to game plan and becomes the sprinter.

Shift Adjustments

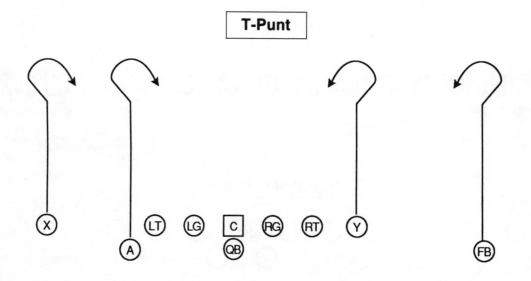

Shifts can be utilized according to game plan. This gives us the flexibility to disguise our punt formation and also to set up a fake.

T-Punt

Kicker

Rules and Mechanics

QB—Call as pass in the huddle—T-punt—74 curl—snap count up—ready break.

Audible—same, live snap count: Zero indicates change to punt!

Line—Block normal 74 protection: If zero is called, block T-punt rules.

T-punt rules: shotgun punt rules

        Center—snap, set, go!
        Guards—block #1
        Tackles—block #2
        A and Y—block #3—contain
        **QB—block most dangerous—
          safety to right
        Kicker—kick and safety to left
        X and FB—sprinters to ball

Pass patterns: On "Curl" call, everyone run curl route. Fight to get open. Deepen route 2 yards beyond marker.

QB—When under center as in T-punt, block to the side of an overload. When no overload, block to the right. Safety responsibilities remain the same.

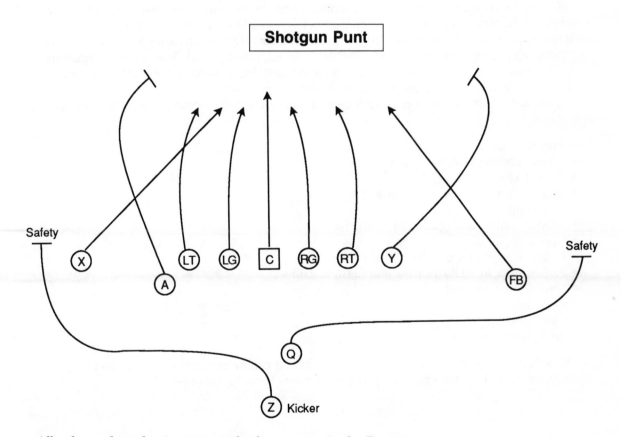

All rules and mechanics are exactly the same as in the T-punt.

PROTECTION AND COVERAGE

Everything in the punting process starts with the long-snap center. The first decision I made for every team I coached was who to play at center. This center snap is the first critical part of the protection package. It must be crisp and accurate; it is the center's prime, and usually his only, responsibility before the actual punting of the ball. Of vital importance, prior to the center snap, is team communication. All players involved in protecting the punter must know and be decisive about whom they are going to block, and verbal communication helps punt units avoid assignment errors and blocked punts.

Once the perfect snap has been made, the punter must get the kick away quickly. In order for the result to be consistent and predictable for the coverage scheme, the punter must work diligently during practice to develop a smooth rhythm and a high kick. Each blocker should butt his man through the numbers and quickly release into his lane to make the transition from protection to coverage. Speed in getting off the line is essential, particularly for the ends. For the blockers, quickness into coverage after the ball has been punted, never following behind or close to a teammate, creates the solid "blanket" required to smother a good return.

Everyone in coverage must exercise good field vision as they cover, being alert for blocking patterns. Coverage men must know when to force and when to contain, knowledge developed in repetitive practice with sound fundamentals. If a player is not in excellent position to force, he must recognize that fact and come under control to contain. Nothing opens wider holes in the "blanket" than a coverage man who is out of control and misses a tackle that he never should have attempted.

Adjust! Each man in coverage needs to learn to adjust to both the width of the field and the flight of the ball. Good communication by the kicker helps coverage men adjust to the flight of the ball, but only good practices can help players learn the right techniques for adjusting to the width of the field. A safe reminder is "When in doubt, get wider!"

Sure tackling and forcing turnovers are the keys to making a punting unit productive as well as efficient. Coverage men must be sure tacklers, and the men with the first shot at the safety must make the tackle to avoid permitting a good broken-field runner to find running room. The best technique is to put the helmet across the torso of the safety when making the tackle, allowing the tackler to focus on the numbers and drive through the man while avoiding a "spearing" call. The second and third tacklers should "tackle the ball" by focusing on the football and making as much contact with it as possible, trying to force a turnover.

In summary, then, the important elements to work on for developing a good punting game are these:

- Proper alignment
- Proper communication on assignments
- Perfect snap
- Kick with a quick, smooth rhythm
- Kick high
- Proper contact and release by blockers
- Speed off the line
- Quickness into proper lanes of coverage
- Adjustment to width of field and flight of ball
- Speed to control point
- Leverage on safety man
- Sure tackling
- Force mistakes

The following formations, plays, and responsibilities can be properly executed, and therefore both effective and productive, only if these elements become instinctive.

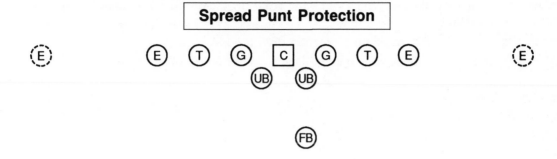

General responsibilities

- We will utilize man protection numbering from the outside in (1, 2, 3, 4, 5). Adjustments will be necessary as problems arise.
- The FB will call the front (8-9-10) and most of the related adjustments.
- The front will be referred to (a) by the number of people on or near the line of scrimmage, and (b) by the numerical rush distribution counting from left to right. With a man on the center, he will be counted to the heavy side (6-4) (7-3/4-6).
- Our normal alignment for our ends will be split 8 yards. Ends will adjust their alignments based upon the call—"Open," "Liz," or "Rip."

Specific responsibilities

Center

- Make a perfect snap every time (0.8 seconds or better).
- The punter gives a directional signal as needed.
- Snap the ball after "Set" and when ready.

Alert: On a delayed count, the FB calls the second "Ready-Set" with only 5 seconds on the clock.

Alert: "Loaded" call—lean block in the direction of the call.

Alert: On a "Hold" call, maintain protection until the ball is is punted.

Don't cover until the ball is punted.

Upbacks

Versus 8- or 9-man fronts—block #3.

Alert: 10-man front—check call ("Liz" or "Rip"), block #4 to side of call—add one and block #5 on the backside of the call.

Alert: When on the backside of a call, you have contain on coverage ("Switch" call).

Alert: On a "2" or "3" call, relay the call to the FB, then add one and block #5 to call side.

Alert: On a "Peel" call, acknowledge receiving the call from FB—block #2 to your side. *Relocate*—switch alignments with guard.

Alert: Versus a 3/4 stack, call "Stack—In" and zone block with the guard—block man to inside #4. Check adjustments.

Alert: On a "Hold" call, maintain protection until the ball is punted.

Alert: "Loaded" call—check adjustments. Don't cover until the ball is punted.

Guards

Versus 8- or 9-man fronts, block #3.

Alert: 10-man front—check for call ("Liz" or "Rip"), block #3 to call side—add one and block #4 to backside of call.

Alert: On a "2" call, relay the call to the UB and FB, then add one and block #4 to call side. UB block #5.

Alert: "3" call—When your blocking assignment forces you to cross a man to block your man, then you can make a "3" call. Utilize the same mechanics as for a "2" call—the FB will block #3.

Alert: Versus a 2/3 stack the UB gives you a "Stack—In" call, in which case you zone block with the UB taking the man outside (#3).

Alert: Versus a 3/4 stack, call "Stack—Out" and zone block with the tackle taking the man to the inside (#3).

Alert: On a "Hold" call, maintain protection until the ball is punted.

Alert: "Relocate"—a term we utilize to indicate a switch in alignments with the UB. Used in conjunction with the "Peel" call.

Alert: "Loaded" call—check adjustments.

Don't cover until the ball is punted.

Tackles

Versus 8- or 9-man fronts—block #2.

Alert: 10-man front—check for call ("Liz" or "Rip"), block #2 to call side—add one and block #3 to backside of call.

Alert: "2" call—when your blocking assignment calls for you to cross a man to block your man, then you make a "2" call. Make the call to the guard, UB, and FB. The FB then blocks #2 and you block #3—guard #4—UB #5. Check adjustments.

Alert: Versus a 2/3 stack the guard calls "Stack—Out," in which case you zone block with the guard and take the man to the outside (#2). Check adjustments.

Alert: On a "Hold" call, maintain protection until the ball is punted.

Alert: "Switch"—a call from the end that tells the tackle to assume the end's coverage responsibility.

Alert: "Peel"—a call used by the FB to instruct the UB to block #2 versus a double "2" call. Check adjustments.

Alert: "Loaded" call—check adjustments.

Don't cover until the ball is punted.

Ends

Basic alignment is 8-yard splits—adjust according to call.

Versus 8- or 9-man front—"Open" call—split out and block through outside number of #1 on snap.

The punter gives a directional signal for release purposes.

Alert: ''Ripple''—when the opponent goes from a 9- to a 10-man front. Adjust to a normal alignment.

Alert: Versus a 10-man front—check call (''Liz'' or ''Rip''), block #1 to call side—add one and block #1 and #2 to backside. (Utilize hinge technique.) Call ''Switch'' to tackle. After blocking, assume near UB's coverage responsibility.

Alert: ''Texas''—a call from the FB that indicates that the end is uncovered. *Alert* for a pass from the punter.

Fullback

Check defensive front and make appropriate calls (8-9-10) (Liz/Rip—Loaded—Ripple—Open—Hold—Texas).

Alert: Versus 8- or 9-man front—call ''Open'' (ends split), block rule most dangerous—make ''Hold'' call according to GP.

Alert: Versus a 9-man front—check for ''Ripple'' that changes the front from 9 to 10.

Alert: Versus a 10-man front, make a ''Liz'' or ''Rip'' call, and block #5 to the call side.

The ''Liz'' or ''Rip'' call is made away from the heavy side of the defensive alignment (6-4 = ''Rip'') or away from the end that is being doubled.

Alert: ''Loaded''—a call made when the defensive front is heavy to the call side (4-6 = ''Rip''). A ''2'' call situation usually develops when a team presents this alignment.

If your man does not come, check backside (hinge).

Alert: ''Peel''—a call made to the UB away from the call side versus a 9-man front when a double ''2'' call situation exists. The UB now blocks #2 to his side.

Alert: ''Texas''—a call made to the punter to make him aware that the end is uncovered. Alert for a pass.

Alert: ''Spy''—a call versus a 9-man front with one LB. Take LB wherever he goes.

Alert: ''Loaded''—a call versus a 10-man (3-7 or 7-3) (4-6 or 6-4) heavy alignment toward the call. Check adjustments.

Fake Punt—check ''Fake Punt'' section.

Cadence—check ''Cadence'' section.

Punter

Align at 15 yards behind center—know the cadence and calls.

Signal the direction of the punt.

''Hold''—check the front—if there is pressure, punt away—if not, hold the ball for two counts, then punt.

''Texas''—be alert that the end is not covered. Use discretion. Possible pass.

Punt in the direction indicated by our splits, scout report, sideline, and weather conditions.

Be alert for a ''Loaded'' call.

Protection Adjustments

8-man front

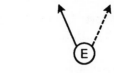

1. Split both ends (open).
2. Utilize "Hold" call to let the ends cover.
3. Ends release in the direction of the punter's signal (left or right).

9-man front

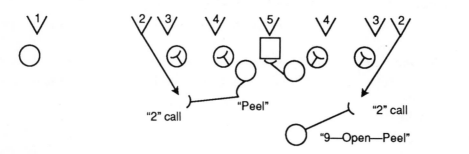

Split both ends according to game plan (open).

Can utilize "2" or "3" call.

Can utilize "Stack" call.

Double "2" call: When this situation develops, the FB declares the direction of the call ("Liz" or "Rip") and then communicates a "Peel" call to the backside UB, who now blocks #2 to his side.

Relocate—The guard and upback switch positions in order to carry out assignment.

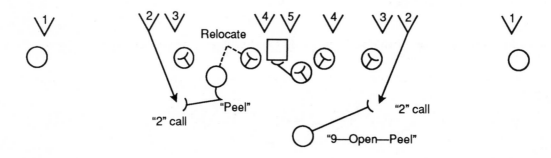

A "Spy" call is made against a 9-man front when one man is in a linebacker position. The FB now calls "Spy" and the number of the LB (#59), and takes him regardless of his alignment. The other members of the punt team treat the front as 8-man and block accordingly. A "Hold" call can be utilized.

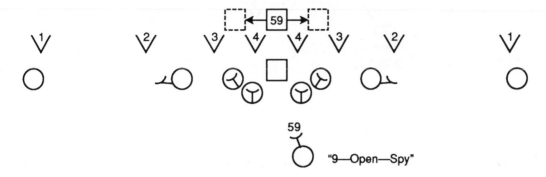

"9—Open—Spy"

A "Ripple" call and adjustment is needed when the front changes from a 9- to a 10-man front. We now call "Ripple" and the FB declares the direction of the call ("Liz" or "Rip"). We then block 10-man-front rules.

"9—Open—Ripple"

Adjustment

"10—Rip"

10-man front

Check for "Liz" or "Rip" call—backside is tight and utilizes a hinge technique. FB blocks #5 to call side.

Hinge ◄---

"10—Rip"

The ''2'' call is utilized when the tackle's assignment calls for him to go through a man to block his normal assignment. The tackle relays the ''2'' call to the guard, upback, and FB, in which case the FB blocks #2—tackle #3—guard #4—upback #5 to the call side.

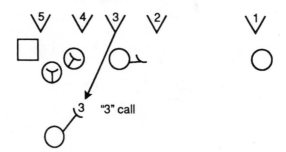

The ''3'' call is utilized when the guard's assignment calls for him to go through a man to block his normal assignment. The guard relays the ''3'' call to the guard, upback, and FB, in which case the FB blocks #3—guard #4—upback #5 to the call side.

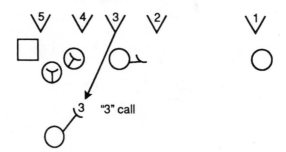

''In'' call refers to a situation where we have a 3/4 stack over the guard or upback. The upback makes the call, then blocks the man to the inside (#3), and the guard blocks the man to the out-side (#4). On the backside of a 10-man call the same mechanics would apply to a 4/5 stack.

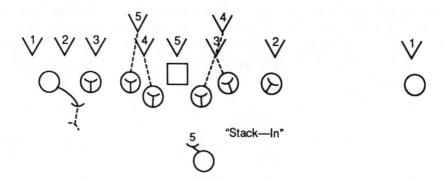

The "Out" call refers to a situation where we have a 2/3 stack over the guard or tackle. The guard makes the call, then blocks the man to the inside (#3), and the tackle blocks the man to the outside (#2).

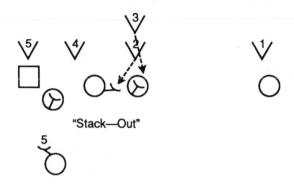

"Stack—Out"

The "Loaded" call refers to a situation where we have a (3-7) (4-6) heavy defensive alignment toward the direction of the call ("Liz" or "Rip"). First adjustment: We will automatically utilize a "2" call to the call side and then block according to our rules. If time permits, we will normally check the call and adjust back away from the heavy side or go quick count if they are jumping late.

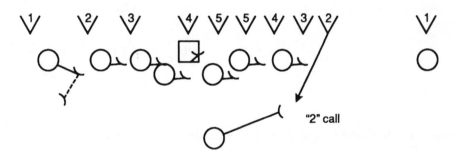

"2" call

Second adjustment: We take a minimum split between the guard and center. The upback to the call side calls "Double" to the loaded side. The backside upback calls "Mannie" (man protection). The upback to the call side now utilizes a "double" technique (lay out), and the center lean blocks in that direction. The guard pivots on his inside foot and blocks his rule (#4). The backside blocks man protection.

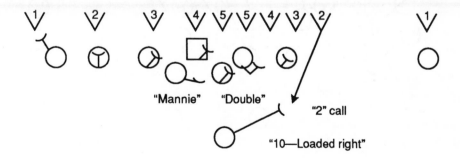

"Mannie"   "Double"

"2" call

"10—Loaded right"

Hinge—This is the technique utilized on the backside of a call by the end. It is necessary in order to block two people when we are outnumbered against a 10-man front.

Maintain normal 3 to 4 foot split.

Anticipate the snap—check with peripheral vision.

Jump back off line of scrimmage and slightly to the inside (1 × 1 yards behind tackle). Keep the shoulders square to line of scrimmage.

Jam the inside rusher by violently extending both arms (must stop or flatten his charge). Now catapult off the inside rusher and extend to the outside rusher—force him off his path.

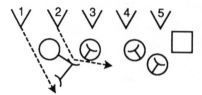

Always protect the inside first.

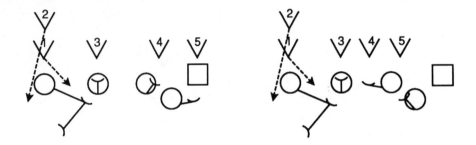

Call "Switch" to the tackle and upback, to adjust the coverage pattern.

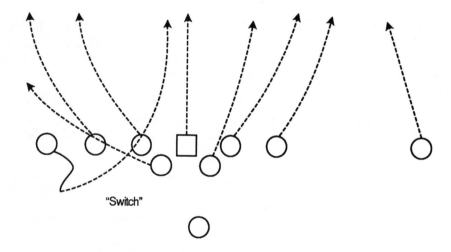

"Switch"

We also have the ability to get into a wing alignment away from the call to help stretch that side of the line and put the end in a better position to execute his responsibility. The tackle can now cover on the snap, blocking through his responsibility.

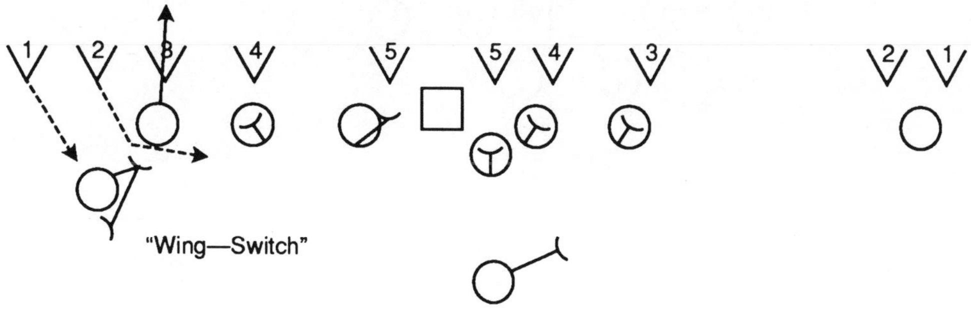

"Wing—Switch"

11-man front

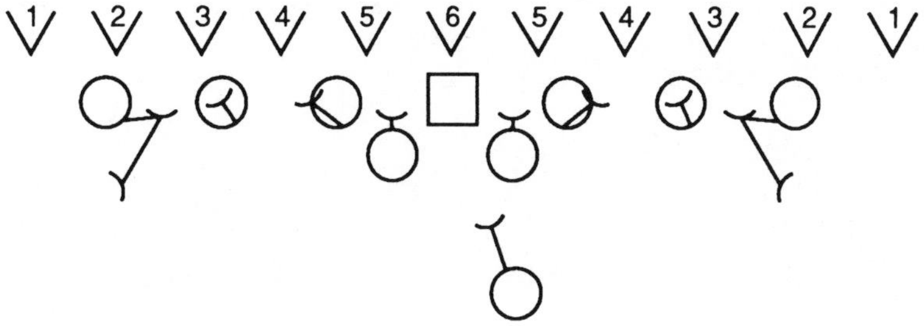

Call "eleven"—both ends align tight and execute a hinge technique on #1 and #2 to their respective sides. Both sides add one and block accordingly. The FB blocks #6. Protection is primary.

8 man (4-4)

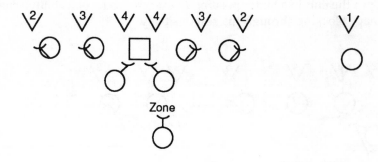

8 man (3-5)

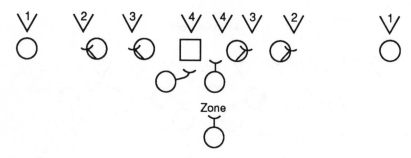

8 man (4-4)

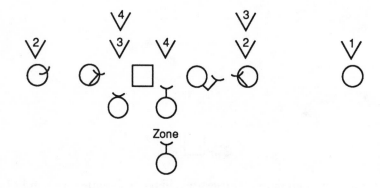

9 man (4-5)

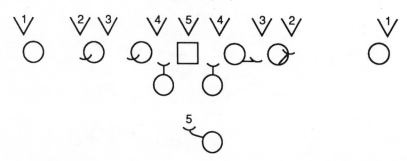

9 man (4-5)

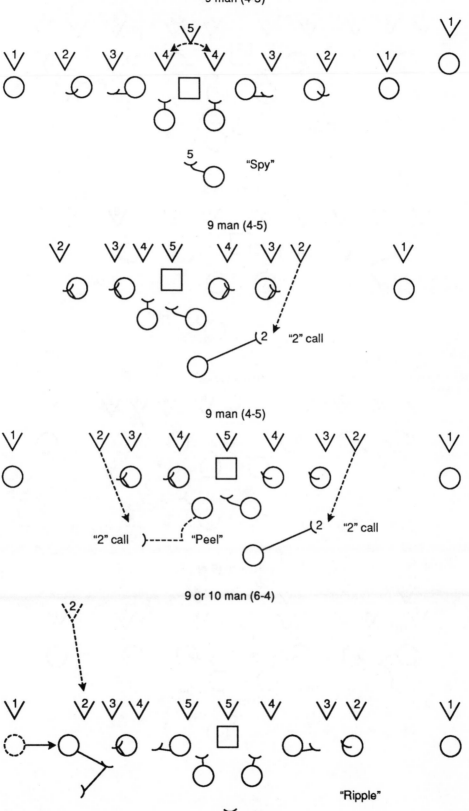

"Spy"

9 man (4-5)

"2" call

9 man (4-5)

"2" call   "Peel"   "2" call

9 or 10 man (6-4)

"Ripple"

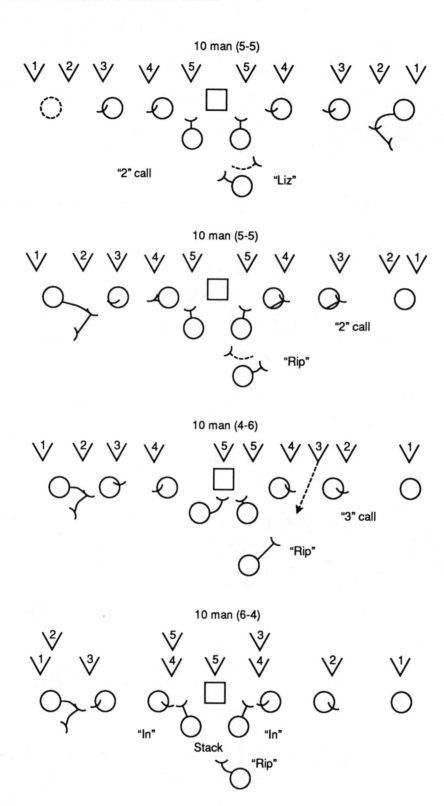

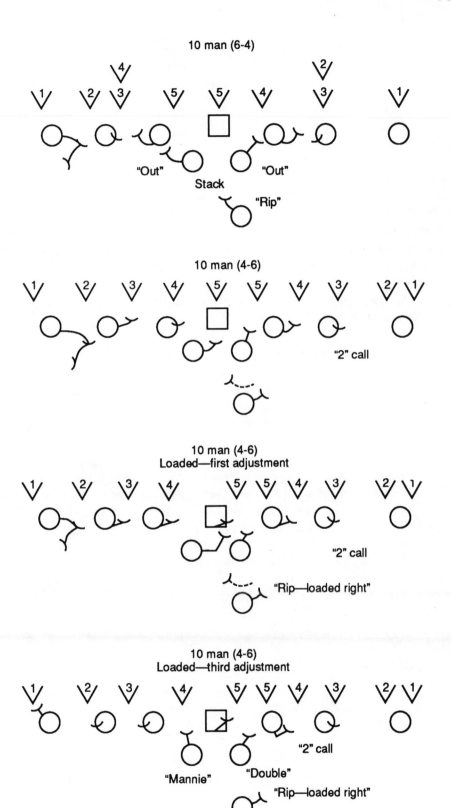

10 man (6-4)

"Out"   "Out"

Stack

"Rip"

10 man (4-6)

"2" call

10 man (4-6)
Loaded—first adjustment

"2" call

"Rip—loaded right"

10 man (4-6)
Loaded—third adjustment

"2" call

"Mannie"   "Double"

"Rip—loaded right"

Punt Coverage

General principles

On snap, set back and block your area of responsibility until the ball is punted. We will establish a rhythm. (2.0 seconds) Ends block outside through your man's outside number and cover on the snap.

Stop rushers' penetration. "Stick" rusher down the middle. Force him to outside. Use hands.

Don't follow a teammate downfield. When you see a teammate crossing in front of you, work outside to his open lane. This principle enables a man escaping off the line of scrimmage before you to sprint to the ball knowing that his lane will be taken up. Maintain approximately a 5-yard horizontal separation.

Sprint all out to the "breaking point" (a point on your side and in front of the football) then "come to balance" (get in a hitting position). The breaking point is approximately 5 to 7 yards in front of the ball.

Maintain outside-in leverage on the ball. In other words, if you are covering from the right side of the formation, keep the ball inside your left shoulder.

On *spread punt* the tackles are responsible for *contain* and *leverage* on the ball. On *fan* coverage the upback will *contain* and maintain *leverage* on the ball. On a 10-man front we use both principles.

If you are the first man to the ball, take an all-out shot at the carrier, attempting first to make the tackle, second to cause a fumble, or third make him change his course. This will give your teammates time to get there and "clean up."

If the return man fair-catches, the first man should sprint on by him. *Don't* interfere with the catch. The remainder of the coverage should *keep coming*. Expect a fumble!

If the return man doesn't field the ball, the first man down should faceguard the ball. Also, the ball should be downed when rolling toward your own goal line. If the ball is rolling to your opponent's goal line, let it roll until it stops, then down it properly. (Listen for the whistle.)

When covering a punt kicked from a position from which the ball might roll into the end zone, sprint to get into a position to down the ball prior to its entering the end zone. The punter will call "Pop up" on the sideline to alert the coverage of his intention to kick the ball high. If the punter is going to attempt an out-of-bounds punt, the coverage will be notified on the sideline.

When within the 2-minute period and trying to run the clock out, do not down a punted ball. Keep the clock running as long as possible. Just defense the ball and be alert for a man picking it up and returning it!

Fullback: After the ball is kicked, continue downfield—get into the coverage—get behind any wall formed.

Punter: After you kick the ball, become the safety. *Be aware of block from the blind side.*

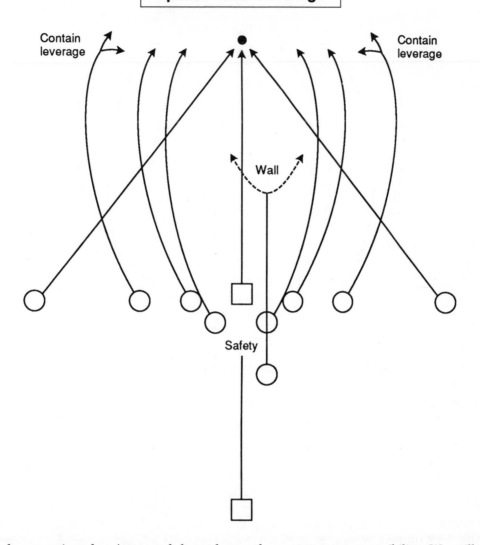

Spread Punt Coverage

Our ends are assigned *sprinters* and *do not* have a lane coverage responsibility. We will utilize a signal from the punter to help you determine the direction of the punt. Sprint to the ball through the inside shoulder.

Our tackles have contain-leverage. With the ball coming toward you, maintain contain—with the ball going away, maintain leverage.

Our guards will force-contain, maintaining outside-in leverage. When the ball goes away, take the position of contain.

Our upbacks will force, maintaining outside-in leverage.

Our center will sprint directly to the ball.

Our FB will cover behind the wall.

Our punter becomes the safety—directly in front of ball.

Attempt to maintain approximately a 5-yard distribution across the field.

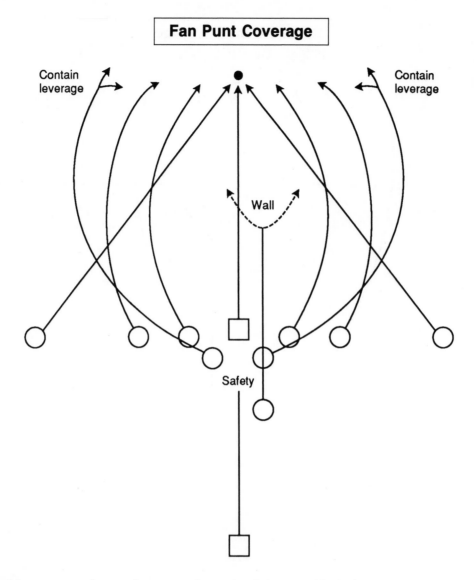

Fan Punt Coverage

Our tackles are now free to force-contain, maintaining outside-in leverage.

Our upbacks now have *contain-leverage*. With the ball coming toward you, maintain contain—ball going away, maintain leverage.

All other coverage is the same as for the spread punt.

This coverage is used when rushers are holding up our upbacks. This call can be made in the huddle or on the line by the upback calling "Fan" to the tackle on his side. He should make the call when using a double technique because he will be late in the coverage or on the backside of a 10-man front—"Switch" call.

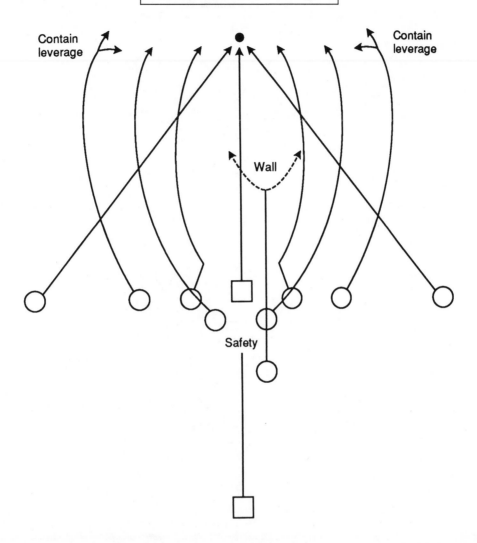

Switch Punt Coverage

Contain leverage

Contain leverage

Wall

Safety

Our guards now release inside and then work back outside.

Our upbacks cover outside through the guards' normal coverage pattern.

All other coverage is the same as for the spread punt.

This coverage is used when rushers are holding up our upbacks and the guards have only one rusher in this area. This call can be made in the huddle or at the line by the guard turning to the upback and calling "Switch."

FAKE PUNTS

In all my years as a head coach, I have never attempted a fake punt that did not work. That sounds like, and is, a pretty outstanding achievement—however, it is something that you can achieve as well. If you are willing to commit the time required for detailed scouting and preparation to properly *execute* all phases of the kicking game, the respect your special teams demand will allow you to take advantage of strategic situations that permit fakes to work.

Following are diagrams and rules on the basic *fake spread punt pass* and *fake punt formation run*. The countless variations on the fake punt are much too extensive to include here. However, you can develop your own innovations based upon the talent and ability in your program by following the rules outlined below.

Fake Punt

Loaded

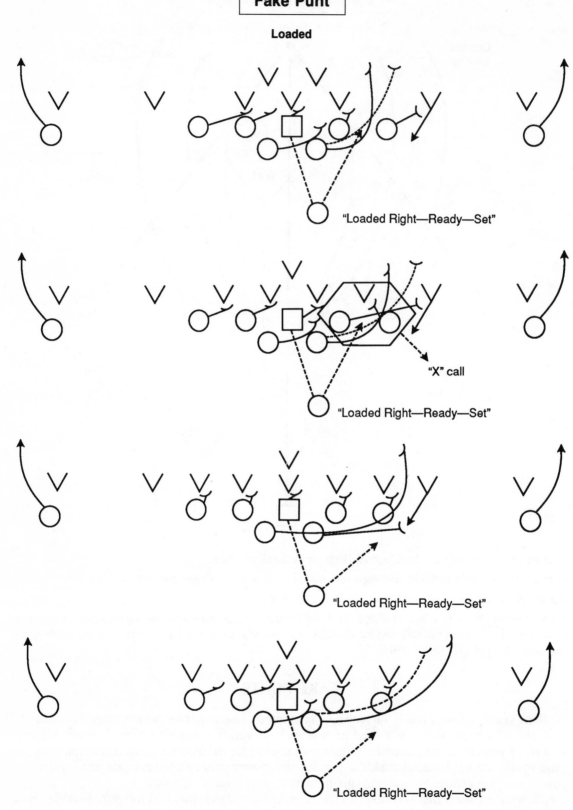

"Loaded Right—Ready—Set"

"X" call

"Loaded Right—Ready—Set"

"Loaded Right—Ready—Set"

"Loaded Right—Ready—Set"

Run Off Tackle or Outside

Sideline call: The predetermined play is called on the sideline. A directional call is made at the line of scrimmage: "Loaded right/left." The play is executed on the command "Ready—Set."

Audible: The alert for the fake play is "Red" (run), or "Blue" (pass). The directional call is then made: "Loaded Right/Left." The play is then executed on the command "Ready—Set."

Omaha: If "Omaha" is called, the fake is now off, and we will *punt*.

Fake Run ("Red")

Assignments:

Ends: Split out and release outside.

Tackles: *Onside:* Block on outside. If there is no one on your nose, check the inside for a possible "Swap" call—cross block with guard.
Backside: Block over outside.

Guards: *Onside:* Block on outside. If the tackle gives you a "Swap" call, acknowledge call—then, on snap, pull and trap block from the tackle outside.
Backside: Block over outside.

Upbacks: Onside: Pull—key off of tackle's block outside-in.
Backside: Pull-block color over outside.

FB: Check front—determine whether fake can be run. Adjust alignment according to call (right or left). Call cadence. Look the snap into the hands. Run off of onside upback's block.

Punter: Fake punt—follow play as safety.

Base

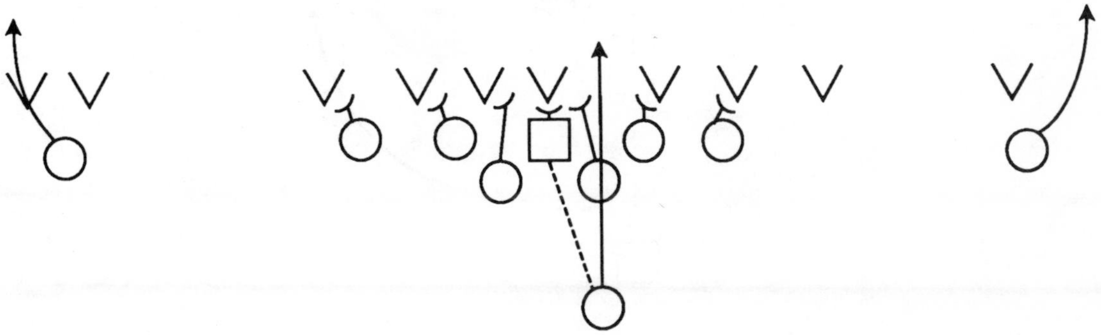

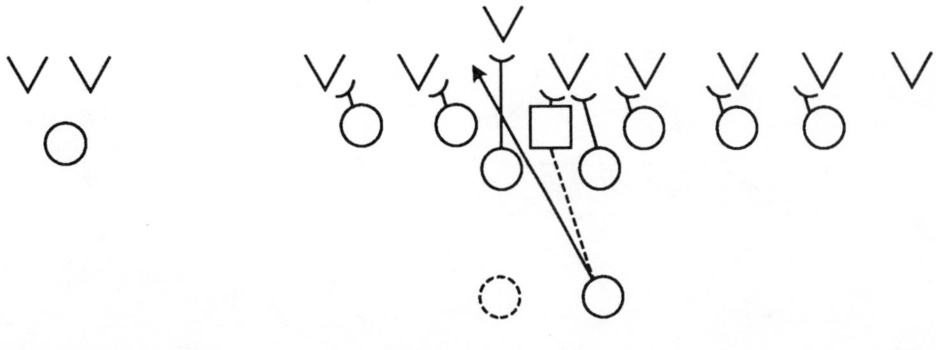

Run Between the Tackles

Sideline call: The predetermined play is called on the sideline. The direction of the play is identified by calling the name of our player at the point of attack, (POA). The play is executed on the command "Ready—Set."

Blocking rule: Head up to outside—away from POA. If there is no one in your area, block most dangerous.

Audible: The alert for the fake play is "Red" (run) or "Blue" (pass). The directional call is then made (*base—player's name—repeat*). The play is then executed on the command "Ready—Set."

Omaha: If "Omaha" is called, the fake is now off, and we will punt on the first "Ready—Set."

Base—player's name—"Ready—Set"

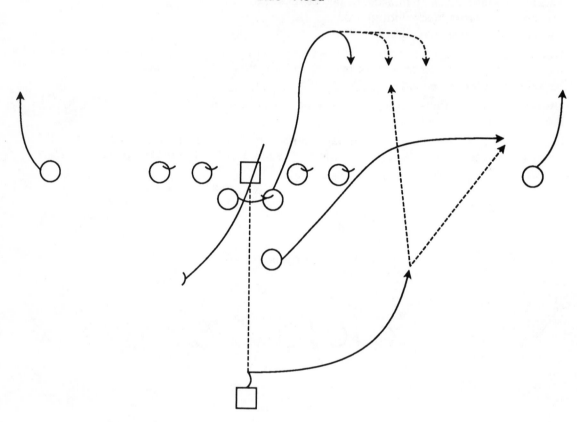

Fake Pass

Blue—Flood

Utilize the same mechanics as for a fake run.

Blue—Screen

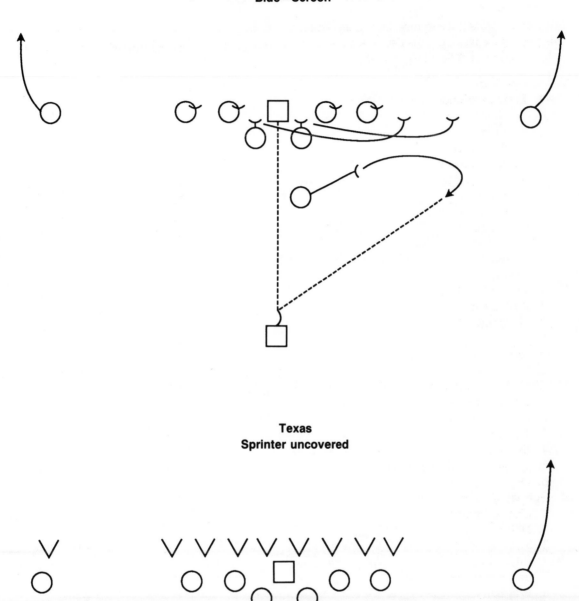

Texas
Sprinter uncovered

Alert:

The FB checks to see whether our ends are covered. If they are not, he calls "Texas," which alerts the punter and end to be ready for a pass. The punter must use his best judgment to determine whether the end is still uncovered after the snap and whether we can make a first down.

PUNTING GAME CHECKLIST

For further assistance in developing as detailed and extensive a punting game as possible, use this personal checklist. This list took a lifetime of coaching, from high school to professional football, to refine and develop—use it well!

A. Spread punt
  1. Basic protection against
     a. 8-man
     b. 9-man
     c. 10-man rush
  2. Hinge protection against
     a. 8-man
     b. 9-man
     c. 10-man rush
  3. Coverages
     a. spread
     b. switch calls—guards, upback, end tackle
     c. fan
B. Tight punt
  1. Protection
  2. Coverage
C. Fake punt
  1. Run
  2. Pass
D. Special situations—Team
  1. Out of end zone
  2. Out of bounds
  3. Taking a safety
  4. Downing the ball inside the 10
  5. Coverage against fair catch
  6. Delayed snap
E. Special situations—Punter
  1. Out of bounds
  2. Hanging ball
  3. With wind
  4. Into wind
  5. Bad snaps—high, low, wide
  6. Wet ball
  7. Taking a safety
  8. Following a safety
F. Special situations—Snapper
  1. Wet ball
  2. Changing snap rhythm
  3. Holding the snap after a defensive shift
G. Changing formations
  1. Regular
  2. Wing
  3. Slot
  4. Man in motion

George Allen's Best

Centers

Ted Fritsch—*Washington Redskins*

Larry Strickland—*Chicago Bears*

George Burman—*Los Angeles Rams*

Len Hauss—*Washington Redskins*

Ken Iman—*Los Angeles Rams*

Charlie Ane—*Detroit Lions*

Jim Ringo—*Green Bay Packers*

Ken Bowman—*Green Bay Packers*

Mik Tinglehoff—*Minnesota Vikings*

Tom Catlin—*Cleveland Browns*

Mike Webster—*Pittsburgh Steelers*

Chuck Bednarik—*Philadelphia Eagles*

Dave Dalby—*Oakland Raiders*

John Rapacz—*Baltimore Colts*

Jim Otto—*Oakland Raiders*

Frank Gatski—*Cleveland Browns*

Punters

Ray Guy—*Oakland Raiders*

Bobby Joe Green—*Chicago Bears*

Mike Bragg—*Washington Redskins*

Yale Lary—*Detroit Lions*

Tommy Davis—*San Francisco Forty Niners*

Bob Waterfield—*Los Angeles Rams*

Norm Van Brocklin—*Los Angeles Rams*

Pat Studstill—*Los Angeles Rams*

Sam Baker—*Dallas Cowboys*

Horace Gillom—*Cleveland Browns*

Jerrel Wilson—*Kansas City Chiefs*

Del Schofner—*New York Giants*

Bobby Walden—*Minnesota Vikings*

Dave Jennings—*New York Giants*

Danny Villanueva—*Los Angeles Rams*

Don Chandler—*Green Bay Packers*

John James—*Atlanta Falcons*

Kickoff and Punt Coverage Men

Rusty Tillman—*Washington Redskins*

Pat Curran—*Los Angeles Rams*

Louie Giammona—*Philadelphia Eagles*

Bob Brunet—*Washington Redskins*

Alex Hawkins—*Baltimore Colts*

J.C. Caroline—*Chicago Bears*

Mike Hull—*Washington Redskins*

Preston Pearson—*Baltimore Colts*

Don Nottingham—*Miami Dolphins*

Jim Jensen—*Miami Dolphins*

John Sciarra—*Philadelphia Eagles*

Bernie McRae—*Chicago Bears*

Brad Dusek—*Washington Redskins*

Roosevelt Taylor—*Chicago Bears*

Pete Wysocki—*Washington Redskins*

Jeffery Severson—*Washington Redskins*

Larry Glueck—*Chicago Bears*

Rocky Bleir—*Pittsburgh Steelers*

Reggie Garrett—*Pittsburgh Steelers*

Walt Sweeney—*San Diego Chargers*

Morris Bradshaw—*Oakland Raiders*

Jeff Barnes—*Oakland Raiders*

Sherman Plunkett—*Baltimore Colts*

Wendall Harris—*Baltimore Colts*

Mickey Zofko—*Detroit Lions*

Dan Dufek—*Seattle Seahawks*

Wilbur Montgomery—*Philadelphia Eagles*

CHAPTER 4

Punt Defense

The punt defense has the potential to gain significant yardage every time the team is on the field. A blocked punt can immediately change the outcome of a game, even to the point of scoring the winning margin of points in what seems like the blink of an eye. A long punt return, the most exciting play in football, can be emotionally devastating to an opponent, as well as lead directly or indirectly to a score. These game-breaking plays require knowledge and concentration by all members of the punt defense unit in order to ensure success.

IMPORTANT PUNT DEFENSE RULES

There are three general types of plays on punt defense: (a) punt returns with coverage hold-ups, (b) punt blocks, and (c) punt prevents. We suggest that you make the plays of all three types look similar in the initial stages. This will minimize your opponents' effectiveness in covering, protecting, and timing for their punts.

A deadly hazard lurks ominously about whenever the punt defense is on the field. That hazard is *mental mistakes*—errors. There are certain errors against which you must instantly guard—errors that not only negate any positive effect an outstanding play may have on your team, but that also can bring about extremely costly consequences, such as loss of ball possession. For a punt defense unit's plays to be effective and productive, everyone on the unit must be highly conscious of avoiding penalties—penalties which follow these errors:

- Roughing the kicker—15-yard penalty (kicking team will get an automatic first down and maintain ball possession)
- Running into the kicker—5-yard penalty (kicking team may get a first down)
- Offside—5-yard penalty (kicking team may get a first down)

- Clipping on runback—15-yard penalty from point of foul or forward progress, whichever is most damaging to the offending team (that could nullify a score and put you in terrible field position instead)
- Clipping or holding prior to change of possession—penalty, plus kicking team retains possession
- Illegal participation (too many men on the field)—15-yard penalty (kicking team will probably get a first down)

These errors can be costly due to the consequences of the ensuing penalty. Two additional mental mistakes that do not involve rule infractions can be, and usually are, immediately devastating. These errors are the most prominent *do nots* in the punt returner's book:

- *Do not* let the ball hit the ground! As we all know, the football has a funny shape that makes it bounce in unpredictable ways. The biggest danger to the receiving team when the ball hits the ground is that it may bounce into a return team player and be legally recovered by the kicking team for what could amount to a gain of 50-yards or more and a first down deep in your territory.
- *Do not* field a punt inside the 10-yard line! The return man should get away from the flight of the ball, pretending to be preparing to catch it (luring coverage men toward him and away from the ball). You must play the odds that favor the ball's being carried into the end zone by its own momentum, thereby avoiding being tackled deep in your territory, or worse.

By keeping these errors constantly in mind and working hard at eliminating them, you can go on to concentrate on proper execution of sound punt defense plays. Knowing the following punt rules will also help you avoid costly errors and mental mistakes.

- *Do not* call a *time-out* if we have less than 11 people on the return team. This penalty can only be assessed against the kicking team.
- The two outside men can release at the snap; all others must hold until the kick. The outside men can be on or off the line of scrimmage, or can become so by motion.
- If the end man is within 2 yards of the offensive tackle, it is legal to cut him at the line of scrimmage (except in high school football).
- If the end is split, he is entitled to the same rules of protection as a wide receiver. (Can be blocked after the kick.)
- A blocked punt that crosses the line of scrimmage is treated as if it hadn't been touched.
- A blocked punt that does not cross the line of scrimmage is a free ball and can be advanced by either team. The kicking team can run or pass in attempting to reach the first-down yard line.
- A punt that has crossed the line of scrimmage and is first touched by the kicking team belongs to the receiving team at that spot. This is "illegal touching."
- Fair catch rules:
  a. Fair catch signal—One hand only is raised, at full arm's length above the head, and waved from side to side.
  b. A fair catch signal applies to any fielder, not just the player making the signal.
  c. A player who signals for a fair catch may not block until the ball touches another player.
  d. No receiver may advance the ball after a fair catch signal, unless it touches the ground or a member of the kicking team—then the ball can be advanced.
  e. Any receiver has the right-of-way to the ball in the air regardless of any signal. (Return men: Go directly to your best fielding position and do not avoid any coverage man.)
  f. The receiving team has these choices following a fair catch:
     — A free kick (punt, dropkick, or placekick)
     — A snap
- Any foul by the defense before the ball is kicked is enforced from the previous spot.
- Roughing the kicker is enforced from the previous spot. It is not a penalty in any of these circumstances:
  a. The rusher touches the ball.

b. The punter started to run and then kicked.
c. The player is blocked into the kicker (such as by the fullback).
d. The ball hits the turf first.

PUNT RETURNS AND RUSHES

During my years as an active coach in professional football, I have seen and coached some outstanding punt returners. When I was with the Chicago Bears, we had one of the all-time best kick returners in Gale Sayers, a potential game-breaker every time he touched the football. In the late '50s, the Los Angeles Rams had an excellent kick returner by the name of Jon Arnett. Arnett was not a racehorse like Sayers, but he had great hands, good balance, and good agility. When we (the Chicago Bears) came into the Los Angeles Coliseum to play the Rams, we gave up 41 points, mainly because Jon Arnett had a field day on punt returns and kickoff returns. Perhaps we underrated Arnett because he did not have exceptional speed, but he could catch the ball well and had good quickness, which gave him the ability to avoid tacklers and get the job done.

In those years, before special teams were given the importance that they have today, the punt return depended upon having that kind of return man on the roster. Return men like Sayers, Arnett, Lenny Moore, and Hugh McElhenny needed just one key block and they were gone! Today, however, it's quite a different ball game. Some professional football head coaches, like Chuck Knox of the Seattle Seahawks, devote as much as 45 percent of their total practice time to working on various phases of special teams play. Now the punt return is a coordinated team effort with detailed plays and specific assignments similar to those of the offense.

The following punt return plays and punt rushes are suited to a variety of circumstances.

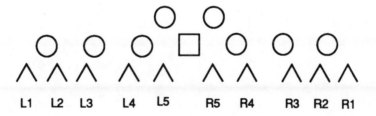

Punt Returns—Rushes

10-man rush

L1 L2 L3   L4 L5   R5 R4   R3 R2 R1

RS

9-man front

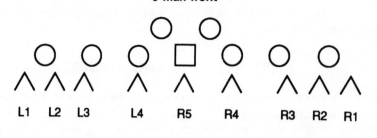

L1   L2   L3   L4   R5   R4   R3   R2   R1

RS

8-man front

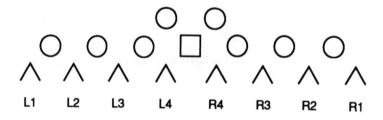

L1   L2   L3   L4   R4   R3   R2   R1

RS

11-man front

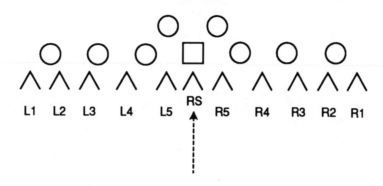

Prevent

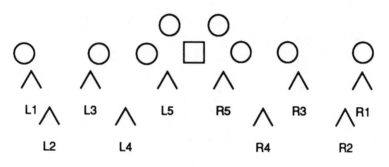

RS

1. We have the ability to utilize 8-9-10-11 or prevent returns.
2. We will refer to our personnel as L1-L2-L3-L4-L5 and R1-R2-R3-R4-R5 and RS (return specialist).
3. Position assignments:

   #1 and #2 positions normally utilize a screen-and-rush technique.

   #3 position utilizes jam, rush, force, contain, and wall techniques.

   #4 and #5 positions normally utilize jam, rush, and wall techniques.

   Blocks will be determined based upon the opponent's blocking scheme.

Punt Returns

Jam return

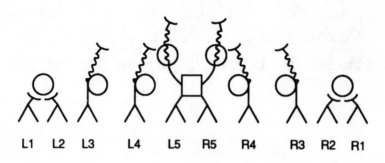

L1   L2   L3   L4   L5   R5   R4   R3   R2   R1

☐

RS

Run from an 8-, 9-, or 10-man front

L1 & L2   Hold up/screen
R1 & R2   Hold up/screen
L3 & R3   Jam/spy/contain
L5 & R5   Jam

Jam right—wall right

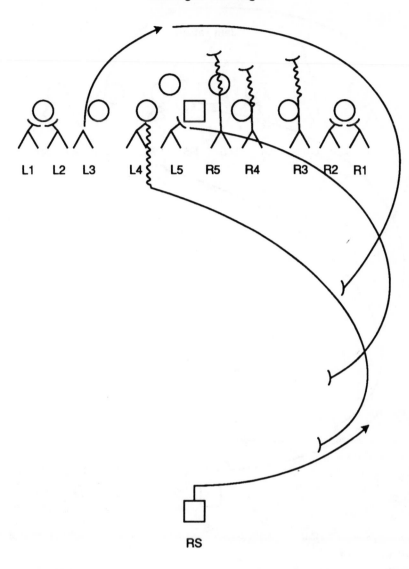

Run from a 9- or 10-man front

L1 & L2 Hold up/screen
L3 Force/wall
L4 Check step/set wall
L5 Jam/wall
R5 Jam
R4 Jam
R3 Jam/spy/contain
R1 & R2 Hold up/screen

Jam left—wall left

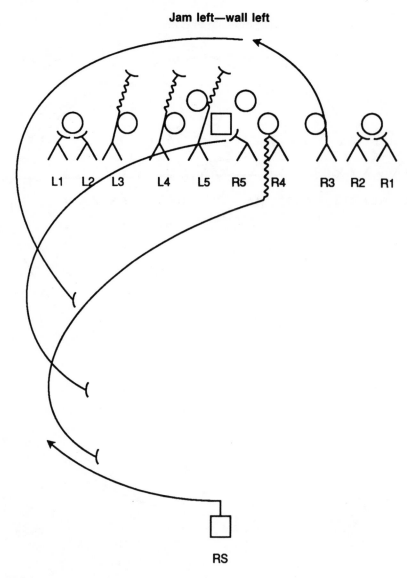

L1 L2 L3 L4 L5 R5 R4 R3 R2 R1

RS

L1 & L2 Hold up/screen
L3 Jam/spy/contain
L4 Jam
L5 Jam
R5 Jam
R4 Check step/set wall
R3 Force/wall
R1 & R2 Hold up/screen

Jam right—rush left

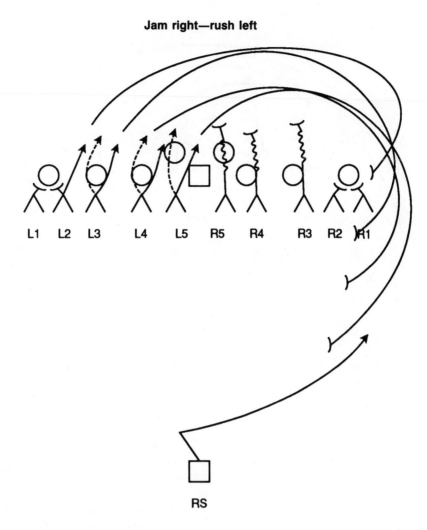

L1 & L2 Hold up/screen rush
L3 Rush/wall
L4 Rush/wall
L5 Rush/wall
R5 Jam
R4 Jam
R3 Jam/spy/contain
R1 & R2 Hold up/screen

Jam left—rush right

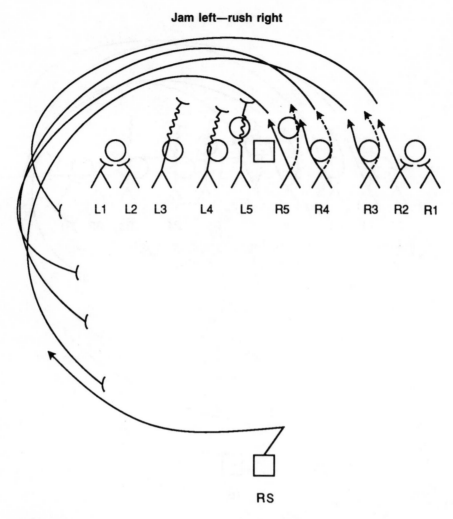

L1 L2 L3   L4 L5 R5 R4   R3 R2 R1

RS

L1 & L2 Hold up/screen
L3 Jam/spy/contain
L4 Jam
L5 Jam
R5 Rush/wall
R4 Rush/wall
R3 Rush/wall
R1 & R2 Hold up/screen/rush

Rush right—wall right

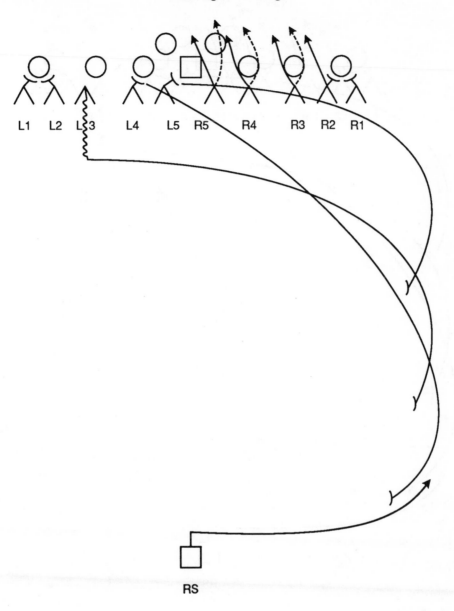

Run from a 9- or 10-man front

L1 & L2   Hold up/screen
L3   Check step/spy/wall
L4   Check step/set/wall
L5   Jam/wall
R5   Rush
R4   Rush
R3   Rush
R1 & R2   Hold up/screen/rush

Rush left—wall left

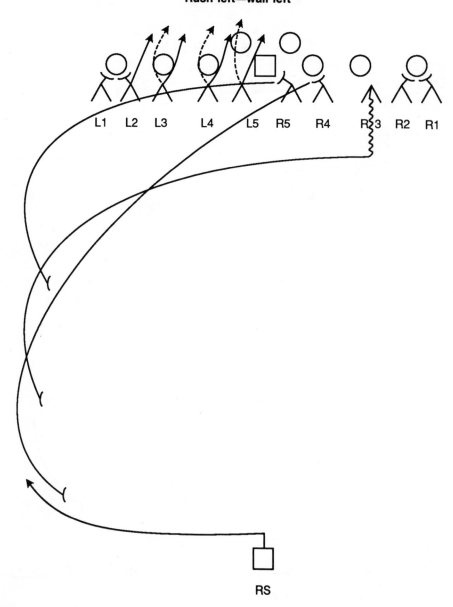

L1 & L2   Hold up/screen/rush
L3   Rush
L4   Rush
L5   Rush
R5   Jam/wall
R4   Check step/set wall
R3   Check step/spy/wall
R1 & R2   Hold up/screen

Middle return

Used from an 8-9-10–man front

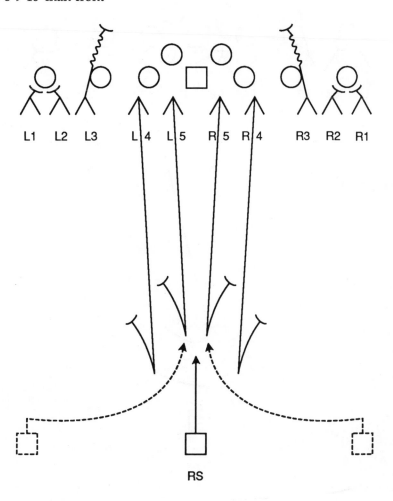

L1 & L2 Hold up/screen
L3 & R3 Jam/spy/contain
L4 & R4 Set return/wedge
L5 & R5 Check step/spy/wedge
R1 & R2 Help up/screen

Middle return right

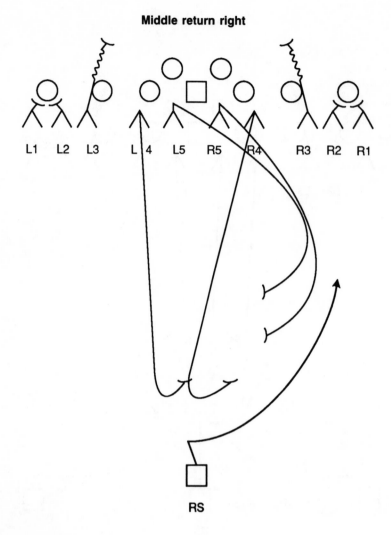

L1 & L2   Hold up/screen
L3 & R3   Jam/spy/contain
L4 & R4   Set wedge right
L5 & R5   Check step/spy/set wall
R1 & R2   Hold up/screen

Middle return left

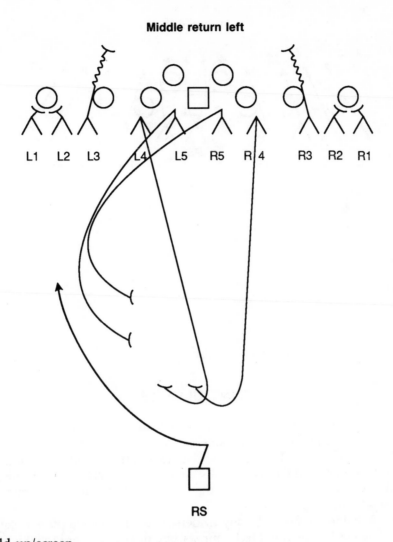

L1 & L2 Hold up/screen
L3 & R3 Jam/spy/contain
L4 & R4 Set wedge left
L5 & R5 Check step/spy/set wall
R1 & R2 Hold up/screen

11-man rush

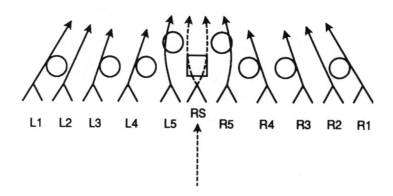

L1 & L2   Rush
L3 & L4   Rush
L5 & R5   Rush
R4 & R3   Rush
R2 & R1   Rush
R5   Rush

PUNT BLOCKS

After a 104-yard kickoff return by Travis Williams of the Green Bay Packers in the 1967 season's second Rams-Packers game, the Rams' sideline was like a morgue. If we lost that game, we would be out of the playoffs. We (the Rams) had to beat the Packers who held the championship, and then the undefeated Baltimore Colts the following week, to reach the championship game. As head coach of the Rams, I thought that we needed an heroic effort by someone to win this game—time was running out on us.

With 54 seconds left in the game, Donny Anderson, the left-footed punter, came in to punt. We had worked all week with Tom Mack, our starting offensive guard (who was *not* a punter, but was the only left-footed player on the squad), trying to imitate Anderson. The work paid off as Tony Guillory came up the middle scott-free, as we had planned, and with perfect form, to block the punt. Claude Crabb picked up the loose ball and returned it to the 5-yard line. Then, with 34 seconds remaining, Roman Gabriel hit Bernie Casey with the winning touchdown pass. In 25 seconds had we turned a devastating loss into an urgently needed win—with a punt block!

The following punt block plays present opportunities for your team to take advantage of your opponent's punt team weaknesses and create overloads and mismatches that can work for you in preparing punt blocks for each game.

There are a few things to stress during the practice of punt block plays. First, remember that if the opponent gets his punt away against a punt block attempt, you must automatically convert to a return. While practicing this, get your players to hustle to their designated positions.

Next, in certain situations, particularly on partially blocked punts and shanked punts, you often will not want to risk fielding the ball. With the Redskins we used to use the call ''Peter,'' which meant we did not want to touch the ball downfield. During practice, teach your players when they hear ''Peter'' (or any call you wish) to look for the ball and get away from it.

Finally, many punt block situations will require a 10-man front committed to the rush on a single safety with no blockers. These situations may require a precalled fair catch. Be sure that your safety is aware of these situations and knows whether an unblocked or partially blocked punt should be fair caught or avoided.

81 Punt Block

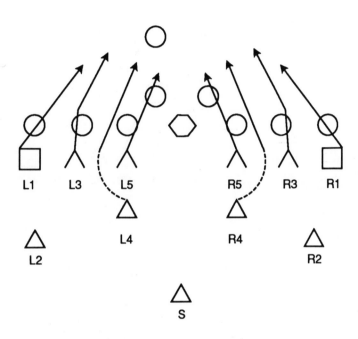

L5 & R5 Drive hard through the gap just to the inside of the guard.

L3 & R3 Drive hard just outside the shoulder of the tackle.

L1 & R1 Drive hard either inside or outside of the end.

L4 & R4 Stem to the guard-tackle gap and drive through it hard on the snap.

L2 & R2 Dog the ends and block them inside-out. They are your responsibility on a pass. If the ends block, you can adjust and block the middle coverers if they are downfield first.

Safety: Field the punt.

82 Punt Block

Overload right

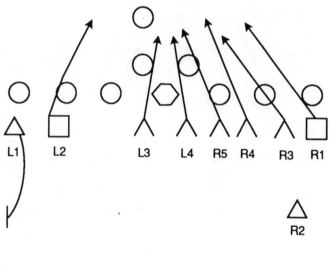

R1   Drive the gap inside the end.

R3   Drive through the area vacated by the tackle if he blocks down on the right tackle or R4.

R4   Drive the gap between tackle and guard.

R5   Drive the gap between guard and upback.

L4   Line up to your right of center. Drive the gap between center and upback.

L3   Line up to your left of center. Drive the gap between center and upback.

L2   Rush the punter just ouside of the tackle.

L1   Line up on the end. Dog him from the inside out. He is your responsibility on a pass.

R2   Key the end. Cover him on a pass. Block him from the inside out if he releases on coverage. If he blocks, you can pick up a man covering up the middle.

Safeties: Field the kick if it comes to you. Block if it goes to the other safety.

Overload left

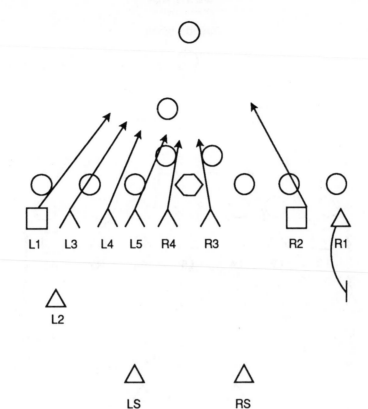

L1   L3   L4   L5   R4   R3   R2   R1

L2

LS   RS

L1   Drive the gap inside the end.

L3   Drive through the area vacated by the tackle if he blocks down on the left tackle or *L4*.

L4   Drive the gap between tackle and guard.

L5   Drive the gap betewen guard and upback.

R4   Line up to your left on center. Drive the gap between center and upback.

R3   Line up to your right of center. Drive the gap between center and upback.

R2   Rush the punter just outside of tackle.

R1   Line up on the end. Dog him from the inside out. He is your responsibility on a pass.

L2   Key the end. Cover him on a pass. Block him inside-out if he releases on coverage. If he blocks, you can pick up a man covering up the middle.

Safeties: Field the kick if it comes to you. Block if it goes to the other safety.

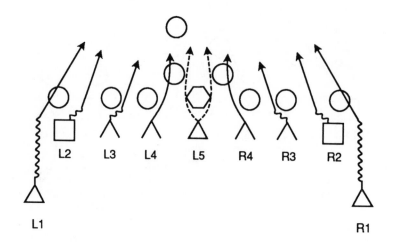

L4 & R4 Drive through the gap between guard and upback.

L3 & R3 On stem shade the inside shoulder of the tackle. Drive the gap to his inside.

L2 & R2 Stem to the gap inside of the end. Drive the gap inside of the end.

L5 Drive the gap to either side of the center.

L1 & R1 Stem to the line of scrimmage. Rush hard through the area vacated by their end if he blocks.

Safeties: Field the punt if it's to you. Block if it's to the other safety.

Inside block

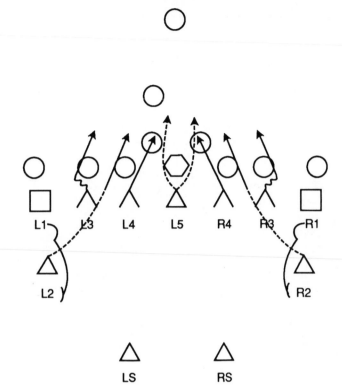

L4 & R4   Drive through the gap inside of the guard.

L3 & R3   Drive through the area just outside of the tackle. Stem out just before the snap.

L1 & R1   Fake a rush. Dog the ends from the inside out. They are your responsibility on passes.

L2 & R2   Stem to the gap between guard and tackle. Drive hard through this gap on the snap.

L5   Drive the gap to either side of the center.

Safeties: Field the punt if it's to you. Block if it's to the other safety.

Gut block

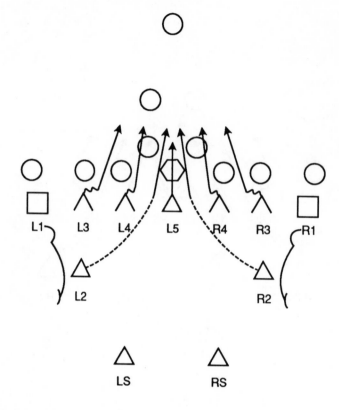

L4 & R4 Stem to the inside shoulder of the guard. Drive the gap between guard and upback.

L3 & R3 Stem to the inside shoulder of the tackle. Drive the gap just inside of the tackle.

L5 Drive *hard* over the center. Tee off on him in order to force a bad snap.

L1 & R1 Fake a rush. Dog the end from the inside out. He is your responsibility on a pass.

L2 & R2 Stem to the gap just to your side of the center. Drive the gap between the center and upback.

Safeties: Field the ball if it comes to you. Block if it is to the other safety.

10-Man Punt Block

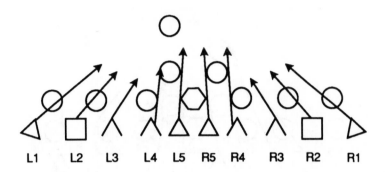

| L1 | L2 | L3 | L4 | L5 | R5 | R4 | R3 | R2 | R1 |

△

S

L4 & R4 Drive the gap between guard and upback.

L3 & R3 Drive the gap between guard and tackle.

L2 & R2 Drive hard through the area vacated by the tackle if he blocks down.

L5 & R5 Drive hard through the gap between center and upback.

L1 & R1 Drive hard through the area vacated by the end if he blocks down.

Safety: Field the Punt.

9-Man Punt Block

Overload left

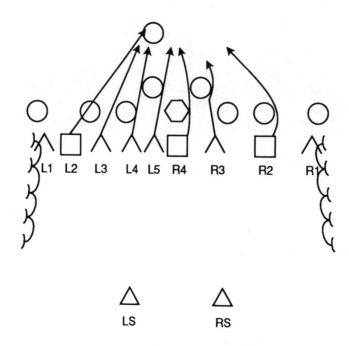

L2   Charge over the outside foot of the tackle.

L3   Charge over the outside foot of the guard.

L4   Sprint between the UB and guard.

L5   Line up between the center and right guard, and sprint between the VB and center.

R4   Sprint to the right of the center.

R3   Sprint to the outside of the UB.

R2   Force from the outside of the tackle.

L1 & R1   Fake rush. On the snap, cover the ends. When the ball is kicked, block the ends out.

Safeties: One safety will designate the receiver.

Blockers: Extend for block.

Everyone: *Do not rough kicker.* Don't clip, and don't be offside.

Don't forget that once you have carried out your punt block responsibilities, you now switch to a punt return possibility.

Overload right

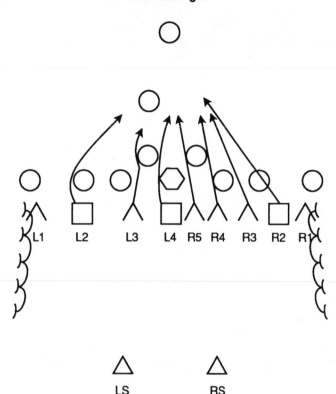

L2   Charge through outside shoulder. Cover the outside for run.

L3   Charge through the outside shoulder of UB, and cover to the outside for run.

L4   Charge to the outside and left side of center; continue to the outside of FB, trying to make him commit to you.

R5   Charge to the inside of UB; continue to FB, trying to make him commit to you.

R4   Charge at FB, and make him commit to you. If FB is blocking someone else, continue for block.

R3   Sprint through the gap between guard and tackle. Sprint for a spot 3 or 4 yards in front of the kicker. Be prepared to block the punt.

R2   Sprint for a spot 3 or 4 yards in front of the kicker. Be prepared to block the punt.

L1 & R1   Fake rush—drop back and cover the end. Block him when the ball is kicked.

Safeties: One safety will designate the receiver. Blocker will block the first man downfield.

Note: If the punt is not blocked, return is automatically to the right.

Blockers: Extend for block.

Do not rough kicker—don't clip—don't be offside!

Don't forget that once you have carried out your punt block responsibilities, you now switch to a punt return responsibility.

PUNT PREVENTS

The prevent is to be used when you have the game won, or in any situation when you want to *ensure* that your opponent punts the ball and you avoid committing any errors. You are essentially allowing your opponent to punt the ball—and nothing else!

The following prevent plays present variations on the concept of forcing a punt.

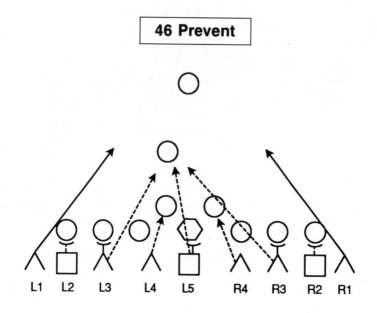

46 Prevent

L1 L2 L3 L4 L5 R4 R3 R2 R1

LS   RS

L1 & R1 Line up wide—drive for the punter, under control. Contain the ball and ensure that the ball is kicked on rhythm.

L2 & R2 Key the ends—you are responsible for them on a pass.

L3 & R3 Key through the tackles to the FB. Alert for a fake.

L4 & R4 Key the upbacks—you are responsible for them on a pass. Also, they will frequently take you to the ball on a fake run.

L5 Key through the center to the FB—play the center softly.

Safeties: Field the punt only if there are no problems: rushers near you, easy kick, etc.—otherwise let the ball go.

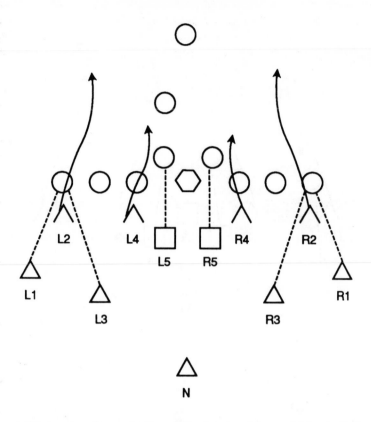

40 Nickel Prevent

L2 & R2 Pressure the punter through the ends, forcing him to kick on time. Contain him in the event of a fake. *Do not think in terms of blocking the kick, and be certain to keep containment leverage on the punter!*

L4 & R4 Rush the punter through the guards. Think in terms of reacting to a fake.

L5 & R5 Cover the upback on your side man to man. He is your responsibility on a pass. If the ball is kicked, dog the upback, blocking him at your discretion.

L1 & L3 Play inside-outside coverage on their RE. If the ball is kicked, block him.

R1 & R3 Play inside-outside coverage on their LE. If the ball is kicked, block him.

Nickel back: Field the ball.

Coaching points:
1. This is a *prevent* defense. We want them to punt, and we are *not* thinking in terms of blocking it.
2. When ball is punted, our return will be to the wide field. If in middle of the field, the return is automatically to the right.

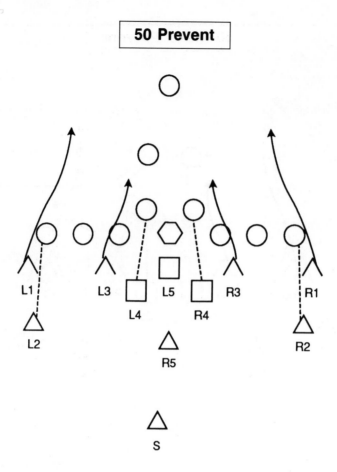

L1 & R1   Pressure and contain.

L3 & R3   Force the kick.

L5   Hold up the center—alert for run.

L4 & R4   Key upbacks for pass possibility. If the ball is kicked, block them.

L2 & R2   Key the ends for pass possibility. If the ball is kicked, block them.

R5   Free inside to back up L4 & R4—protect S if the ball is punted.

Safety: Field the ball if it is punted. Back up L2 & R2 if a pass is attempted.

Note: If the ball is punted, the return will be to the wide field and to the right from midfield.

George Allen's Best

Punt Returners

Eddie Brown—*Washington Redskins*
Jon Arnett—*Los Angeles Rams*
Alvin Haymond—*Los Angeles Rams*
Johnny Morris—*Chicago Bears*
Willie Wood—*Green Bay Packers*
Billy Johnson—*Houston Oilers*
Speedy Duncan—*Washington Redskins*
Eddie Meador—*Los Angeles Rams*
Rick Upchurch—*Denver Broncos*
Mike Nelms—*Washington Redskins*
Terry Metcalf—*Saint Louis Cardinals*

Charlie West—*Minnesota Vikings*
Bob Hayes—*Dallas Cowboys*
Tommy Casanova—*Cincinnati Bengals*
Bill Dudley—*Washington Redskins*
Jack Christiansen—*Detroit Lions*
Johnny Roland—*Saint Louis Cardinals*
Emlen Tunnell—*New York Giants*
Greg Pruitt—*Oakland Raiders*
Joe Arenas—*San Francisco Forty Niners*
Lynn Swan—*Pittsburgh Steelers*

Punt and Kick Returners

Alvin Haymond—*Washington Redskins*

Bruce Harper—*New York Jets*

Punt Blockers

Tony Guillory—*Los Angeles Rams*
Bill Malinchak—*Washington Redskins*
Matt Blair— *Minnesota Vikings*
Erich Barnes—*Cleveland Browns*

Ted Hendricks—*Green Bay Packers*
Gary Lewis—*Green Bay Packers*
J.T. Thomas—*Pittsburgh Steelers*
Nolan Cromwell—*Los Angeles Rams*

CHAPTER 5

Kickoff

A kickoff, any kickoff, is the purest form of defense. There are four basic types of kickoffs: deep, squib, pop-up, and onside. In each case, the kicking team will try to control the return possibilities by the placement of the kick (left, middle, or right) in combination with the type of kick used. However, the key to any successful kickoff is the coverage. The onside kick is generally used as a surprise tactic or in desperate circumstances in an effort to maintain possession of the football after a score (most often because the kicking team is behind late in the game), but even this kick requires the same type of planned coverage to safeguard against a return.

Certain kickoff formations may occasionally be a factor in the overall success of a kickoff unit, but no matter how you disguise it or where you kick the football, unless the coverage is good, the kickoff will not be successful.

THE LEADERSHIP SQUAD

One year, when I was coaching the Pro Bowl, we scored a go-ahead touchdown late in the fourth quarter and were leading the Tom Landry–coached all-star team by only three points. I was on our sideline getting the kickoff coverage team together (in those all-star games, coaches rarely have their starting linemen covering kicks). "Deacon" Jones, one of the best defensive ends ever to play the game, came up to me, accompanied by Merlin Olsen, Alan Page, Karl Eller, and Jim Marshall, also all perennial all-pros, and said they would like to cover this kickoff. They had all agreed that it was very important not to allow our opponent to get good field position. You must understand that "Deacon" Jones and Alan Page could run with anyone, and the others were only a short step behind; when you place your best players, particularly great defensive linemen of this caliber, on a kickoff coverage unit, they do not get blocked very often. I also felt it was an extremely important kickoff situation (particularly because the difference between winning and losing the game was, at that time, $2,500 per man), and I agreed to let them do it.

These players went down the field, stayed on their feet, and worked for the tackle. The opposing team returned the ball up the middle, and the runner was stopped inside the 20-yard line. Some of the players on the opposing return team told me after the game that they couldn't believe all these all-pro superstars were covering that final kickoff, which we won as a result by a score of 10 to 7.

I have always had a great deal of admiration for athletes with this kind of leadership. Whether they are motivated by pride, money, or simply the desire to be the best at what they do, leaders like David "Deacon" Jones always know that *critical situations* demand the positive attitude and commitment of "take-charge" players. The kickoff coverage unit of that situation, in that pro-bowl game, is the same as any kickoff coverage unit anywhere (high school, college, or pro), at any time, in any game. Every kickoff is a *critical situation* and, as a head coach, you have a mandate to develop a group of athletes for your coverage unit who reflect the positive attitude and commitment required for success—a leadership squad!

If you properly develop this kind of leadership in some of your better athletes (whether starters or backup players) to man a kickoff coverage team, that coverage team will become a source of pride for the entire team, making it an honor to be selected for that special unit. It is just such team unity and pride that spell the difference between mediocrity and excellence in kickoff coverage team play, specifically, and overall team play in general.

KICKOFF RULES AND PRINCIPLES

One of the first things required of leaders, particularly on a football special team unit, is that they know the rules and principles for that specific area of play. This helps them guide others to reach the level of execution required for excellence.

Rules

The following rules should be clearly known and understood by all of your leadership squad.

- If a kick does not travel 10 yards, it is an invalid kick and must be recovered by the kicking team, or the ball will belong to the receiving team if they recover it at that point.
- If the ball is touched by the receiving team, including before it has traveled 10 yards, it is a free ball.
- If the kickoff goes out of bounds, or is recovered by the kicking team before traveling 10 yards, it is kicked again following a 5-yard penalty.
- Once a kickoff travels 10 yards, it is a free ball and belongs to the recovering team at the point of recovery.
- If the ball is recovered in the end zone by the kickoff team, it is a touchdown.
- On a kickoff, the kicking team may catch the ball in midair, if no receiver is in the area. However, the kicking team may not advance the kick.
- If there is a receiver in position to catch the ball in the air, he has right-of-way to the ball.
- The kickoff receiving team may fair-catch the ball, and all fair catch rules apply.
- Before the last 2 minutes, the clock starts when the ball is kicked; during the last 2 minutes, the clock starts when the ball is legally touched in the field of play.
- A punt is allowed after a safety; a placekick or dropkick is allowed after a field goal or touchdown.
- A free kick after a fair catch calls for lineup just as on any kickoff. However, no tee may be used, and a field goal can be scored. After such a free kick, treat the ball downfield exactly like a field goal attempt. (The kicking team cannot gain possession unless the ball is first touched by the receiving team.)

Principles

In addition to knowing kickoff rules, there are certain principles that the kickoff team must follow.

- Covering a kickoff requires an all-out sprint. Speed is important, but the intent to make the tackle is even more important!
- Stay in the assigned coverage lanes if at all possible!
- Initially defense the field. Once the return has been defined, defense the football!
- If you are forced out of your lane, get back into it as soon as possible or fill a vacant lane ahead of you!
- If you are knocked down, become a linebacker and back up the front line!
- If a man inside of you is knocked down, move in and fill his lane. He will get up and fill the vacant lane!
- It is not a shame to get knocked down, but it is a *crime* to stay down! Many tackles are made by a man who has gotten up after being knocked down!
- Approach the ball through your inside shoulder.
- The first man down very seldom makes the tackle, so keep coming! Usually all the first tackler will do is set up the ball carrier for the hit! Create the fumble!
- Come to balance as you get to the breaking point 4 to 5 yards in front of the ball carrier. If you are the first man to get to a wedge, cut down as many of them as possible!
- Do not overrun the ball.
- A tackle should never be made by one man!
- The coverage goal is, first to keep the ball inside the 20-yard line and, second, to create a turn-over!
- *Remember*. Any ball that has traveled 10 yards is a *live* ball. You cannot advance it, so ensure its recovery!
- *Never* assume a ball will not be returned out of the end zone.
- Be alert to down a ball in the end zone if for some reason the safety lets the ball roll dead and fails to down it himself!

FUNDAMENTAL ELEMENTS OF COVERAGE

Once you have selected and developed your leadership squad, you can begin to teach the fundamental elements of kickoff coverage. Developing controlled aggression, basic attack fundamentals, and sound plays are essential for effective kickoff coverage.

Controlled Aggression

This is the most aggressive play in football, so the first element to be developed is a *controlled aggression*, which combines physical aggressiveness with carefully trained mental control.

The following coverage techniques should be taught for proper kickoff coverage. This is a concise list of important coaching points to be used in the teaching process.

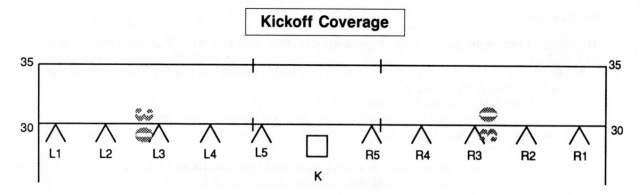

Note: For high school and college the ball will be kicked from the 40-yard line and the team should line-up on the 35-yard line. All other assignments apply, allowing for the 5 yard difference (throughout this chapter).

Types of kickoffs

1. Deep, with emphasis on hang time and distance.
2. Deep, with squib emphasis on action on ball creating problems in handling.
3. Pop-up, with emphasis on accuracy into a void area.
4. Onside, with emphasis on action and direction.
5. Punt, following a safety, with emphasis on hang time and direction.

Alignments

#1 3 yards from sideline, inside foot on 30-yard line.

#2 3 yards outside numbers, inside foot on 30-yard line.

#3 On inside numbers, inside foot on 30-yard line.

#4 4 yards outside hash, inside foot on 30-yard line.

#5 On inside hash, inside foot on 30-yard line.

Mechanics

Stance: Turned at 90 degrees with hands on knees.

Takeoff: Anticipate kicker's rhythm and be 1 yard behind him when the ball is kicked—sprint.

Vision: Cover with speed, maintaining good peripheral vision and anticipation of where the ball is going.

Coverage: Anticipate where the ball is going, but do not start to converge until you are up the field through your lane and we have covered the field (approximately 35 yards).

Note: If your own color crosses in front of you, anticipate moving outside to cover that void—don't follow your color—own your lane!

Converge: After covering through your lane and up the field, start to converge to the ball by attacking through the blocker's shoulder in the appropriate direction of the return man—attack the ball carrier with your inside shoulder—keep the ball in front of you as you close the gap.

Contain: The assigned people for contain must be disciplined to maintain their course and be sure that nothing gets outside them.

Safeties: Sprint up the field through your lane—start to come to balance at approximately the 35-yard line—maintain leverage on the ball and don't get caught up in the traffic—hand fight and maintain a cushion until you get to the ball—as the safety *you must* make the stop.

Contact: The first man down makes an all-out effort to make the stop—let it all out. The second wave should come to the balance point (4-5 yards from ball) maintaining the converge principles. The third wave or cleanup should emphasize knocking the ball carrier back and stripping the ball.

Attack Fundamentals

The second element to be developed is basic *attack fundamentals* essential to good coverage, with particular emphasis on "attacking the wedge" on a middle return. Breaking up the wedge, particularly on a strong middle return, is the key to stopping the returner before he can break out into the open field. These basic coverages include almost every contingency and tie into the wedge-busting technique in the first diagram.

Attacking the Wedge—Middle Return

Responsibilities

#1 Contain—if the ball is outside the wedge to your side.
Leverage—if the ball carrier turns toward the far hash.
Safety—if the ball is between the far hash and sideline—cover your two thirds of the field.

#2 Force—if the ball is within the wedge—attack outside-in.

#3 Attack the ball outside-in. Hand fight across and behind wedge busters when the ball is away from you—close gaps between #4 and #5 as you move across the wedge

#4 and #5 Attack through the wedge gaps to the ball.

Kicker Maintain a 15- to 20-yard cushion to wedge and play safety. Follow the movement of the ball carrier on proper pursuit angle.

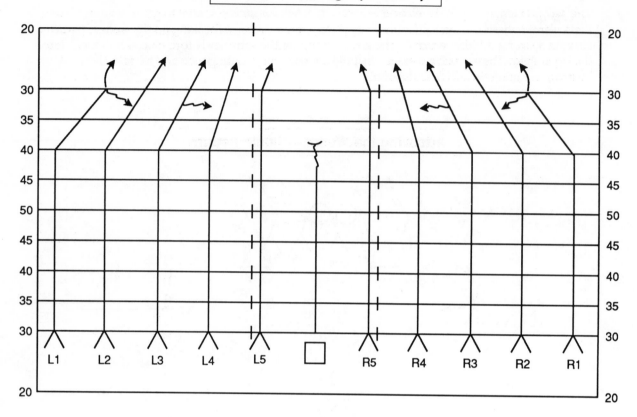

Responsibilities

#1 Contain—if the ball is outside the numbers leverage.
Leverage—if the ball is between the onside number and the far hash.
Safety—if the ball is outside the far hash and sideline—cover two thirds of the field.
L1 & R1—You will spot the ball (wind problem), then assume responsibilities.

#2 Force—if the ball is outside the numbers.
Force/contain—if the ball is inside the near number. Don't let the ball outside you—attack outside-in.

#3 Attack the ball outside-in. Hand fight across and behind the first wave when the ball is away from you (become linebacker). Hard fight the wedge and close gaps behind #4 & #5.

#4 and #5 Own your lane! You must penetrate beyond your intended blocker. Watch for cross blocks. Attack through the wedge to the ball. You set the tempo for our coverage.

Kicker After the kick be aware of blindside blocks. You are our middle safety with the ball between the numbers. If the ball is outside the number you become the safety to that side and responsible for one third of the field. Maintain an approximate 15- to 20-yard cushion from our front line. Hard fight—don't get knocked off your feet—buy time—make the tackle.

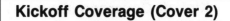

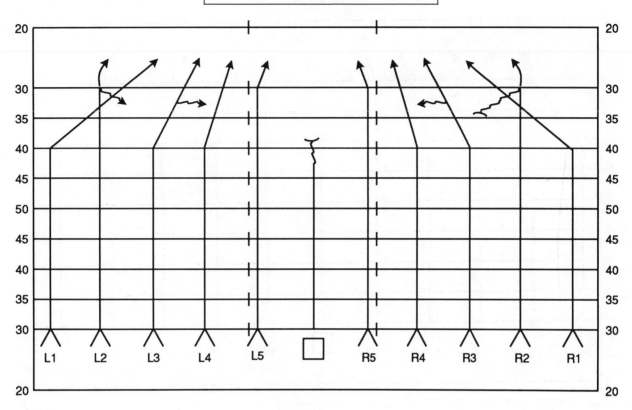

Responsibilities

The responsibilities are the same as for cover 1 except that we switch alignments between #1 and #2. #1 aligns in #2 position, and #2 aligns in #1 position. #1 must cross in front of #2 but only after covering up the field 20-25 yards.

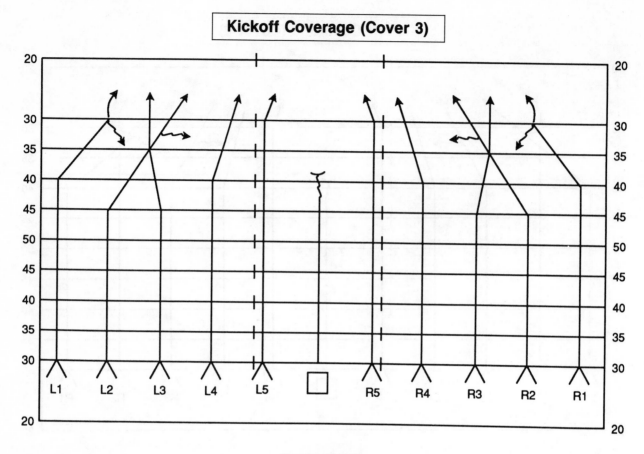

Responsibilities

The responsibilities are the same as for cover 1 except that we switch alignments between #2 & #3. #2 aligns in #3 position, and #3 aligns in #2 position. #2 must cross in front of #3 but only after covering upfield 20-25 yards. #2 aligns in #3 position, and #3 aligns in #2 position. #2 must cross in front of #3 but only after covering upfield 20-25 yards.

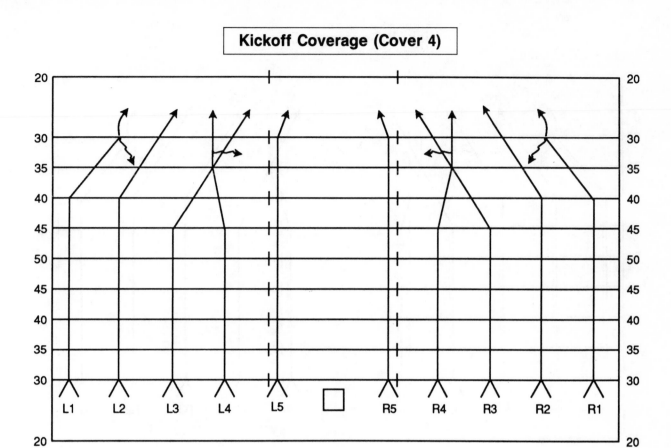

Kickoff Coverage (Cover 4)

Responsibilities

The responsibilities are the same as for cover 1 except that we switch alignments between #3 and #4. #3 aligns in #4 position, and #4 aligns in #3 position. #3 must cross in front of #4 but only after covering upfield 20-25 yards.

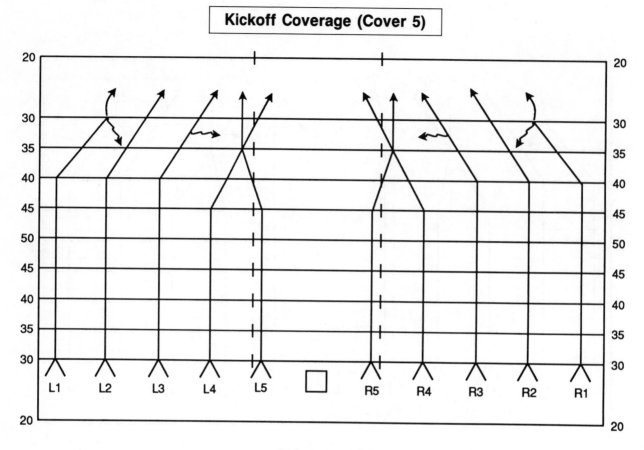

Kickoff Coverage (Cover 5)

Responsibilities

The responsibilities are the same as for cover 1 except that we switch alignments between #4 and #5. #4 aligns in #5 position, and #5 aligns in #4 position. #4 must cross in front of #5 but only after covering upfield 20-25 yards.

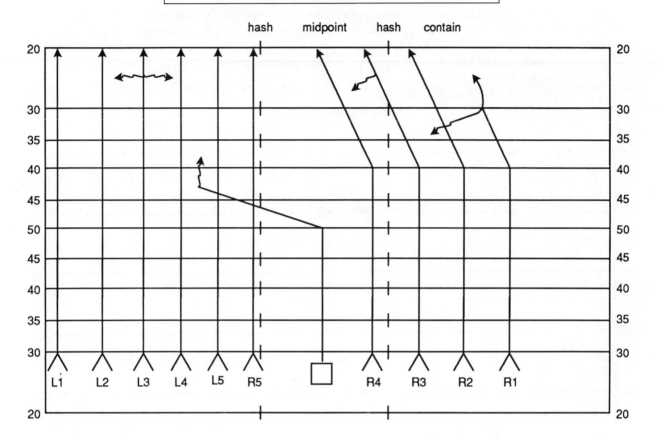

Kickoff Coverage (Sideline Left or Right)

Responsibilities

The responsibilities are the same as for cover 1 except that we now slide over one man in the predetermined direction of the kick. We will slide over on the kicker's command so that the opponent can't adjust at the last moment. With six people working from the hash outside, the ball carrier normally will attempt to get outside by crossing the field. Therefore, #5, #4, #3, and #2 to the backside *must* go to their respective sprint spots before converging on the ball.

Constant and repetitive work should be done until the following actions become instinctive for all coverage personnel:

- Get a good takeoff; all coverage men, except the safeties, should be running full speed 1 yard behind the ball when it is kicked.
- Maintain a good lateral relationship; lane protectors must maintain the integrity of their areas; early in coverage they may run around blocks, but deep in coverage they must take on the blockers.
- Contain men must be sure to keep the play to their inside; they must never be lured to the inside of a potential blocker.
- Go all out; do not slow up or let up; get to the return man as deep in his territory as you can—full speed all the way.
- Close and tackle; know when to "settle" and square up and when to "rocket" into a tackle.
- Explosive tackling; develop proper technique for exploding into a tackle—it can create turnovers.

Sound Plays

The final fundamental element of kickoff coverage is the development and practice of *sound kick-off plays*. The following plays and assignments can form the basis for any number of variations that you wish to create. They will work equally well for deep kicks or squib kicks and provide a sound concept of kickoff protection for you to use in developing a complete kickoff package.

Kickoff—Middle

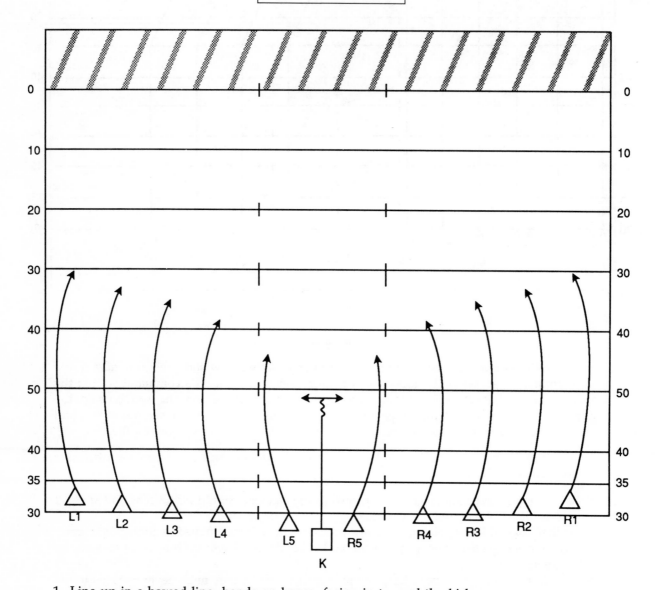

1. Line up in a bowed line, hands on knees, facing in toward the kicker.
2. Spacing is 3-1/2 yards between each man. L1 and R1 are 3-1/2 yards in from sideline.
3. When the kicker passes your line of vision, take off in pace closely behind the kicker. No one offside.
4. Go down as fast as possible, maintaining proper lateral spacing. Be ready to react to the ball.
5. Swing the gate closed on the returner.
6. Kicker pull out as safety. Slide laterally to stay in a direct line between the ball carrier and your goal line.
7. L1 and R1 must not let runner get outside. Keep him contained.

Kickoff—Double Sprinter

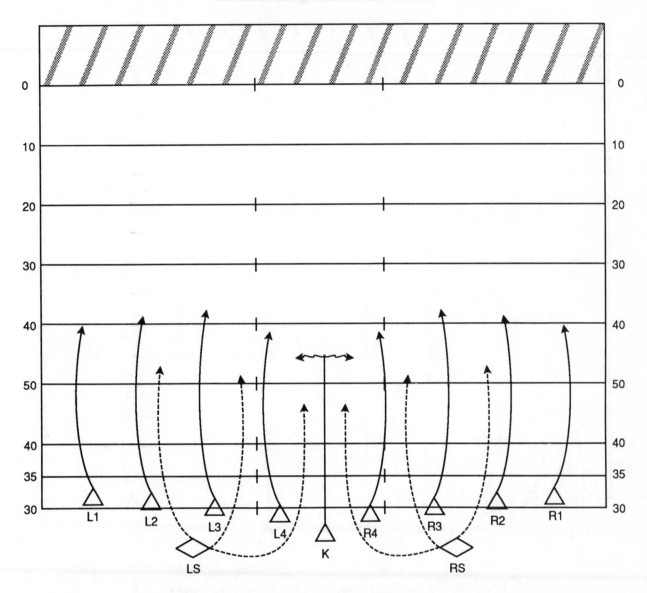

1. Line up in a bowed line, hands on knees, facing in toward the kicker.

2. Sprinters—line up approximately parallel to the kicker in a fluid position between #2 and #3 on your side. Move about to disguise your intentions.

3. L1 and R1 line up 4 yards from sideline.

4. Coverers on each side line up 5 yards from each other. Kicker is lined up 3 yards from L4 and R4.

5. Sprinters—time your forward move so that you are gaining forward momentum when the kicker moves toward the ball.

6. Sprinters will cover through the lane between #2 and #3, #3 and #4, or #4 and kicker on their side. Other coverers adjust to maintain good lateral spacing as they cover.

7. Sprinters can go directly to the ball from the outside in.

8. The kicker is a safety. Pull out and get on a line directly between the ball carrier and your own goal line.

9. L1 and R1 must not let the ball carrier get outside. Keep him contained.

Kickoff—Right Hashmark

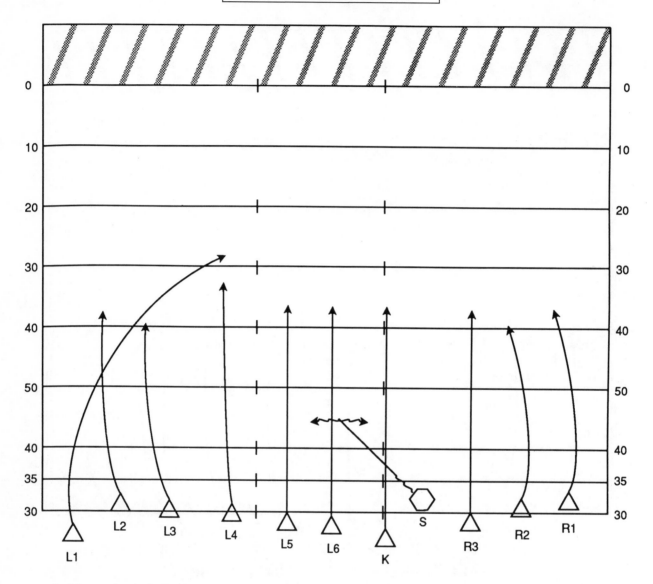

1. Line up in a bowed line, hands on knees, facing in toward the kicker.

2. Spacing is 4 yards between all numbered men (this includes the kicker).

3. The safety lines up in a position to approach the ball for an onside kick but not obstructing any coverer.

4. Numbers L1 and R1 line up 4 yards from the sideline.

5. The sprinter is L1. He lines up parallel with the kicker so he can get more of a running start.

6. The sprinter takes a course whereby he swoops outside-in at the ball carrier.

7. Numbers L2 and R1 are the contain men. Do not allow the ball carrier to get outside.

8. The safety approaches the ball in timing with the kicker, to threaten the onside kick. After a regular kick, the safety must stay on a line between the ball carrier and our goal line.

9. All coverers maintain good lateral relationship.

Note: Numbering on hashmark kickoffs is straight across, counting from the side from which we are kicking.

Note: On the left hashmark, kickoff personnel will flip-flop, and we'll count from left to right.

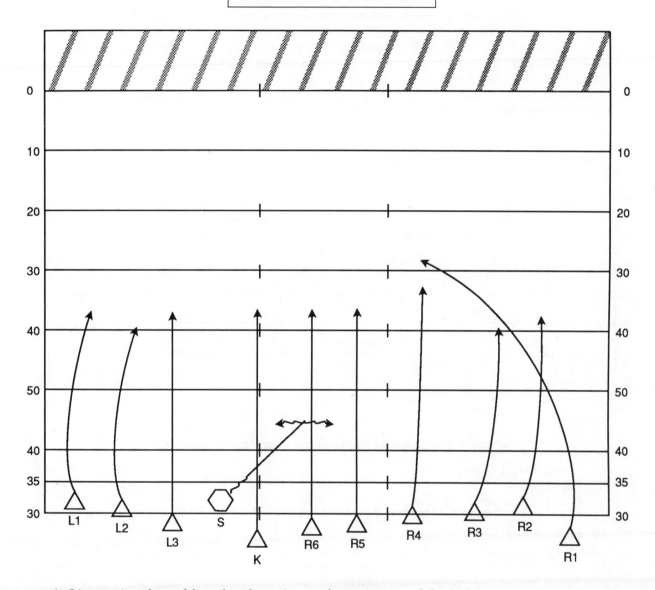

Kickoff—Left Hashmark

1. Line up in a bowed line, hands on knees, facing in toward the kicker.
2. Spacing is 4 yards between all numbered men (this includes the kicker).
3. The safety lines up in a position to approach the ball for an onside kick but not obstructing any coverer.
4. Numbers L1 and R1 line up 4 yards from the sideline.
5. The sprinter is R1. He lines up parallel with the kicker so he can get more of a running start.
6. The sprinter takes a course whereby he swoops outside-in at the ball carrier.
7. Numbers L1 and R2 are the contain men. Do not allow the ball carrier to get outside.
8. The safety approaches the ball in timing with the kicker, to threaten the onside kick. After a regular kick, the safety must stay on a line between the ball carrier and our goal line.
9. All coverers maintain good lateral relationship.

Note: Numbering on hashmark kickoffs is straight across, counting from the side from which we are kicking.

Note: On the right hashmark, kickoff personnel will flip-flop, and we'll count from right to left.

ONSIDE KICKOFF

You may note that to this point we have not included any onside kicks in play form. Frankly, our feeling is that the outcome of an onside kick depends more on luck than on either skill or execution. The bounce of the ball has more influence on the result than any controlling factor, and therefore the type and design of onside kick plays should be left primarily to the imagination of the head coach, based on what he feels confident in and comfortable with. However, as a guide to those of you who wish to design some onside kickoff plays for your program, we have outlined the basic elements and responsibilities.

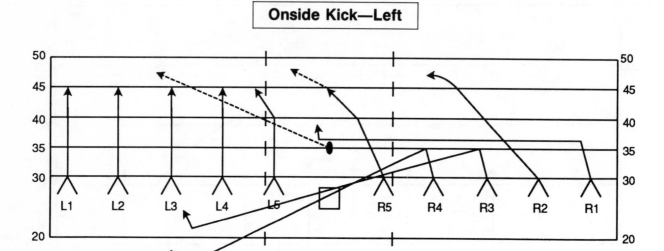

Responsibilities (onside left) (also run from sideline alignment)

L1 Sprint, keep ball in bounds.
L2 Sprint to ball.
L3 Sprint to ball.
L4 Sprint to ball.   Closest man recovers the ball. Others block and protect recovery.
L5 Sprint to ball.
R5 Sprint to contain point—alert for ball or return.
R4 Sprint behind first wave—alert for ball or return.
R3 Sprint behind first wave—become safety.
R2 Sprint to contain spot—don't let ball outside.
R1 Maintain leverage—become safety.
K   Aim at the left number—the ball must go 10 yards—cover to sideline.

Onside Kick—Right

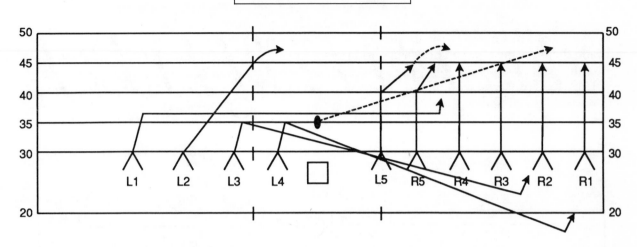

Responsibilities (onside right) (also run from sideline alignment)

L1 Maintain leverage—become safety.
L2 Sprint to contain spot—don't let ball outside.
L3 Sprint behind first wave—become safety.
L4 Sprint behind first wave—alert for ball or return.
L5 Sprint to contain point—alert for ball or return.

Closest man recovers the ball. Others block and protect the recovery.

R5 Sprint to ball.
R4 Sprint to ball.
R3 Sprint to ball.   Closest man recovers the ball. Others block and protect the recovery.
R2 Sprint to ball.
R1 Sprint, keep ball in bounds.
K   Aim at the right number—ball must go 10 yards—cover to sideline.

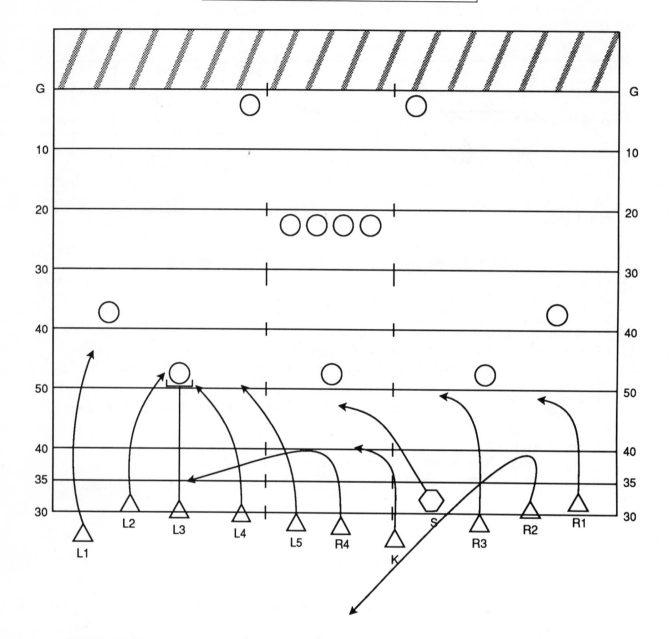

Right Hashmark—Onside Kickoff

L3 You are the "wipeout" man. Block their guard. If the end has moved up to the restraining line, block him.

L2, L4, & L5 Go for the ball.

L1 Go for the ball if it comes your way. Keep it from going out of bounds.

R4 You are the short safety.

K, R1, & R3 Fake a regular kickoff and then swerve toward the ball after it has been kicked.

R2 You are the deep safety.

S Approach the ball in timing with the kicker. Kick the ball so it bounds toward a spot at the junction of the far sideline and the opponent's 40-yard line.

ORGANIZATION AFTER A SAFETY

The reason we refer to this as an "organization" after a safety as opposed to a kickoff is that, even if your offensive team has intentionally taken a safety, it is the only circumstance in the game of football in which you must kick off or punt after you have been scored upon. Although every player and coach is fully aware of the rules for this situation, it occurs rarely and is at best unsettling.

The rules require that the ball be kicked without the use of a kicking tee, which is why most teams use their punter to get sufficient height and hang time. Otherwise the coverage is the same as for kickoff. The head coach must bring his kickoff team together after a safety to dispel any negative emotions and revitalize the energies of *controlled aggression* needed to cover a safety kickoff. Because the ball is kicked from the kicking team's 20-yard line, the coverage goals must be adjusted. On a normal kickoff the goal usually is to stop the return man inside his own 25-yard line; on a safety kickoff the goal must be adjusted to tackle the return man inside his own 35-yard line. This is much more difficult, and the head coach is the one person capable of motivating the leadership squad to make the extra effort required to achieve this task.

Even though it may rarely be used, the safety kickoff must be practiced regularly each week. The strengths and weaknesses of each week's opponent must be considered when planning the type and placement of kicks to be used, much the same as one would do weekly for the regular kickoff. However, it is the sideline organization and motivation instituted by the head coach that finally determines the degree of success achieved. The following information will help.

Kickoff After a Safety

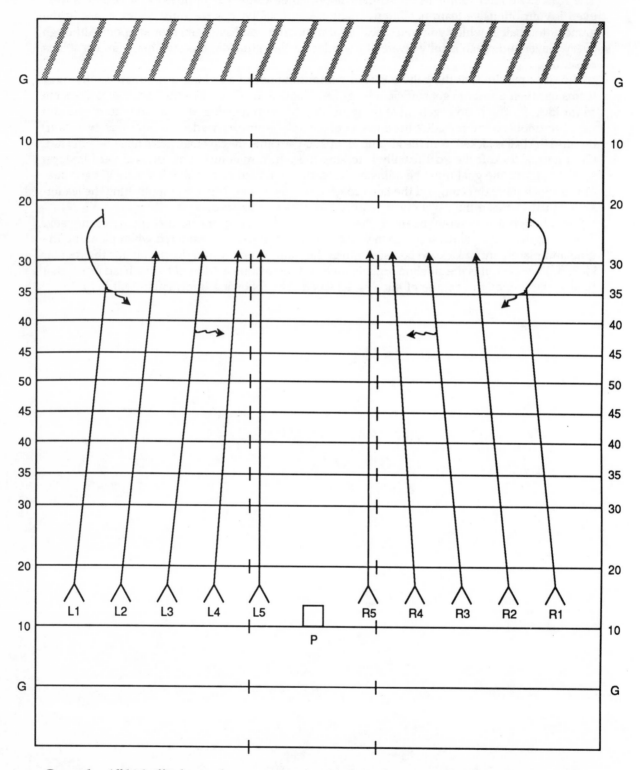

General: All kickoff rules apply, except that we are allowed to punt rather than placekick. Alignment is straight across, even with the punter. Takeoff is on his second step (we will time this out with the punter).

Alert: When kicking in this situation we have just given up 2 points. It's our job to get the ball back and gain momentum!

George Allen's Best

Kickers

Bob Waterfield—*Los Angeles Rams*

Ben Agajanian—*Los Angeles Rams*

George Blanda—*Oakland Raiders*

Lou Groza—*Cleveland Browns*

Jan Stenerud—*Kansas City Chiefs*

Jim Turner—*Denver Broncos*

Bruce Gossett—*Los Angeles Rams*

Mark Mosley—*Washington Redskins*

Fred Cox—*Minnesota Vikings*

Jim Bakken—*St. Louis Cardinals*

Kickoff coverage men

Rusty Tillman—*Washington Redskins*

Alex Hawkins—*Baltimore Colts*

Pat Curran—*Los Angeles Rams*

Bob Brunet—*Washington Redskins*

Preston Pearson—*Baltimore Colts*

Don Nottingham—*Miami Dolphins*

Jim Jensen—*Miami Dolphins*

Louie Giammona—*Philadelphia Eagles*

J.C. Caroline—*Chicago Bears*

Mike Hull—*Washington Redskins*

John Sciarra—*Philadelphia Eagles*

CHAPTER 6

Kickoff Return

No single play can leave a more lasting impression on players, coaches, and fans than a long kickoff return for a touchdown. In 1974 we (the Washington Redskins) dedicated the Buffalo Bills' new Rich Stadium. It was an exhibition game, but even so, I told the team that when you are part of the dedication of an NFL Stadium, it is history in the making, and, exhibition game or not, we would win the game for history's sake. I also said that on historic occasions just winning was not quite enough; the event itself demands an unforgettable play to open the festivities—what could be more unforgettable than a long kickoff return for a touchdown? I told Herb Mulkey, our kickoff return man, ''If we win the toss, that is your assignment.''

We won the coin flip, and the Bills kicked the ball 2 yards deep in the end zone. Mulkey returned it 102 yards for a touchdown, on a spectacular return that had the entire stadium on its feet. We did win the game, and Herb Mulkey, whom we had signed as a free agent, later went on to make the Pro Bowl. Those who saw that game may not remember who won or the name of the return man who ran back the opening kickoff, but they will always remember the 102-yard kickoff return for a touchdown. Even to this day, the owner of the Buffalo Bills, Ralph Wilson, and the great O.J. Simpson remember that game and that play, as they have mentioned to me on various occasions.

GENERAL INFORMATION

A complete kickoff return package should include both returns and defenses. There are six basic kickoff returns; middle, right, left, left hash and right hash (which are precalled), and a special sideline return that is an automatic adjustment. The two kickoff defenses included in the package, for onside and squib kicks, which require special personnel and/or alignments, are predetermined by the game situation and the high probability of either one of these kicks being used.

Basic assignments for each of the returns and defenses can be adjusted each week, if necessary, to take advantage of the specific coverage pattern being used by each opponent. Adjustments might also be warranted to take advantage of an opponent's personnel weaknesses.

For this special unit to be as effective as possible, each player must execute his individual assignment to perfection. Each player on the kickoff return team, to execute error-free football, must know not only his responsibility on the return play or defense called but also the following rules and principles that apply to this phase of the game.

Rules

All members of the kickoff team must understand the following rules:

- The kickoff is to be made from the 35-yard line; the restraining line for the receiving team is 10 yards away, on the 45-yard line (note the 5-yard difference between this and high school and college).
- Once a kickoff travels 10 yards, it is a free ball and belongs to the recovering team.
- A kickoff recovered in the end zone by the kicking team is a touchdown whether or not the receiving team touched it.
- If the receiving team on a kickoff touches the ball before it goes 10 yards, the ball becomes a free ball and belongs to the team that recovers it.
- If the kickoff goes out of bounds, the kicking team must kick again with a 5-yard penalty. The new kickoff line is the 30-yard line, and our new restraining line is the 40-yard line.
- A fair catch can be used by the receiving team. All fair catch rules apply.
- There is *no* blocking below the waist.

Principles

In addition to knowing kickoff rules, players need to follow several basic principles.

- Do not clip—always get into position to block your assignment. If you cannot get him legally, head for another man.
- Front five personnel always be alert for an onside kick.
- Versus a squib kick (predetermined flat kick or line drive) we will *automatically* go to a wedge return.
- When a middle return has been called and the ball is kicked off to one side, the return takes place in front of where the ball was received. The wedge captain has the responsibility to direct the wedge to a frontal position on the ball.
- When a directional return has been called, we will do everything we can to get the ball to the point of the blocking pattern.
- One safety will be assigned to be the ''call'' safety, calling out who should field the ball. Use a ''You'' or ''Me'' call, and do it quickly and loudly.
- Remember—once the ball crosses the 45-yard line, it is a live ball.
- *Down* every ball that rolls dead in the end zone.
- Once the return man leaves the end zone, he cannot return to the end zone and down a ball.
- Our first goal is to *score*, and our second goal is to bring the ball out to the 30-yard line.

KICKOFF RETURNS

Kickoff return specialists are a special breed. They have many styles: blazing speed from the goal line to the wedge like Travis Williams (Green Bay Packers 1966 to 1970); speed, quickness, and great balance like Gale Sayers (Chicago Bears, 1965 to 1969) and Tim Brown (Los Angeles Raiders, 1988 to present); or deceptive speed combined with incredible stop-start acceleration like O.J. Simpson (Buffalo Bills, 1967 to 1977). But whatever the style, the great return specialists, past and present, have several things in common—exceptional peripheral vision, unusual ability to read blocks, good hands to catch and hold the football, excellent judgment, courage, and, most of all, good blockers!

Although the great return men do much of it on their own, the well-blocked, well-executed return plays unquestionably give these specialists their opportunity to excel. The kickoff return, like every other play in football, is an 11-man effort—the better each man executes his assignment, the higher the probability of success.

It is important to keep in mind that kickoffs (unless they are squibbed) should always be fielded in the air. Also, backs other than the safety must be prepared to field short kicks that come to them, but, they must not back up to field a kick if the safety can field it cleanly.

The following kickoff return plays cover the entire spectrum of return situations. Coaches should pay special attention to the notes and alerts.

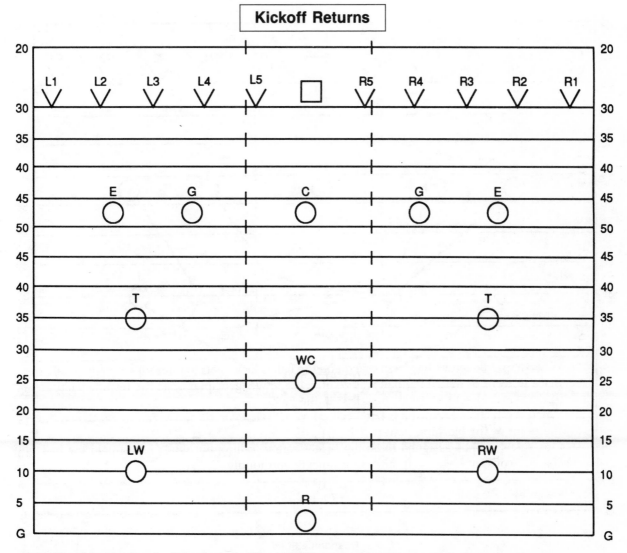

Kickoff Returns

Note: For high school and college the ball will be kicked from the 40-yard line, and the return team should line-up between their 45- and 50-yard lines. All other assignments apply, allowing for the 5 yard difference (throughout this chapter).

Personnel and alignments

Center: Align between the 45 and 50, offset from the ball.

Guards: Align between the 45 and 50, approximately 4 or 5 yards outside hash.

Ends: Align between the 45 and 50, approximately on outside of the number.

Alert: Always check for an onside kick.

Wedge captain: Align on the 25-yard line on the hash unless a special return is called. Disguise alignments.

Tackles: Align on the hash at the 25. Adjust to spread alignment on call.

Wings: Align on the 10-yard line, on the number.

Return man: Align on the goal line between the hashes.

Alert: Weather conditions may cause adjustment on alignments.

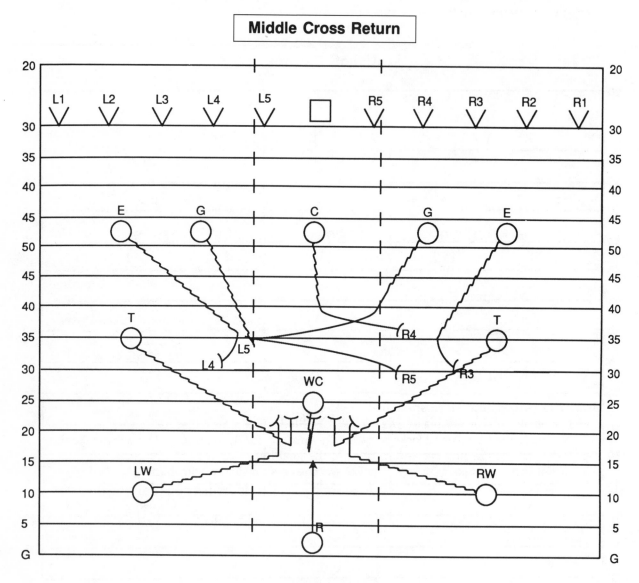

Middle Cross Return

Responsibilities

Ball kicked from the 5-yard line to the goal line (3.8 to 4.0 hang)

Wall (CGs, Es)

1. Adjust to the distance and direction of the kick—*anticipate.*
2. Assuming the wedge is set approximately 12 yards in front of R3, you should initiate your block approximately 10 yards in front of the wedge.
3. *Sprint* to your sprint point—settle—position yourself for the block—make contact from the inside out. *Screen* (chin to chin) block from the inside out. Force your man to widen his coverage lane outside the path of the wedge—*maintain position.*
4. *Finish your block.*

Center: Align between the 45 and 50, offset from ball. Block L4 or R4 as indicated by scout report. (Make huddle call.) Sprint point of the 40-yard line and straight back. *Note:* You might switch blocking assignments with the offside guard as game plan dictates. Take R5 or L5, and guard takes R4 or L4.

Guards: Onside: Align between 45 and 50—split the difference between the hash and number. Block L5 or R5 based on huddle call. Sprint point is at the near hash on the 40-yard line.

Offside: Align halfway between hash and number. Block R5 or L5 or switch with center and block. R4 or L4 as the game plan dictates.

Sprint point is at the near hash on the 35-yard line.

Ends: Onside: Align at the number. Block #3. Sprint point is approximately 5 yards outside the hash and at the 35-yard line.

Offside: Align at the number. Block #4.

Sprint point is at the hash on the 35-yard line.

Wedge (wedge captain, tackles, wings)
1. The wedge captain sets the wedge approximately 12 yards directly in front of the return man. On a sideline kick (outside the number) form the wedge on the near number.
2. Seal the wedge and assume a rocker stance. On the "Go" command, *sprint* up the field keeping the wedge compact. Block straight ahead or from the inside out.

Wedge captain (WC): Align at the 25-yard line between the hashes. *Anticipate* the flight of the ball. Set the wedge approximately 12 yards in front of the return man and never outside the number. The tackles should be no more than an arm's length away. Assume a rocker set. On the "Go" command, sprint straight up the field.

Tackles: Align at the 35 on the number (check for an onside kick). *Anticipate* and *sprint* to get into position on the wedge. Locate WC and establish position one arm's length from him. Assume a rocker stance. *Sprint* up the field, blocking straight ahead or from the inside out.

Wings: Right wing: Align on the number at the 10-yard line. Seal up the wedge. Approximately 1 yard by 1 yard off the outside hit off the right tackle. Give the "Go" command as the RS starts up the field. After giving the command, *sprint* up the field, blocking from the inside out. Don't leave the wedge—opponents will come to you.

Left wing: Same, without giving starting command.

Returners (wings and return specialist)
1. *Communicate*—The RS makes the "You" or "Me" call.
2. Normally the RS takes all kicks between the number and deep outside. The wings take the kicks outside the number and in front of the goal line.
3. When the wing takes the kick, the RS switches responsibility with him.
4. Returner: *Field the ball—sprint* into the pocket created by the wedge—find a crack—run north and south.

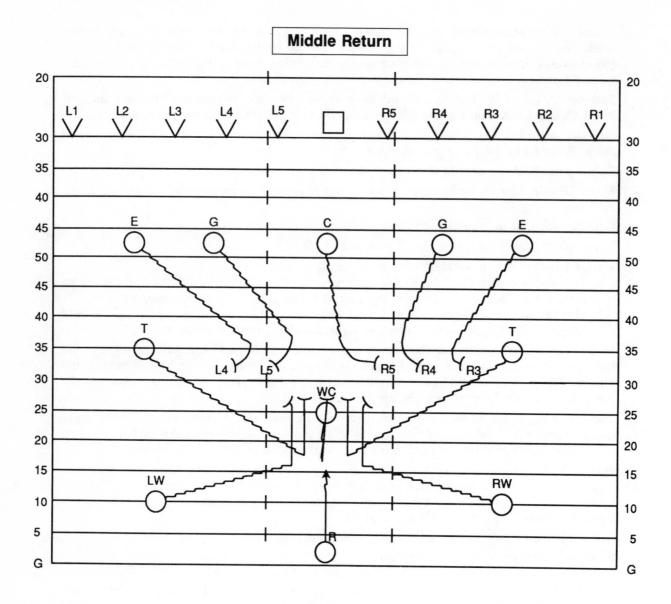

Middle Return

Responsibilities

1. This return is used against teams that do a lot of crossing, or when the kicker kicks high and short, or after an opponent's safety.
2. Must anticipate the depth of the kick and screen according to the position of the wedge (10 yards from wedge).
3. All the same rules apply for the wedge and returners (middle cross).

Sideline Return

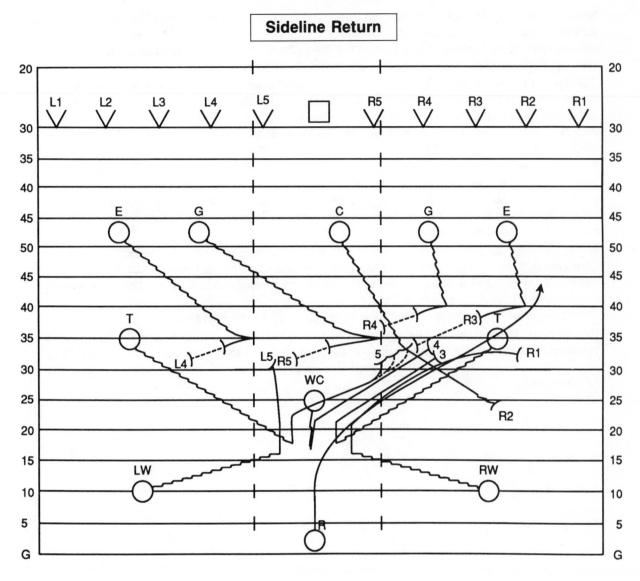

Responsibilities

General

1. *Anticipate* where the ball is kicked and adjust accordingly.
2. Get to your *sprint point—settle*—take up clask—*screen* (chin to chin) your man away from point of attack. Contact rule prevails.
3. Set the wedge just like a middle return.
4. "Break" command by WC changes the course of the wedge to 45-degree angle.
5. The return is on, as long as the ball is kicked from the offside number or in the direction of the call. If the ball goes outside the offside number, we will wedge return up that sideline.

Individual

Center: Sprint back to the right hash at the 40-yard line—spy on the contain man (#2)—maintain inside-out position—initiate your block at approximately the 25-yard line—screen your man inside-out and away from the wedge (trap block).

Guards: Onside—Sprint back to the 40-yard line—establish outside in position on #4—take up slack—initiate block at the 40—*screen* to the inside.

Offside—Sprint back to the far hash at the 35-yard line—establish outside in position on #5 toward the return—take up slack—initiate block at the 35—*screen* away from return.

Ends: Onside—Sprint back to the 40-yard line—establish outside in position on #3—take up slack—initiate block at the 40—*screen* to the inside.

Offside—sprint back to the onside hash at the 35-yard line—establish inside-out position on #4—take up slack—initiate block at the 35—*screen* to the outside.

Tackles: Onside—Set on wedge. On "Go" command start upfield (5-10 yards). On "Break" command go at 45-degree angle toward the number in the direction of the call (under the kick out block by the center). Take the first color that shows. Check #3.

Backside—Set wedge (same as above). On "Go" command start upfield. On "Break" go at 45-degree angle toward number. Take first color that shows. Check R5-L5.

Wedge captain: Responsible for setting the wedge—same as middle return. Can go outside the number in the direction of the return. After getting the "Go" command, start up field 5 to 10 yards. Call "Break" to signal the wedge to alter the upfield course to a 45-degree angle. Block color. Check #4 in the direction of the return. Kicks away from return and outside the number—middle return (communicate).

Wing: Onside—Be alert for "You"/"Me" call. If *"Me"* call, form on wedge (same as middle)—after calling "go—go—go" command start with wedge. On "Break" command go under kick out block and block #1 in the direction of return. *Screen* (prefer inside-out). If *"You"* call, switch responsibilities with return specialist.

Offside—Sprint to wedge, then continue on to block #5 to the backside.

Return man: Responsibile for calling "You" or "Me" (same as middle return). Sprint upfield to establish the threat of a middle return—break with wedge at 45-degree angle. Stay behind WC. Dip inside kick and block, then flatten angle looking for daylight off of wing's block. Get to the 30 plus—*score!*

Reverse Right or Left

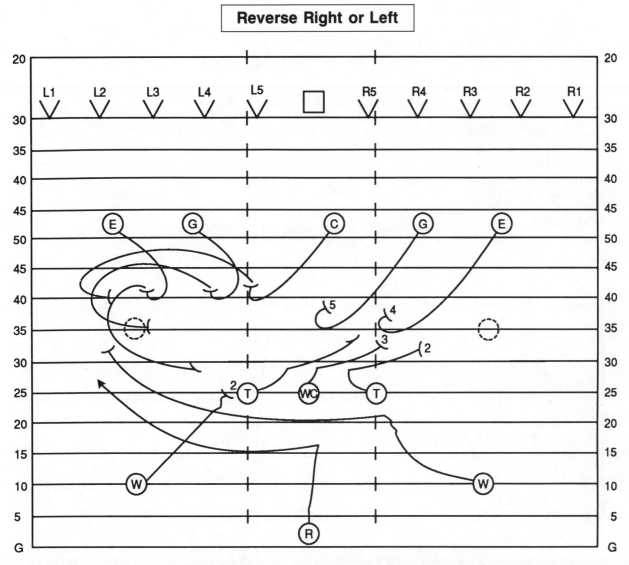

Center: Drop back to the 40-yard line square to #5 in the direction of the call—brush block to the inside—circle and set up picket 5 × 5 yards from the guard's block. Block most dangerous.

Guards: Onside guard: Drop back to 40-yard line square to #4 in the direction of the call, brush block to the inside, circle, and set up picket 5 x 5 yards from the end's block. Block most dangerous. Backside guard: Drop back to 35-yard line, square with #5 away from return, and screen block to the outside.

Ends: Onside end: Drop back to the 40-yard line square with #3 to the onside, brush block to the inside, circle, and set up picket 5 × 5 yards from the wing's block. Block most dangerous. Backside end: Drop back to the 35-yard line, square with #4 away from the return, and screen block to the outside.

Wedge captain: Form wedge at the 25-yard line in front of the return man. On command, start in the direction of a sideline return (under control). Block #3 or color away from the return.

Tackles: Onside: Block color. Backside: Block #2.

Wings: Onside wing: Start as though forming on the wedge—settle and spy on #2. Square with man and screen block to the inside—don't allow penetration—this is the key block. Backside wing: Start as if to form on wedge. Establish approximately a 1 × 3 yard relationship with the tackle on the wedge. Start the wedge early (1 sec.). When the return man gets approximately 5-6 yards from you (8-9 yards from wedge) break across the wedge and lead return outside the picket.

Return man: Start course behind wedge as though running a sideline return in the opposite direction of the return at approximately 5-6 yards from the wing (8-9 yards from the wedge). Break across the wedge and outside the picket.

Alert: On cross side kick, form wedge return.

AUTOMATIC CONVERSIONS

Whenever a ball is kicked down a sideline away from the predetermined return side, an automatic conversion should be made to a special type of return. This special return is run up the sideline where the ball has been kicked. This type of adjustment can and should be used against both a regular deep kickoff and a squib kickoff. The following plays consider both conditions.

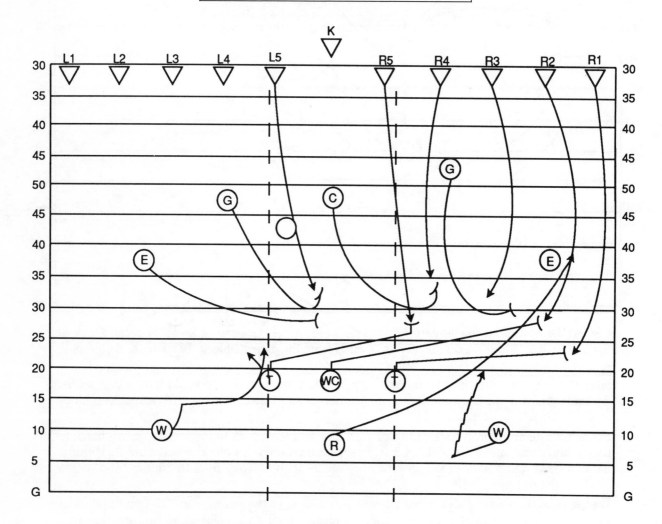

Automatic Right Sideline Return

RG Drop back and block R3 from head-up position.

RE Stalk R3 from outside. Double team along with our RG from outside.

C Drop back and get position to block R4.

LG Drop back and get position to block L5.

LE Drop deeper and come across the field fast, seeking to get in front of the return to lead the play through the hole. Cleanup-block on any leakage as you are on your way.

LT   Move laterally with the wedge. Be prepared to block R5 as he covers.

WC   Move laterally with the wedge. Block out with a hard running shoulder block on R2.

RT   Move laterally with the wedge. Block out with a hard running shoulder block on R1. If R fields the ball, double out on R2.

LW   Start quickly to join the wedge. Veer off to block any coverer coming in behind the wedge from our left.

RW   If the kick is to you, return it through the alley created by blocks on their R2 and R3. If safety fields it, block out on R1. If it goes to our RHB, lead the play up through that alley and clean up on any leakage.

Note   This return is one to which we will convert automatically when we have called a middle or left return and the ball has been kicked near our right sideline.

Automatic Squib Blocking—Right

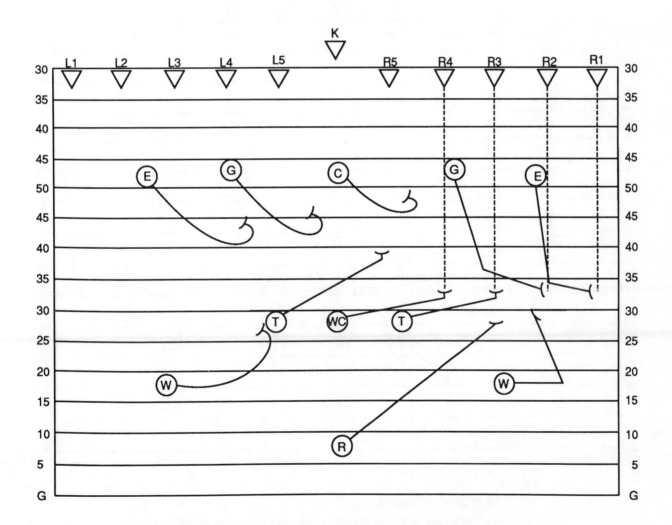

RE   Drop back and block out on R1.

RG   Drop back and block out on R2.

C   Drop back; get position on R5; block away from the ball.

LG   Drop back; get position on L5; block away from the ball.

LE   Drop back; get position on L4; block away from the ball.

RT & LT   Move laterally with the ball; assist with fielding of the ball; if necessary, block R3 and leakage.

RW   Move quickly to field the ball; concentrate on picking up the ball; cut inside the blocks of the RT and RE.

LW   Protect backside.

R   Assist in fielding the ball; lead the blocking up field.

Coaching point   This return is one we will go to automatically versus a squib kicked near our left sideline.

Automatic Squib Blocking—Left

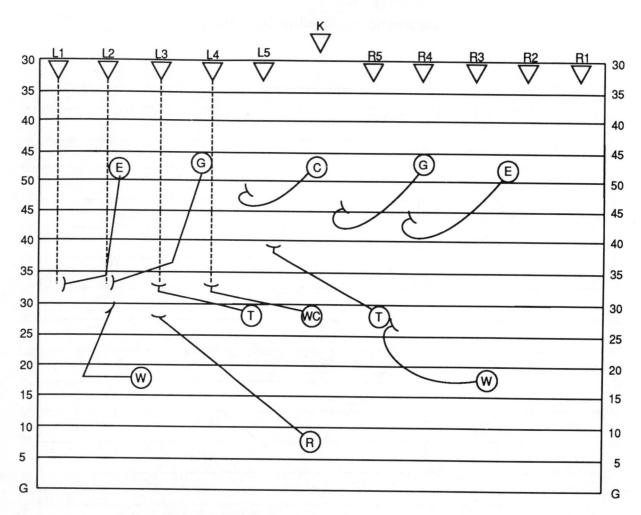

LE   Drop back and block out on L1.

LG   Drop back and block out on L2.

C   Drop back; get position on L5; block away from the ball.

RG   Drop back; get position on R5; block away from the ball.

RE   Drop back; get position on R4; block away from the ball.

LT & RT   Move laterally with the ball; assist with fielding the ball; if necessary, block L3 and leakage.

LW Move quickly to field the ball; concentrate on picking up the ball; cut inside the blocks of the RT and RE.

RW Protect backside.

R Assist in fielding the ball; lead the blocking up field.

Coaching point This return is one we will go to automatically versus a squib kicked near our left side line.

KICKOFF DEFENSES

The use of special personnel and a special kickoff return alignment are required when it is extremely likely that your opponent will attempt an onside kickoff. These special onside kickoff players should all have good hands and quick feet. The bigger people, such as tight ends, fullbacks, and linebackers, should be the frontline personnel, backed up by receivers, halfbacks, and defensive backs.

When the onside kick is a concern, but still less than a 50-percent possibility, it is best to leave the regular kickoff personnel in the game. In this instance, an adjustment in their alignment, in order to defend against the lesser possibility of an onside kickoff, should suffice; a regular kickoff return call can be made, if the opponent does, in fact, kick off deep.

The following onside kickoff defense is, in my opinion, the most consistently effective and the most difficult against which to execute a successful onside kickoff.

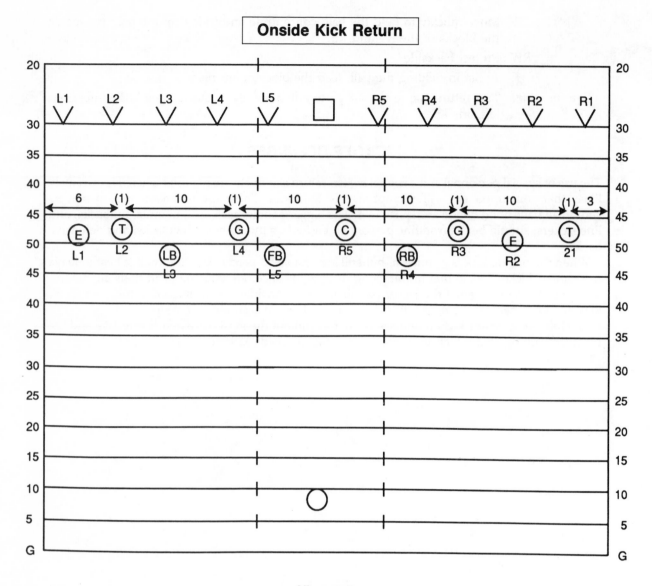

Alignments

1. The width of the field is 160 feet or approximately 54 yards. We want to distribute 10 people staggered across the front approximately 5 yards apart.
2. *Front line*: The center sets the coverage pattern by offsetting left or right (scout report) from the ball approximately 2-3 yards. The front line forms on the center, spaced 10 yards apart. The front line now shifts to approximately 2-3 yards from the near sideline and approximately 5-6 yards from the backside sideline.
3. *Back line*: The back line offsets in the direction opposite to the front line, and they split the difference between them.
4. The front line aligns 18 inches from the 45-yard line, and the back line aligns on the 50-yard line with the exception of the ends. The ends align at the 48-yard line.
5. Assume a hitting position ready to move. Watch the kicking leg to anticipate the direction of the kick. Slightly adjust your alignment if needed in order to see the ball.
6. *Return man*: Align at the 20-yard line—take no chances—fair-catch or down all kicks if in doubt.

Rules

1. The ball must go 10 yards to become a legal onside kick.
   1.1 If the ball is short of 10 yards and the kicking team recovers it, a 5-yard penalty is assessed and the kick goes over.

1.2 If the ball goes out of bounds, an ensuing penalty and kick take place.

1.3 If the ball is short of 10 yards and the receiving team recovers it, the receiving team takes possession of it at that point.

1.4 If the ball is *touched* at any point by the receiving team, the ball becomes *free* to either side.

2. Keeping these rules in mind, we will do the following:

   2.1 If the ball is short and *you are sure* you can recover it—do so. Protect the ball at all costs— Form a wedge.

   2.2 If the ball is short and there is any question about recovering it—back off.

   2.3 If it's a line drive kick, the front line should avoid handling the ball, then block the most dangerous man.

   2.4 If the ball is kicked deep, drop back to the 30-yard line and block your assigned man.

George Allen's Best

Kickoff Returners

Travis Williams—*Green Bay Packers*

Gale Sayers—*Chicago Bears*

Abe Woodson—*San Francisco Forty Niners*

Ron Smith—*Los Angeles Rams*

Hugh McElhenny—*San Francisco Forty Niners*

Lem Barney—*Detroit Lions*

Willie Galimore—*Chicago Bears*

Lenny Lyles—*San Francisco Forty Niners*

Ollie Matson—*Chicago Cardinals*

Herb Adderley—*Green Bay Packers*

Tim Brown—*Philadelphia Eagles*

Mel Renfro—*Dallas Cowboys*

Clint Jones—*Minnesota Vikings*

Eddie Payton—*Detroit Lions*

Lynn Chandnois—*Pittsburgh Steelers*

Clarence Childs—*New York Giants*

Bobby Mitchell—*Cleveland Browns*

Buddy Young—*Baltimore Colts*

Mercury Morris—*Miami Dolphins*

Woodley Lewis—*Los Angeles Rams*

Larry Jones—*Washington Redskins*

Noland Smith—*Kansas City Chiefs*

Dick James—*Washington Redskins*

Johnny Counts—*New York Giants*

Kickoff Return Blockers

Rusty Tillman—*Washington Redskins*

Bob Brunet—*Washington Redskins*

Pat Curran—*Los Angeles Rams*

Alex Hawkins—*Baltimore Colts*

Bill Ring—*San Francisco Forty Niners*

CHAPTER 7

Point-After-Touchdown and Field Goal

If I had to select a single most important player on the Point-After-Touchdown (P-A-T) and field goal team, obviously it would be the placekicker. However, without an excellent center and a good holder, a placekicker is useless, unless of course he can drop-kick.

With the Redskins we put together what, in my opinion, was the perfect "nucleus of three" for the P-A-T/field goal unit. For my kicker, I signed Mark Mosley as a free agent. He had failed with two NFL clubs before he came to us, but I liked his attitude, dedication, and coolness under pressure. He turned out to be an excellent choice, as he usually kicked well, but most of all he was consistent. In fact, he kicked so well against our division rival Dallas that before every game Tex Schramm would file a complaint with the league that Mosley was using an illegal shoe. Tex would even come down on the field before our game and pretend to inspect his shoe, just to upset Mark. I loved it and told Mosley that there wouldn't be any complaints if he kicked poorly. Mark usually made Tex eat his words by being his consistent, accurate self.

When I made the trade for the young Joe Theismann, I told him that the Redskins were an ideal team for him. We had two veteran quarterbacks in Billy Kilmer and Sonny Jurgensen who would be the best teachers a young quarterback could ever hope to learn from, and eventually Theismann would be the number one. In the meantime, he would be able to play and contribute on special teams as a punt and kickoff returner and, most especially, as a holder for the P-A-T/field goal unit. Joe Theismann became one of the best field goal holders I ever had, and the reason he was so good was because he was quick, he could run with the ball, and he had good hands. The fact that Joe was a quarterback with a strong arm gave us an added dimension on fake field goals or busted plays.

Finally, I made a trade with the Atlanta Falcons for Ted Fritsch, a long-snap center for punts and field goals, and that completed my trio. Without a doubt, Fritsch was the best long-snapper in the league at that time. His snaps were precise, and he could put the laces exactly where you wanted them almost every time. With Ted Fritsch, I was always confident that every field goal attempt (and also every punt) would begin with a perfect snap.

We surrounded our "nucleus of three" with the best blockers and coverage people we could find on our football team; as a result, the Redskins' overall kicking game was consistently among the NFL's best. What happens when a P-A-T/field goal unit has a great center, an excellent holder, solid blockers, and top coverage people is that the success of this unit falls solely into the hands (or, in this case, onto the foot) of the placekicker. If the kicker is confident, dedicated, and cool under pressure, the team will be highly successful.

GENERAL INFORMATION

There is no other area of the kicking game, or in the game of football, that demands more consistent precision than the P-A-T/field goal. On the P-A-T/field goal team, precision + consistency = success! A consistent "nucleus of three" is the key to that success.

The kicker and the holder must be certain that the holder depth, every time, is 7 yards from where the ball is placed by the referee. To ensure this, the kicker should make the initial spot for the placement of the ball while lining up his angle. Then the holder must visually verify the depth of the ball spot (or tee) as he gets down into his ready position.

The center must practice to develop a precise snap every time. The ball must always arrive exactly at the location the holder feels most comfortable with (never above the holder's numbers), and the laces should consistently be delivered to the same location relative to the holder's top hand. Something any long-snapper must keep in mind is that bad snaps that are high or away from the holder are not simply bad—they are potential disaster. *Always keep the ball down and in the direction of the holder's body.*

The holder is the fulcrum of the placekick action on which the success or failure of the kick usually turns. A sure-handed catch of the snap, quick adjustment of the location of the laces, and a precise spot of the football with the proper angle and attitude must all be accomplished with split-second timing on a consistent basis for the placekicker to develop the confidence he requires in the holder, thus eliminating hesitation or anxiety.

The kicker himself must develop a consistent, precise placement of his "plant" foot, an exact angle and location of his kicking foot at the point of contact with the football, and a clearly delineated leg swing (from backswing to follow-through). Repetitive practices and total concentration are the only means by which to consistently accomplish the precision required to execute successful place-kicks.

Rules and Principles

Strict adherence to the following general rules and principles will increase the consistency of the placekicking unit's performance.

- Our center, holder, and kicker must work as a unit. Strive for perfection. Total time for the snap and kick is 1.2 to 1.4 seconds.
- We will huddle unless we are fighting time. If there are no time-outs remaining, we must be prepared to sprint into position—we need approximately 15 seconds to get the kick off under these circumstances.
- Players aligned out of proper number position *must* report to the referee.
- The holder acts as the quarterback for the unit. He must check to see that we have 11 people. If we do not, use best discretion in taking a time-out—a penalty may not make a major difference. The holder must always check the time on the clock.
- Line—Assume a three-point stance immediately.
- Be alert for audibles ("Red" or "Blue").
- Be alert for "Fire" call.

- On field goals, cover after the kick.
- Do not be drawn offsides.
- If you are uncovered, always check for a leaper—block him in midair.
- Alert: Be ready to go in for a field goal any time the ball is inside the opponent's 50.
- Alert: We will also have the ability to punt out of the field goal formation—protect and cover.
- *You* are responsible to see that you are substituted for, if you cannot participate.

Add to these elements precise attention to detailed blocking schemes and consistently aggressive, disciplined coverage, and it is possible to develop a P-A-T/field goal unit with credibility—one that demands attention and respect.

POINT-AFTER-TOUCHDOWN PROTECTION

Protecting for the P-A-T kick is basically one-dimensional—protection only. The prime objective is to defeat an all-out, 11-man attempt to block the kick. In this circumstance it is wise to use the best blockers on the team up front, without concern for coverage ability. Basic protection technique (for both P-A-T and field goal) should include adjustments to corner stunts, interior stunts, and attempts to draw offensive linemen offside. This will require the most disciplined blockers on the team, to avoid compromising the integrity of the protection. The following information illustrates the proper P-A-T protection formation and basic assignments.

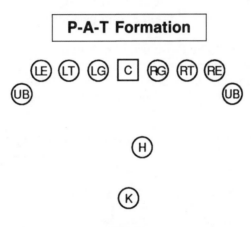

Mechanics

Sideline call: P-A-T or field goal on the ball—alert for fire!

Stance: A three-point—upbacks a two-point.

Cadence: There will be no cadence called at the line of scrimmage. Therefore, when the team is set the holder will call "Ready—Set." There will be no movement after "Set." The center will snap the ball *any time* after "Set."

Assignments

Center: The ball is snapped when the center is ready, any time after "Set." Pass the ball accurately and with zip, then set and raise slowly. Use head movements like a pitcher holding a man on first base. Do not permit a man to pull you to permit a lane to block the kick. Be solid and hold your ground.

LT-RT:

LG-RG   Set step to inside and raise. You are responsible for your inside. Do not move so far inside that you make it difficult for the man outside of you. Do not permit a man to pull you to establish a lane for a blitzer to block the kick.

LE-RE: Drop-step with outside foot and set with power to your inside, which is your responsibility. Do not be faked to the outside so a man goes through to your inside. Alert for "Fire" call!

UBs: Take position facing outward so that drop-stepping end's outside foot will form a wall with you. You are responsible for your inside. When you are certain of the inside, try to bump anyone coming near you on your outside. Do not be faked to the outside to permit a blitzer to go unmolested after the kick. Keep formation as wide as possible. Alert for "Fire" call!

Holder: Always work with the same center and kicker. You are as responsible for a good kick as the kicker. Be certain you are 7 yards deep. *Know your kicker*. Call the cadence after you have checked that your kicker is ready. *"Fire" call* for a mechanical breakdown. Alert: Time on the clock.

Time Elements: Strive for a 1.2 kicking time.

Fake field goal

Sideline call: On the sideline or in the huddle we call a fake field goal. We then execute the predetermined fake upon the command "Set." We first give the directional call *"Load* Right/Left," then the snap call "Ready—Set."

Audible: At the line of scrimmage the holder gives an *alert* call of "Red" (run) or "Blue" (pass), then the directional call *"Load Right/Left,"* then the snap call "Ready—Set."

Omaha: When "Omaha" is called, the fake is *off*, and we revert to the field goal.

FIELD GOAL PROTECTION AND COVERAGE

The primary difference between a P-A-T and a field goal, other than the field goal generally being a longer kick, is that it is essential to cover a field goal after the ball has been kicked. If the kick is not blown dead by an official, it is a live ball and can be returned by the opposing team. A secondary difference, due entirely to additional responsibilities, is the use of some different personnel.

The players required are much like those used on the punt team—good, disciplined blockers with the quickness and aggressiveness to cover and tackle well. Coverage on a field goal kick is similar to that used in a tight punt formation (see chapter 3). From the basic protection formation, the following assignments apply to field goal protection and coverage.

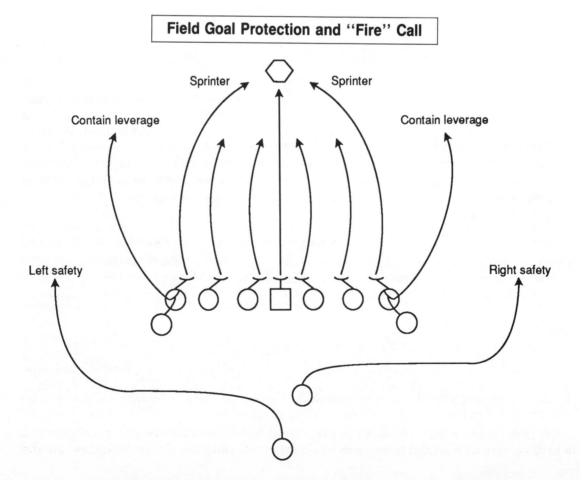

Field Goal Protection and "Fire" Call

Sprinter · Sprinter
Contain leverage · Contain leverage
Left safety · Right safety

Protection and assignments: Same as for P-A-T

Coverage: Field goals kicked from outside our 20-yard line should be covered as diagramed above. The important thing to remember is *protection #1, coverage #2.*

"Fire" Call: Mechanical breakdown in execution of kick!

Results in an automatic fake field goal!

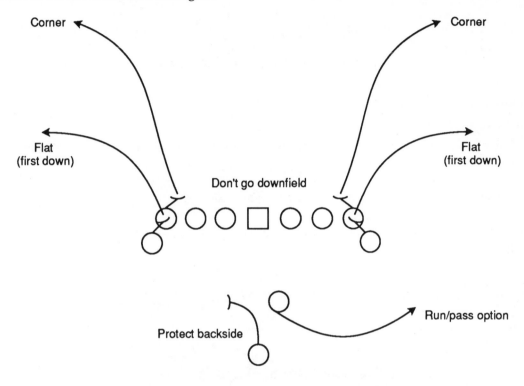

FAKE FIELD GOAL AND AUTOMATIC

There is no limit to the number and methods of field goal fakes attempted in football each year. This seems to be the singular area of creative expression of football coaches everywhere. There is unanimity among fans that field goal fakes are fun to watch. But the fact is, field goal fakes work only if the field goal team has credibility and respect as a consistently successful kicking unit. If a field goal team can attain that type of respect, a fake based on the simplest of precepts will work. The secret to a successful field goal fake or an "automatic" on a bad snap, like anything else, is execution.

One year when I was with the Redskins we played the Chicago Bears in Chicago. At the time we were in first place, a game ahead of my beloved Dallas Cowboys. The Bears had just scored a touchdown and set up for the extra point that would give them the lead. The snap from the center went high and wide of the holder, Bobby Douglass, and bounced all the way back to the 40-yard line on the synthetic playing surface at Soldier Field.

Douglass was an excellent runner and scrambler, for a quarterback, and he retreated to recover the ball. In some of the most incredible broken field running since the days of Red Grange, Douglass ran the ball back to about the 25-yard line. There, while avoiding tackles, he threw a pass on the run to the corner of the end zone, which I thought was going out of bounds. Instead Dick Butkus, the outside blocker, had released to the corner and made a spectacular over-the-shoulder catch, keeping both feet inbounds, for the extra point. We lost 17 to 16, and as a result Dallas won the Eastern Division Championship by one half a game.

The odds against a spontaneous play of this type being successful have to be about 1000 to 1 (a predetermined fake reduces the odds to almost even). However, the point is, these are the reasons *that* play worked in *that* game: (a) The automatic was based on sound field-goal—fake pass principles, and (b) two outstanding athletes never quit on the play and made it work with determination and great effort.

The following fake field goal plays are basic and sound. One of them could very well have been the play that ended our season back in Soldier Field on that December day several years ago.

Fake Field Goal—Run/Pass

Sideline call: Fake field goal on "Set."

Directional call: "Load right" = right; "Load left" = left.

Cadence: "Load right"—The ball will then be snapped on "Set" of the command "Ready—Set."

Audible: "Red" or "Blue"—"Load right" or "Load left"—"Ready—Set."

"Load right" call

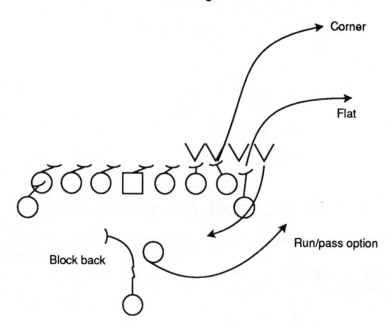

''Load left'' call

''Omaha'' call: Calls off the fake—everything goes back to normal field goal procedure.

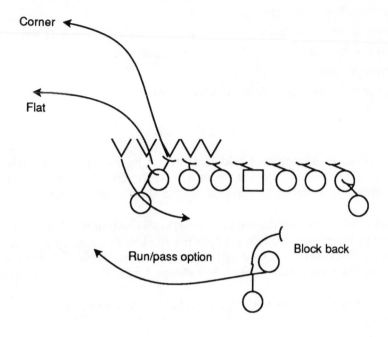

Corner

Flat

Run/pass option

Block back

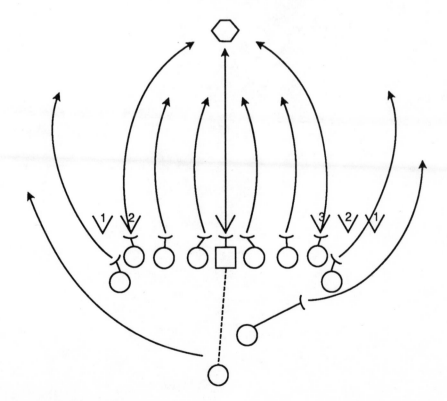

Fake Field Goal—Punt

Sideline call: Fake field goal.

Punt **cadence:** Normal mechanics.

Center: Snap the ball directly to the kicker.

Holder: Block #1 to the rush side.

UBs: Upback to the rush side block #2. Upback to the backside block #1 after checking inside.

LE-RE: End to the rush side block #3. End to backside block #2.

Gs and Ts: Normal protection.

Kicker: Punt the ball using one step. Punt away from the return man or out of bounds.

FREE KICK

A free kick is just that, an uncontested field goal attempt following the fair catch of either a punt or a kickoff. The rare times it is used are generally at the end of a half or game, after a short punt from the opposing team's end zone, or after a short safety kickoff.

The first time I ever used a free kick, I was head coach of the Rams and we were playing the Detroit Lions in Tiger Stadium. I didn't have my full kickoff coverage team in the game. That was a huge mistake that almost cost us the game, because Lem Barney (whom I mentioned earlier) almost ran the ball back for a touchdown. We stopped him, but we were lucky.

If you ever have the opportunity to use a free kick, be sure to put your regular kickoff coverage team in the game!

George Allen's Best

Centers

Ted Fritsch—*Washington Redskins*
Larry Strickland—*Chicago Bears*
George Burman—*Los Angeles Rams*

Len Hauss—*Washington Redskins*
Ken Iman—*Los Angeles Rams*

Holders

Joe Theismann—*Washington Redskins*
Richie Petitbon—*Chicago Bears*
Bob Chandler—*Buffalo Bills/Oakland Raiders*
Bobby Layne—*Detroit Lions*
Bart Starr—*Green Bay Packers*
Paul Krause—*Minnesota Vikings*
Sonny Jurgensen—*Washington Redskins*

Elroy Hirsch—*Los Angeles Rams*
Tommy James—*Cleveland Browns*
Joe Scarpetti—*New Orleans Saints*
Tom Flores—*Los Angeles Raiders*
Ken Stabler—*Los Angeles Raiders*
Bobby Boyd—*Baltimore Colts*
Jim Zorn—*Seattle Seahawks*

Kickers

George Blanda—*Oakland Raiders*
Lou Groza—*Cleveland Browns*
Mark Mosley—*Washington Redskins*
Bruce Gossett—*Los Angeles Rams*
Bob Waterfield—*Los Angeles Rams*
Ben Agajanian—*Los Angeles Rams*
Jan Stenerud—*Kansas City Chiefs*
Fred Cox—*Minnesota Vikings*
Jim Turner—*Denver Broncos*
Jim Bakken—*St. Louis Cardinals*
Paul Hornung—*Green Bay Packers*

Tom Dempsey—*New Orleans Saints*
Garo Yepremian—*Miami Dolphins*
Roy Gerela—*Pittsburgh Steelers*
Pete Gogolak—*New York Giants*
Dan Crockroft—*Cleveland Browns*
Lou Michaels—*Pittsburgh Steelers*
Ray Wersching—*San Francisco Forty Niners*
Chester Marcol—*Green Bay Packers*
Earl "Dutch" Clark—*Detroit Lions*
Doak Walker—*Detroit Lions*
Pat Summerall—*New York Giants*

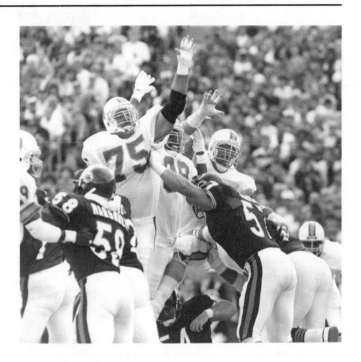

CHAPTER 8

Point-After-Touchdown and Field Goal Defense

In professional football it is possible to use an all-out 11-man rush on P-A-T situations. However, in high school and college football, due to the 2-point conversion, it is not advisable to commit all 11 men to the rush unless it is a "desperate block" situation.

We will be including a broad range of P-A-T and field goal defensive plays in this chapter, and among them will be some 11-man, maximum rush situations to be used for desperate block situations in both circumstances.

GENERAL INFORMATION

Most teams are extremely lax when attempting to block a P-A-T or field goal. Many more place-kicks can be blocked if teams are determined to do so. Kick-blocking success provides a tremendous margin for winning those close games that determine championships.

On field goal defense there are a variety of situations a team must prepare for regularly:

- *Maximum rush,* to be used in a positive kicking situation where all resources are committed to the rush with no concern for the fake or the return
- *Basic P-A-T/field goal block,* which has built into it elements of rush, normal precaution against fake, and provision for a return
- *Field goal rush with added precaution against the fake,* which is similar to the basic block, adjusted to move the middle linebacker back off the line to key and contain the holder to watch for fake
- *Field goal prevent,* used to encourage an opponent to kick, when the main concern is guarding against the fake

137

Proper defense against the field goal also requires being prepared for the possibility of returning the field goal by setting a blocking wall on the same side as the rush, recovering and advancing a blocked field goal, reacting to the partially blocked field goal, and games (internal and corner group) on the rush. Preparation on these elements takes practice, so allow generous practice time to execute them properly—it will pay off, I promise you!

Rules

The following rules will help you in preparation:

- Field goal attempt from 20-yard line and missed—our ball at the line of scrimmage.
- Field goal attempt from inside 20-yard line and missed—our ball at the 20-yard line. Provided: The receiving team does not touch the ball in the field of play on our side of the line of scrimmage.
- Field goal attempt is touched on the offensive side of the line of scrimmage and then crosses the line of scrimmage: no change in the above.
- Field goal attempt following a fair catch (free kick lineup): no change.
- Field goal is blocked and does not cross the line of scrimmage: Either team can advance it.
- Field goal made: The team scored on has the choice to kick or receive. Do not talk.

Principles

Players should learn the following P-A-T and field goal principles:

- A field goal or P-A-T is never routine. Concentrate on your assignments. Know the personnel you align on. Be alert for any change in personnel alignment that tips off a fake field goal attempt. Be alert for a safe field goal call from the bench.
- We must avoid any penalty. A penalty on a field goal or P-A-T can be the most costly and decide the ball game.
  a. Too many men on the field. Know when you belong on the field. If you are a substitute, be alert if regular is not able to be in the game.
  b. Alert to a safe field goal. Only *regular* defensive personnel should be on the field if a safe field goal is called.
  c. Do not be offside.
  d. Roughing the kicker. When you take your proper course to the "sweet spot" you should never rough the kicker or holder.
- Avoid touching the ball on the defensive side of the line of scrimmage.
- Exceptions:
  a. The opponent attempts a tie-breaker field goal with time expired—return it for a touchdown.
  b. A poorly kicked or partially blocked ball on which the return possibility clearly exceeds the line of scrimmage or the 20-yard line. This is particularly true at the end of a half or game when we are behind. Field such a kick and get out of bounds in order to save a few seconds.
- If the opponent's field goal kicker is in the game, and the opponent lines up in (or shifts to) a regular formation, our audible is "Star" coverage outside the danger zone at the Red 15-yard line and "Free" coverage inside the Red 15-yard line.
- If they have motion by the holder or the kicker, it is a spread formation toward the motion. The audible is "Star" outside the Red 15- yard line and "Charlie" inside the 15-yard line.
- If either wing goes in motion, the man with coverage on him goes with him, and the original call stays on.
- Fake field goals
  a. Tips
     1. Any change in posture of the holder
     2. Any change in #1 and #2 personnel

3. Any outside movement by any blocker at the snap

4. Release by #1 or #2

- Reaction

    a. Coverage element: Lock on men or take force key from your man.

    b. Contain man: Contain ball. Cover the kicker or holder if either attempts to release as receiver.

    c. Rush element: Zip and Plug. Come off rush force on the ball as quickly as possible. Defensive line widens to the ball.

    d. Do not allow the man with the ball to reverse his direction and scramble.

- Broken play, bad snap, muffled hold, and so on

    a. Treat like a fake field goal.

    b. Apply assignments and reactions.

MAXIMUM RUSH

If the game situation suggests that a positive kicking circumstance exists, for either the P-A-T or the field goal, consider using the maximum rush. These situations generally occur toward the end of a half or on the last play of the game; however, clever disguising of the initial alignment may permit jumping into a maximum rush at the last second without telegraphing the intent, thereby gaining an element of surprise. The following maximum rush plays are our specific recommendations for every team's kicking game playbook.

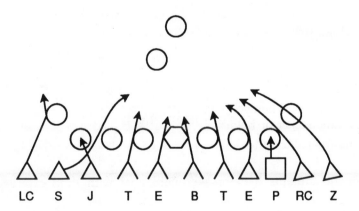

Maximum Rush Right

Z   Drive hard outside the hip of HB. Flatten your course and lay out in the kicking lane.

RC   Drive hard through the gap just outside their end. Flatten your course and lay out in the kicking lane.

P   Line up head-on with their end. Drive into him hard, breaking down his protection base.

RE   Drive the end-tackle gap.

LT & RT   Drive the tackle-guard gap.

B & LE   Drive hard over the shoulder of the center. Knock him deep into the backfield. Get hands high.

J   Line up on the inside shoulder of the end. Drive into him hard, opening the lane.

S   Loop behind the charge and drive the end-tackle gap.

LC   Drive the outside shoulder of HB, seeking to occupy him. *Do not* attempt to rush the kicker.

Maximum Rush Left

Z   LC   P   E   T   B   E   T   J   S   RC

Z   Drive hard outside the hip of HB. Flatten your course and lay out in the kicking lane.

LC   Drive hard through the gap just outside their end. Flatten your course and lay out in the kicking lane.

P   Line up head-on with their end. Drive into him hard, breaking down his protection base.

LE   Drive the end-tackle gap.

LT & RT   Drive the tackle-guard gap.

B & RE   Drive hard over the shoulder of the center. Knock him deep into the backfield. Get hands high.

J   Line up on the inside shoulder of the end. Drive into him hard, opening the lane.

S   Loop behind the charge and drive the end-tackle gap.

RC   Drive the outside shoulder of HB, seeking to occupy him. *Do not* attempt to rush the kicker.

Kamikaze Right

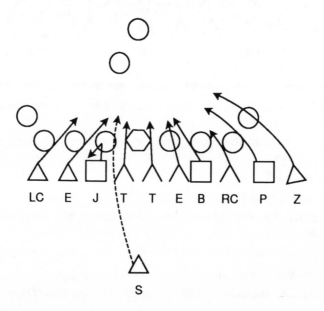

LC   E   J   T   T   E   B   RC   P   Z

S

Z   Drive hard outside the hip of HB. Flatten your course and lay out in the kicking lane.

P   Drive hard over the outside foot of the end. Flatten your course and lay out in the kicking lane.

RC   Line up on the inside shoulder of the end. Drive hard through the outside foot of
(LC for left)   the tackle.

B   Line up on the tackle. Drive hard through the gap to the inside of the tackle.

RE   Line up shading the outside shoulder of the guard. Drive hard over the guard, knock-
(LE for left)   ing him into the backfield. Get hands high.

RT & LT   Drive hard over the shoulder of the center. Knock him deep into the backfield. Get your hands high.

J   Line up on the guard. Seek to pull him out.

LE   Line up on the tackle. Drive hard over his inside foot.
(RE for left)

LC   Line up on the end. Drive hard over his inside foot.
(RC for left)

S   Stunt through the gap.

Note: You can arrange pull stunts with different rushmen.

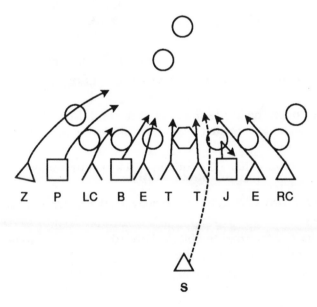

Kamikaze Left

FIELD GOAL BLOCK

The field goal block is a game saver. Teams with a full complement of field goal block plays in their playbook can select one or two to practice for upcoming opponents each week. Detailed film analysis and scouting reports will allow the staff to determine an opponent's vulnerability to a particular type of block or game. The opponent's field goal unit should be duplicated in practice and their mistakes or weaknesses exploited by the block play or game that takes the most advantage of these flaws. Repeated practice against these possibilities develops the players' ability to immediately recognize developing situations and react quickly and properly to block the field goal using the predetermined play.

The basic field goal block must be executed flawlessly until it is instinctive for the players. This play (both left and right) must be among the very first special teams plays to be practiced in the early days of preseason. Without consistent proper execution of this play, the threat diminishes and all other variations lose their effectiveness. The basic field goal alignments and assignments are as follows.

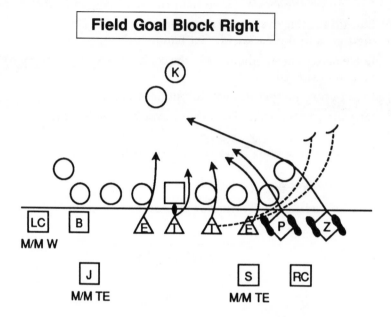

Field Goal Block Right

Z Key the ball—get fast through the hip of the wing. Lay out over the sweet spot.

P Key the ball—align one foot deeper, drive through the hip of the end. Force the wing to block down on you.

E Key the ball—drive through the inside shoulder of the end. Make him block you. Alert for switch call from the tackle; on "Switch" call draw block the swing to contain. Look for a screen or the first back out.

T Key the ball—draw the block—then take contain—on kicker or holder. Look for a screen or the first back out.

T Align nose on the center. Drive through the gap between the center and guard, getting hands high to block the kick.

E Align nose on the guard away from the block. Drive through the gap between the center and guard, getting hands high to block the kick.

B Contain—cover the kicker or holder—be alert for a screen.

LC M/M wing

S M/M TE

J M/M TE

RC M/M wing

Block Right Footwork of Zip and Plug

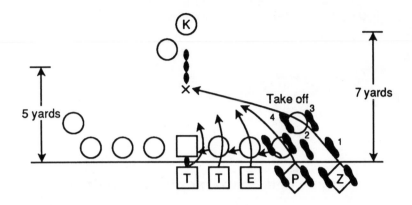

Z   Align *cocked to inside* outside foot back. Align wide enough to get a good close angle to the sweet spot, 4-1/2 yards from the ball. Take first step with outside foot across line of scrimmage; second step with inside foot; third step, drive off with outside foot to inside, adjusting course; fourth step, take off on inside foot and lay out body with arms out, eyes open, moving hands to block ball.

P   Align—cocked to the inside on the inside shoulder of the wing. Take first step with outside foot to cross the line of scrimmage with first step. On second step, jump over the step through the gap between TE and wing to get to the sweet spot, or force the wing to block down hard on you to give the zip a clean course to block.

Field Goal Block Left

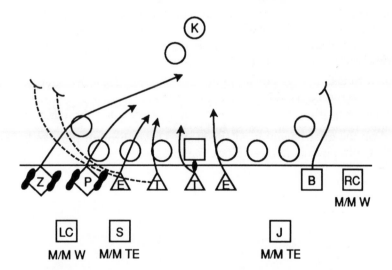

Z   Key the ball—get off fast through the hip of the wing and lay out over sweet spot.

P   Key the ball—align one foot deeper, drive through the hip of the end. Force the wing to block down on you.

E   Key the ball—drive through the inside shoulder of the end. Make him block you. Alert for "Switch" call from the tackle; on "Switch" call draw block the swing to contain. Look for screen or first back out.

T   Key the ball—draw the block—then take contain on the kicker or holder. Look for a screen or the first back out.

T   Align nose on the center. Drive through the gap between the center and guard, getting hands high to block the kick.

E   Align nose on the guard away from the block. Drive through the gap between the center and guard, getting hands high to block the kick.

B   Contain—cover the kicker or holder. Be alert for a screen.

LC M/M wing

S   M/M TE

J   M/M TE

RC M/M wing

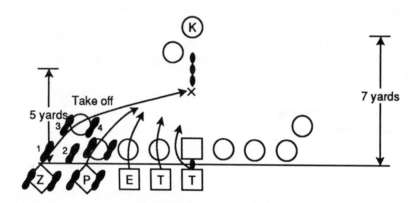

Block Left Footwork of Zip and Plug

Z   Align. *Cocked to inside* outside foot back. Align wide enough to get a good close angle to the sweet spot, 4-1/2 yards from the ball. Take first step with outside foot across the line of scrimmage; second step with inside foot; third step drive off the outside foot to the inside, adjusting course; fourth step, take off on inside foot and lay out body with arms out, eyes open, moving hands to block ball.

P   Align. Cocked to inside on inside shoulder of the wing. Take first step with outside foot to cross the line of scrimmage with first step. On second step, jump over and step through the gap between TE and wing to get to the sweet spot, or force the wing to block down hard on you to give the zip a clean course to block.

Field Goal Block Middle Jump

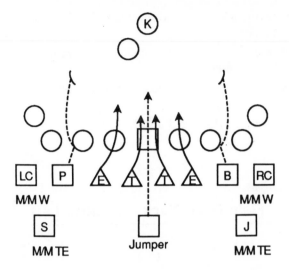

Jumper   Get lined up. So your jump will be in the path of the ball, time your jump to get over the defensive line; get to the ball as it comes off the ground.

ETTE   Drive the offensive line back well on aggressive charge. We must get linemen low and drive back off the ball.

P & B   Stick the tackle so he cannot block down on the jumper, then go to contain.

Field Goal Block—In-Close Right

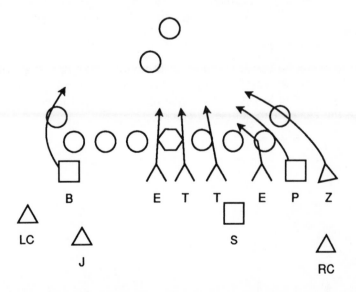

Z   Rush hard outside the hip of HB. Flatten course and lay out in the kicking lane.

P   Drive over the outside foot of the end. Flatten course and lay out in the kicking lane.

RE   Pull the end inside. Do not let him out! He is your responsibility on a pass.
(LE for left)

RT   Drive the gap between the guard and tackle.
(LT for left)

LT & LE   Drive hard over the shoulder of the center. Knock him deep into the backfield. Get
(RT & RE   hands high.
for left)

B   Rush from the outside. *Do not* attempt to block the kick! Contain the holder. Tackle
him if he rolls out.

S   Line up opposite their tackle on the side of the rush. Key the holder. Contain him
if he rolls out on a fake.

RC   Cover HB on a pass. Play the pass first. If HB blocks and the end releases, cover
(LC for left)   the end.

LC & J   Cover in and out on their end and halfback.
(RC & J for
left)

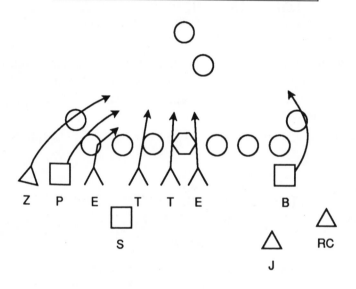

Field Goal Block—In Close Left

PAT Block

Z Key the ball, get off fast through the hip. Wing—lay out over the sweet spot.

B Key the ball, drive through the hip of TE. Make the wing block you.

P Key the ball, drive through the inside shoulder of the end. Make him block you.

T & E Drive the center and guards back off the ball to get penetration and give jumpers a chance to get the ball behind the line of scrimmage.

DB Keep OT from blocking down on the jumper. Be alert for a fumbled snap.

DB Keep TE from blocking down on the jumper. Be alert for a fumbled snap.

J Get lined up, get a running start, and line up over the course of the ball. When the ball is kicked, get high up over the line of scrimmage to bat it down.

Finally, after the basic field goal block and its variations are thoroughly absorbed, the various games can be easily taught. These games allow a P-A-T/field goal block unit to exploit the weaknesses of individual opposing team players. Start with the rushman games, then the corner games, and finally the combination games, teaching them first as part of the general special teams repertoire, then concentrating on one aspect intensely for a specific practice period; this will best etch the games into the players' minds.

After the players know the fundamentals and mechanics of each game, the details can be easily reactivated for use against a specific team and executed properly within the practice time allowed in preparation for playing that team.

The following games include the best that any teams of ours have ever used.

P-A-T and Field Goal Rushmen Games

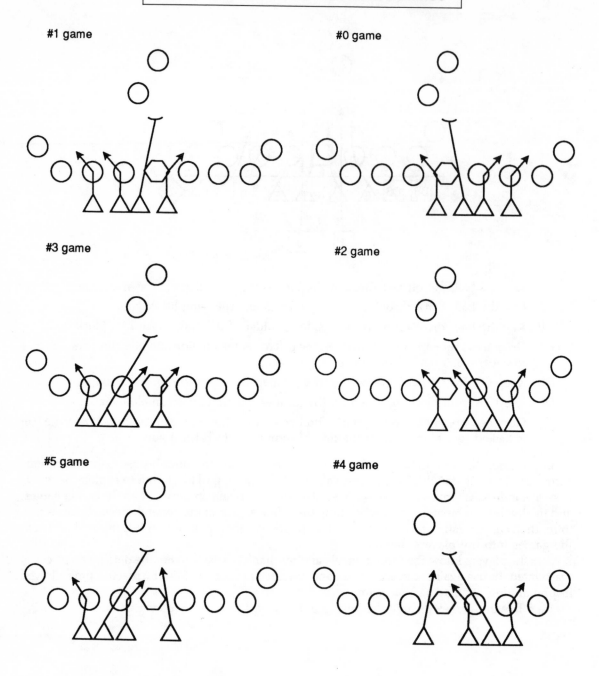

#7 game

#6 game

#42 game (10 and 32)

#12 game (1 and 2)

#30 game (3 and 0)

#12 game (1 and 2)

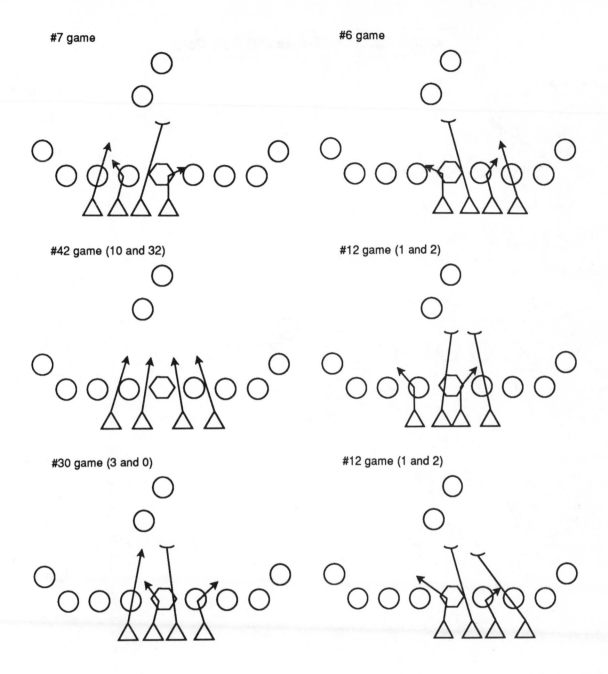

Corner Games on P-A-Ts and Field Goals

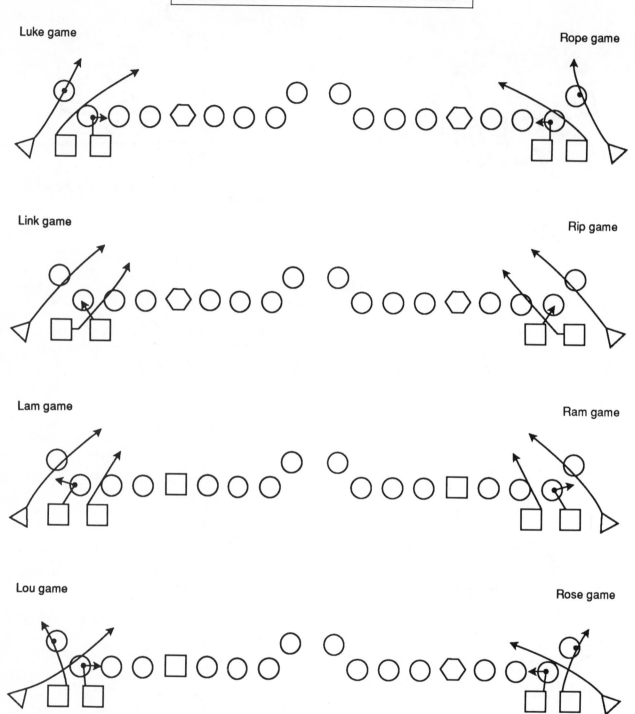

Luke game

Rope game

Link game

Rip game

Lam game

Ram game

Lou game

Rose game

Combination Games—Rushmen and Corners

41 luke   42 rope

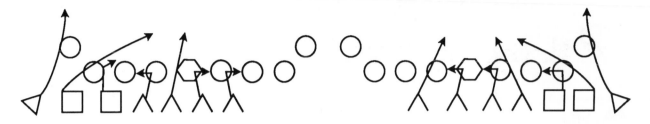

43 link   40 rip

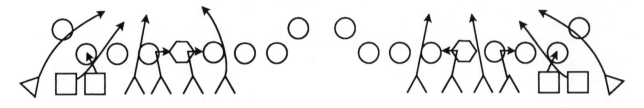

43 lam   40 ram

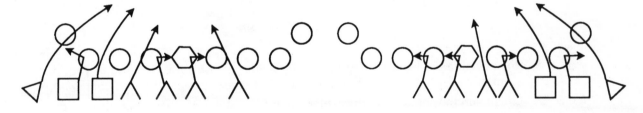

41 lou   42 rose

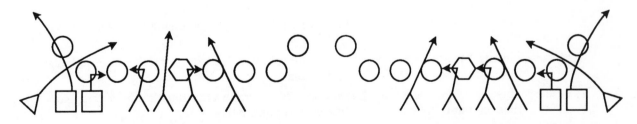

FIELD GOAL PREVENT

Given a game situation in which a field goal by your opponent will not hurt, but a touchdown or a first down that could lead to a touchdown might spell defeat, the best course of action is to invite the opponent to kick the ball. This prevent alignment discourages and most often defeats a fake field goal.

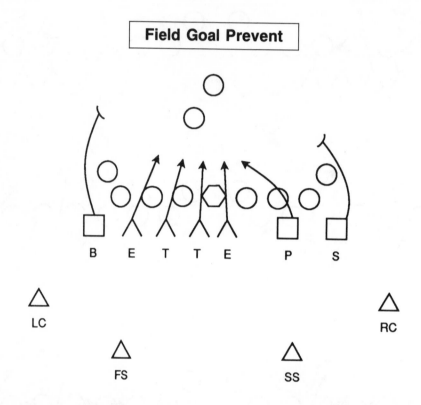

Field Goal Prevent

B & S	Rush outside the halfback. Do not let the holder (passer) roll out around you on a run or pass. Do not try to block the kick, but stress keeping the play contained.
RT & RE	Line up on the shoulder of the center. Charge hard into the backfield, driving the center back with you. React to the play (kick or fake).
LT	Drive hard through the guard-tackle gap. React to the play.
LE	Line up on the inside shoulder of the end. Drive hard over the outside foot of their tackle. React to the play.
P	Line up just outside their tackle, and rush hard over his outside foot. React to the play.
Safeties	Line up 8 yards deep, opposite the inside shoulder of the offensive end. You have in-out coverage on their end and halfback.
Cornerbacks	Line up 6 yards deep and 4 yards outside the halfback. Effect in-out coverage on their end and halfback. Coordinate with your safety.
Note to DBs	Play your receiver and not the kicker. Play pass responsibilities first.

FIELD GOAL RETURN

If your opponent is about to attempt a long kick, either in desperation or near the end of a half, and it is a kick that you feel has little or no chance of success, you might consider using your basic prevent personnel. Adjusting the prevent to the following field goal return alignment may allow you to return a short or errant kick (that does not reach the goal line) into a return for positive yardage.

Field Goal Return

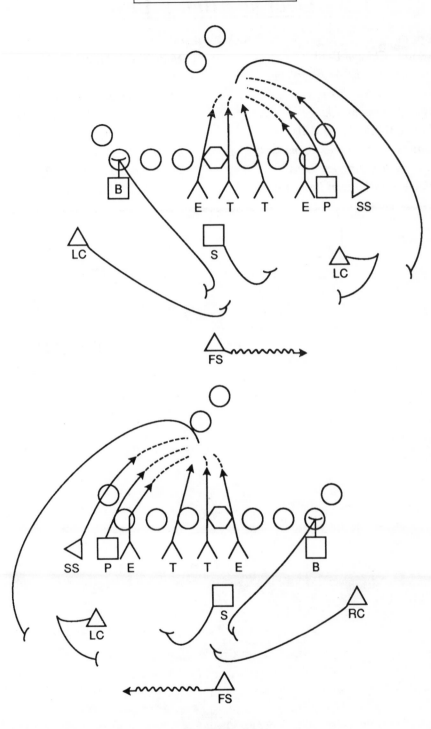

General rules

1. Go through with your block attempt and pass defense responsibilities.
2. Peel back toward the side from which you rushed, because these offensive men will be the ones more likely to be tied up.
3. S should pick up the first coverer to release inside.
4. Backside backer and halfback should get in position to keep the backside end and sprinter from getting to our safety.
5. Onside halfback should take the first wide coverer on the side of our return.

George Allen's Best

Kick Blockers

Doug Atkins—*Chicago Bears*

"Deacon" Jones—*Los Angeles Rams*

Carl Eller—*Minnesota Vikings*

Alan Page—*Minnesota Vikings*

Gino Marchetti—*Baltimore Colts*

Lamar Lundy—*Los Angeles Rams*

Merlin Olsen—*Los Angeles Rams*

Ron McDole—*Washington Redskins*

Matt Blair—*Minnesota Vikings*

Dick Butkus—*Chicago Bears*

Lester Hayes—*Los Angeles Raiders*

"Big Daddy" Lipscomb—*Baltimore Colts*

Diron Talbert—*Los Angeles Rams*

Dave Butz—*Washington Redskins*

Bill Brundige—*Washington Redskins*

CHAPTER 9

Special Teams Drills

Agility, conditioning, and reaction play a very important part in the development of players and therefore in team success. The drills in this chapter will improve these areas, particularly in relatation to the kicking game. We have presented 25 kicking drills that are, in our opinion, the most proven drills used today.

Every coach has an encyclopedia of drills, some of which date back to Knute Rockne's time, and some of these drills are still valuable. However, we believe there is a definite need for every coach, regardless of his experience or the level of football he is coaching, to update his repertoire of drills to keep pace with the latest trends. This chapter provides an up-to-date catalog of the most useful and successful kicking drills available to coaches today.

PUNTING DRILLS

Stance and Steps Drill

The first job is to set the stance, to discover how the feet should be placed at the beginning of a kick.

Before making any kind of punt, the kicker should stand with the kicking foot forward. Most kickers will find they need to take only one step with the nonkicking foot before they kick with the other. This eliminates the unnecessary extra step most untrained kickers take.

Have the kicker take his stance until he feels comfortable and solidly set; while he is in this position, push him forward, back, left, and right. If his feet are poorly placed, the kicker will easily be pushed off balance. Balance is an integral part of each good, accurate kick.

After the kicker has found his correct stance, have him practice making his kicking steps and go through the motions of kicking the football. No ball is needed in this drill for steps. He is just trying to get the feel of the act.

Sometimes it helps to outline the position of the feet throughout the kicking procedure. Chalk marks or dye can be placed on the grass. In this way the kicker can check himself as he practices the dry-run kick. Soon the footwork will become second nature.

Foot Position Drill

This is more of an exercise. Not everyone can point his foot to full extension at first. Kickers should practice pointing their toes daily. This means really bringing the heel up and the toes down. During warm-up, the kicker should sit on the ground and have a teammate (or manager) grab his toes and depress them, keeping the heel solidly on the ground. He should also take 10 to 15 short jab-steps each day, stressing the point of the toe.

Kicking Without Center Snap Drill

Punters will want to practice kicking many times when a center is not available. They should get several balls together at one place. They want to simulate the ball striking the hands. An important part of the kicking performance is the quick manipulation of the ball in the hands. This is necessary to get the laces up and to extend the ball forward, ready to place it on the foot.

An excellent drill for this is done by tossing the ball a few inches into the air, quickly adjusting it the moment it strikes the hands, then going through all the motions of kicking the football.

After the kicker has kicked all the balls, he goes to the other end of the field and shags the balls so he can kick them back.

Drop Drill

Faulty punting usually results from a poor drop from the hands to the moving foot. Have the punters go through the kicking procedure, but don't let them kick the ball. Check the drop. Another way to do this is to just "bunt" the ball. Kickers will quickly see a good drop, and rhythmical leg swing will get unusual distance without much force.

Foot and Ball Relationship Drill

Have the kicker mark the middle seam on the underside of the ball with soft white chalk before he kicks the ball. After the kicker has completed his follow-through, observe the line made by the chalked middle seam on the instep. If that line is at a slight angle to the inside of the kicking shoe and crosses the laces about midway, you should have a good punt.

Form and Accuracy Drill

Distance is not a concern in this drill. Make sure the kicker understands that. This is a drill for kicking short at a set target.

Have the kicker work with another player about 10 yards away. The kicker just meets the ball and practices until he gets it to the other man. The receiving player should hold his hands up as a target. The kicker should always check his stance, see that his running foot and the nose of the ball are pointed in the direction of the target. Always see that the ball is held properly.

This is a good time to practice raising or lowering the point on the drop to gain loft or kick a line drive. Gradually lengthen the distance in this drill.

Rhythm and Speed Drill

The action of the kicker can be timed quite accurately by a stopwatch. First, clock the time from when the center passes to when the ball reaches the kicker's hands. Next, time the speed with which the kicker kicks the ball after it has reached his hands. Third, time the whole process. In this manner you can determine just when the kicking action is being delayed. These are the common causes of delay:

- The center snap is slow or arches like a rainbow.
- The kicker didn't move into the ball when receiving it.
- The kicker fiddles with the ball too much, getting it set for the drop.
- The kicker takes too many steps.

Be sure you time this from the exact distance your kicking formation dictates. If you punt from the spread punt, the kicker should align at 14 yards.

Punt Under Pressure Drill

This is a good drill for a center, punter, and defenseman who are logical punt blockers (Figure 9.1). Place the rushers on either side of the center, out about 7 yards. Allow only one rusher from either side to come on the snap and try to block the kick. The kicker kicks without any blocking. If the kicker is back 14 yards, the center snap is perfect, and the kicker kicks quickly and on rhythm, the blocker will have to get a real jump on the snap to block the kick. This forces kicker concentration. It also makes the center realize his importance in the kicking game. Further, the rushers learn to go for the ball out in front of the kicker. There is nothing more frustrating than to finally get your opponent stopped, force him to punt, and then have one of your defenders rough the kicker.

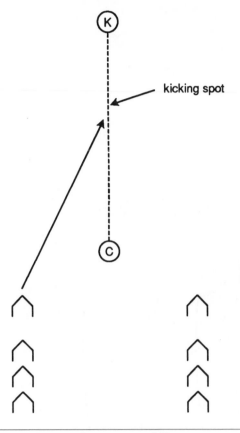

Figure 9.1. Punt under pressure drill.

Punter Concentration Drill

Have two centers side by side. The first center is the real center and snaps first. After the punter receives the ball, have the other center rifle another ball at the kicker. The second ball may cause the kicker to lose balance or draw his eyes off the ball he is supposed to kick, or both.

Suddenly cross in front of the kicker when he is about to kick.

Get up a crowd around the kicker with only a narrow opening to kick through. Have them shout and try other distractions.

Once in a while center back a wet ball without the kicker's knowledge.

At first some of these things will bother the kicker, but they can be applied to benefit him tremendously.

Bad-Pass Drill

Take the offensive team to their own 1-yard line and declare fourth down. The kicker is now lined up on the restraining line. Go through the kicking procedure, but do not allow defenders to block the kick if they break through the protection. The center purposely snaps bad passes high, low, and to either side. The passes are receivable, but just off enough to cause problems.

Another bad-pass drill involves just the kicker and a coach. Use this as a pregame warm-up drill. The coach rolls back bouncing balls to the kicker, who must field the ball and get the kick away. You must always drill for the unexpected.

Team Punting Drill

Use a full offensive team in a kicking situation. Against them have seven or eight rushers and one safetyman (Figure 9.2). Make the punt rush full-speed and the punt coverage full-speed up to the tackling point. The idea is to protect the kick and cover the kick, but reduce the injury possibility that would exist if you allowed full-speed punt returns. Without defensive blockers in the way, you can more easily check the covering team to see whether they are in lanes. Also, the covering team must come to collection as they move in for the tackle. Station a coach down by the punt receiver to call the coverage to collection as they near the ball.

PUNT RECEIVING DRILLS

Every time the punters are punting, the punt return men should receive. They should work mostly around the 10-yard line, and a coach should be with them to correct mistakes. The following points are checked:

- Get under the ball.
- Don't try to field a ball you are not "under."
- Catch the ball in the hands and then bring the ball in to the body.
- When the ball hits the hands, the elbows and knees give a little with the drop of the ball.
- Put the ball away and start to run.

Fair Catch Drill

Always have practice time for fielding fair catches. The procedure is the same as for catching punts for return, except that when the ball reaches the receiver's hands and the elbows and knees give, go right to the ground with the left knee. This leaves the right knee directly under the "basket" made by the hands and arms. This prevents the ball from slipping through and reduces the fumble possibility.

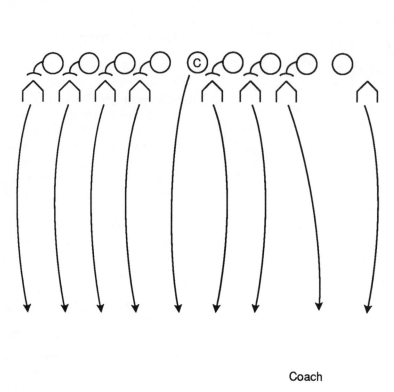

Coach

S

Figure 9.2.   Team punting drill.

Team Punt Return Drill

The scout team punts to the defense. The rush may be full-speed; sprint to the blocking pattern, but knock off the contact at that point (Figure 9.3). A good way to keep this realistic is to have the blockers grab the covering team in both arms as a signal to stop. Be sure to kick from both hashmarks as well as from the middle of the field.

Every punt return has points that must be followed:

- There must be someone to force the kicker to kick. Usually the offside rush will force the kicker to kick the ball to the side you wish to return to.

- Occupy as many kick covers as you can for as long as you can.
- Form a blocking wall that is equally spaced from receiver to line of scrimmage.
- The three deep men should be placed to receive short or squibbed kicks but still be in the blocking pattern.
- One deep man always insures the catch by being a personal guard against the first man down.
- On sideline returns, the returner should always head upfield first to draw in the coverage.
- There should always be a man in the wall assigned to check the area between the wall and the sideline for ''lurkers.''

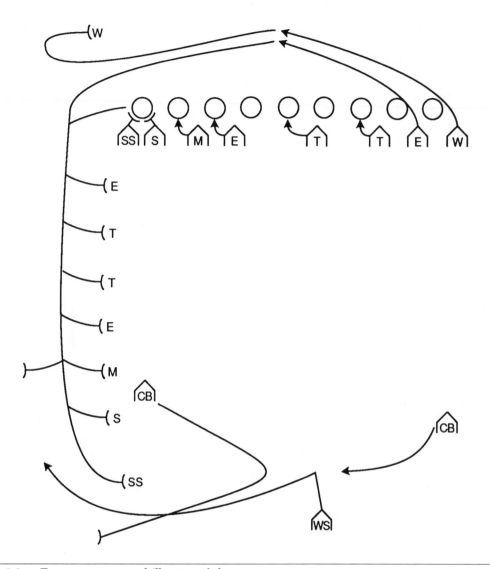

Figure 9.3a. Team punt return drill, return left.

Team Punt Return Drill Against the Wind

In order to save time and avoid confusion, set up a kicking team in position to punt. Alternate the two defensive units against this setup. When the ball is snapped, the offense remains passive and does not cover. The defense goes through their assignments of rush and delay and forms the downfield pattern. The punt receiver catches and runs the play out. The next team jumps in and executes the return.

PLACEKICKING DRILLS

Individual Kicking Position Drill

In placekicking, the kicker is approaching a fixed object: the ball. The kicker must have his steps down so pat that every time he makes an approach his feet will fall in exactly the same pattern and have precisely the same spacing. He can't expect to accomplish this by guesswork. He must mark his steps.

To mark his steps, the kicker stands with the kicking foot as it would contact the ball when the kick is made, and puts a marker (piece of canvas or white cardboard) under the nonkicking foot. Then he takes a long step backward to measure the distance covered by the forward hop. He brings the feet together so that the marker may be put underneath the kicking foot. Then he takes another, but shorter, step backward with the nonkicking foot. Next he brings the kicking foot alongside it and should now be in starting position. The kicker is now ready to kick.

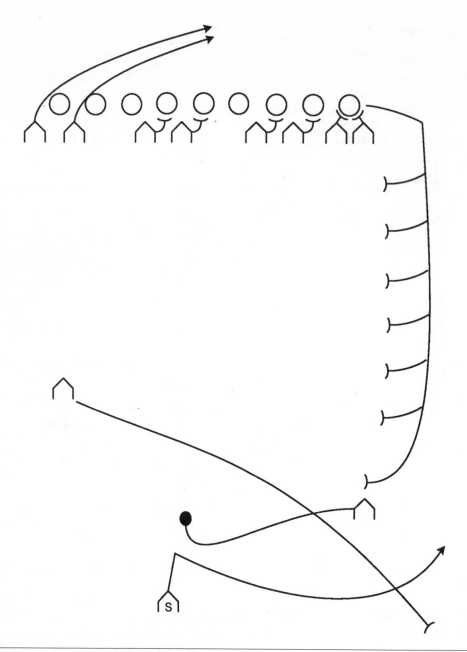

Figure 9.3b. Team punt return drill, return right.

Placekicking Contact-Point Drill

In practice, the ball should be marked with an inverted pyramid centered on the seam in the lower half of the ball. The bottom point is placed on the rear middle seam, just 3 inches up from the bottom end of the ball. The top line is 3 inches higher (6 inches up from the bottom end of the ball) and is 3 inches long, drawn at right angles to the middle seam, extending out 1-1/2 inches on each side of it. Mark it with dark-colored chalk. Mark a white dot on the front of the kicking toe.

The white dot will show up on the ball when it is kicked. After each kick, note carefully just where the foot hit the ball. Having determined this, wipe the area within the triangle clean for the next kick. Be sure not to erase the triangle or the line on the rear seam of the ball, because they may give additional information as to just how the kicker is contacting the ball by the lines they leave on the kicking foot.

The exact spot where the placekicker's toe should hit the ball is about 5 inches from the bottom tip of the ball and directly on the rear middle seam.

Placekicking Practice Drill

Use a skeleton unit of a center, holder, placekicker, and two rushers. The rushers line up 5 yards on either side of the center and alternate rushing the kick on the snap of the ball. It is better to use only one rusher at a time. Also, the rushers should be started from 5 yards deep in the secondary (Figure 9.4); this added distance allows for the kick to get off, but it is close enough to be a mental factor.

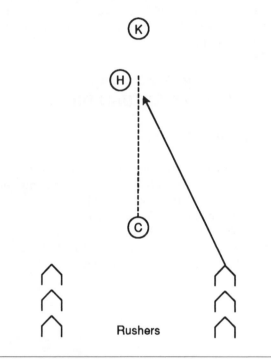

Figure 9.4. Placekicking practice drill.

On this drill, you work on the center snap, holder, placement, and kick. The timing between these three players is most important. Use at least five balls. A manager or spare player should catch the balls and pass them back to a spare rusher who places the ball by the center. Five minutes a day is sufficient time for this drill.

Field Goal Drill

Use exactly the same setup as in the preceding drill, only keep moving the ball back farther and farther. Also, move it from hash to hash. It is a good idea to keep records on successful kicks from the different distances. Not counting the wind factor, you should pretty well know the chances for a successful kick from anywhere from the 40-yard line on in.

Multiple Field Goal Drill

Use your best three field-goal kickers, each with a center and holder. Place the groups in various positions on the field. This drill is designed to save time. Use a stopwatch to time each group. Three to 4 seconds between each group should be acceptable. Also, you'll need several managers to catch all these balls.

Team Rush on Extra-Point Attempts Drill

The defensive unit should always rush with at least nine men when trying to block extra-point attempts. There should always be two points of penetration: one from the outside and one up the middle (Figure 9.5). The reason for not coming from both outsides at once is the injury factor to the rushers. One man will be more reckless when he knows he is not on a collision course with a teammate. The penetration points are areas where you put more rushers than there are blockers. Outside is the more successful, because you can force the offense to block in, avoiding a jammed situation, and spring one man clean. However, this one man is fairly wide by this time. He must get a super start and lay out, stretching his whole body in the air. His arms are outstretched, and if he times it right he has a chance to get his hands on the ball. The middle penetration is a question of finding a crack in the blocking and powering through.

Team Rush on Field Goal Attempts Drill

Rushing field goal attempts is a different situation for two reasons. First, there is much more likelihood

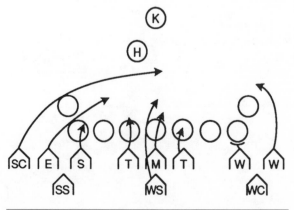

Figure 9.5. Team rush on extra-point attempts drill.

of a fake field goal and a run or pass; and second, you always need a safety to field short kicks. This leaves a maximum front line of eight. Of the eight who line up to rush, two must fake a rush, cover the flats, and be containers in the event of a run. You can still try to penetrate at the same two points. The third man is on the left side, and the second man in on the right side should draw blocks and then escape into the flat, looking for screens, flat passes, or a run, as in the three deep play zone pass defense (Figure 9.6).

KICKS WITHOUT A CALLED RETURN

It is a good idea to have a set return on all kicks other than those kicks where a return has been called. Let's take these situations:

- A punt rush is on.
- A team comes out on third down and aligns in punt formation.
- A field goal is attempted.
- Your opponent quick-kicks.

All these situations should have a stock return. Your team will never remember a variety of returns. A good coaching expression is, "All surprise kicks are left returns."

Punt Rush Drill

There are as many punt rushes as there are imaginations to dream them up. For simplicity, it is a good idea to plan your punt return and punt rush from the same front. There are a couple of exceptions, however. You may want a special rush to take care of a weakness noted in the punt protection of a particular opponent. Also, once in a while you may want to risk everything and go with a 9- or 10-man rush. Whatever your plan or scheme, this drill is hardly ever done at full speed. You train your players and rehearse the action. Figure 9.7 shows a 10-man rush.

KICKOFF AND
KICKOFF RETURN DRILLS

Basic Kickoff Drill

Use the portion of the field between the hashmark and the sideline from the far 40-yard line into the goal line. Take your two best kickoff men, and place one on the far 40 and one on the goal line. The kicker on the 40 has two footballs, and the kicker on the goal line has one already teed up. The kicker on the 40 tees up one ball and kicks it.

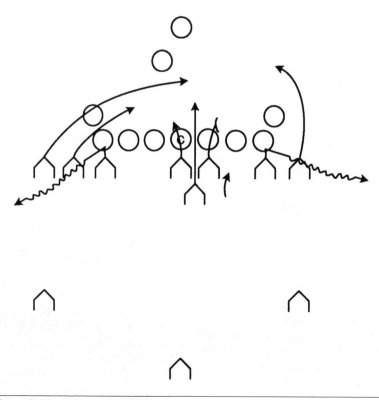

Figure 9.6. Team rush on field goal attempts drill.

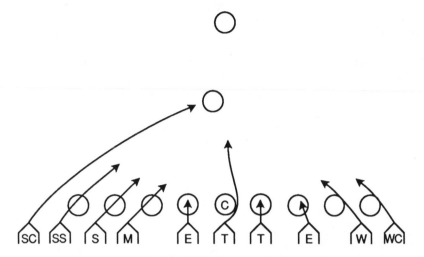

Figure 9.7. Punt rush drill.

The kicker on the goal receives the kick while the first kicker tees up his second ball. The receiver then kicks back toward the far 40-yard line (Figure 9.8). In this fashion each kicker has a teed-up ball waiting. A couple of managers are helpful to field stray kicks. Eight kicks a day are enough. Kickers can swap sides if the wind is a big factor.

Kickoff Return Drill

This is always a team drill. Much time is lost if your kickoff man is a poor one. To make sure the time spent on kickoff returns is meaningful, use a strong passer to simulate the kickoff. This way you can time the reception with the blocking pattern. If your passer can't get the ball high and deep enough, move him 20 yards out in front of the covering team (Figure 9.9). As with punt returns, you don't want this drill with full-speed blocking. Have the receiving team use a two-arm grab to simulate a block.

Combination Drill

This drill combines centering, kicking, kick rushing, kick coverage, passing, and receiving. Use two or three sets of five interior linemen to go one at a time. Also use three kickers in a single file. Set up three sets of defensive ends 5 yards off the line (this is because there is no blocking for the kicker). Punt receivers are downfield for the reception of the punts.

The sequence works like this: The first set of interior linemen take position; the center snaps to the kicker, and the ends rush the kick; the kicker kicks to the punt receivers; the linemen cover in lanes and break down in tackling position when near the punt returner; the punt receiver throws a long pass to one of the linemen, who returns the ball to the next center. Offensive ends can also be

Figure 9.8. Kickoff drill.

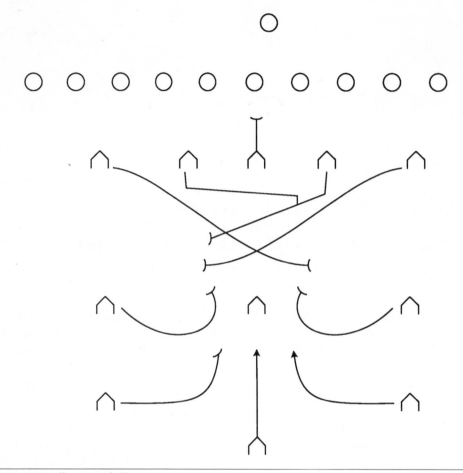

Figure 9.9. Kickoff return drill.

used if you have enough offensive personnel (Figure 9.10).

Kickoff Cover Drill

The most dangerous thing you can do is get your 11 fastest men, put them on the kickoff cover team, and let them all go for the ball. Kickoffs should be covered in waves. There should be three fast, reckless men who go for the ball any way they can get there, as fast as they can get there. The kicker should not be one of these men. It is best to have one of these men next to the kicker and one from each side. The next wave includes everyone but the two safetymen. The second wave tries to stay in lanes and keep containment. Two safetymen back up each side. The ball may be placed anywhere between the hashmarks. Even spacing is promoted by placing the tee in line with one of the uprights of the goal post. This means you can have a kick coverer 5 yards from each sideline and place the others at 5-yard intervals between these two. This leaves the safetyman and the kicker (Figure 9.11).

A good way to drill kickoffs is to start practice with them, just as they start the game. Right after warm-ups, go to four or five kickoff covers, then proceed with the practice schedule. You do not have to have a full receiving team. Kickoff coverage can be timed against the wind. If personnel exist for a scout receiving team, line them up as your next opponent aligns to receive kickoffs. They can form the return, but this should not be done live.

Surprise Kick Return Drill

Your opponent may surprise you with a kick in one of two situations: (a) It's third down, your opponent has the ball in back of his own 30, the yards remaining may be short or long, your defensive signal caller has called one of your regular defenses, your opponent comes out in punt formation; or (b) your opponent quick-kicks. In both cases, you've got to go with the defense called, except that your secondary must react. The easiest adjustment is for the strong safety to move to middle safety, the weak safety to retreat to a punt-receiving position, and the two corners remain the

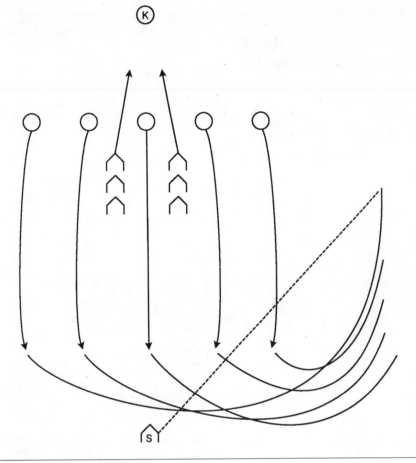

Figure 9.10. Combination drill.

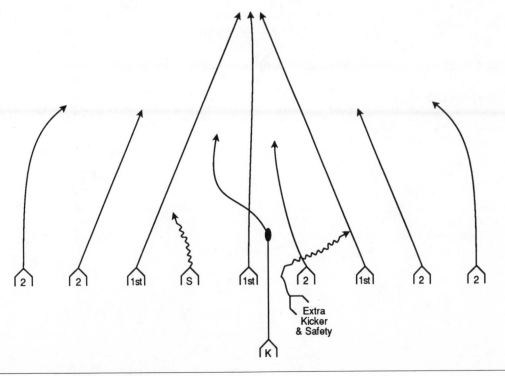

Figure 9.11. Kickoff cover drill.

same. The three remaining secondary men play zone.

Three-deep schemes must rotate back. The best way to drill on this is to have the scout team occa-

sionally pull a surprise kicking situation during your signal drill. Figure 9.12 shows a four-deep reaction.

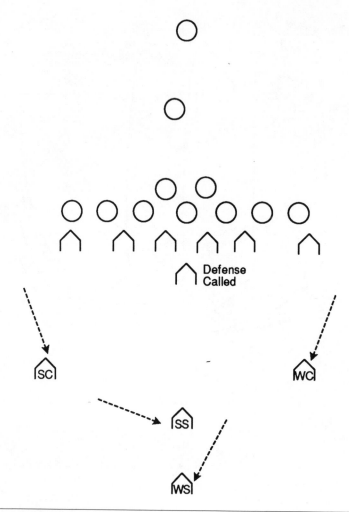

Figure 9.12.   Surprise kick return drill.

CHAPTER 10

George Allen's Special Teams Hall of Fame

This chapter is divided into two areas. The first area is a hall of fame for special teams players and coaches who were in professional football before 1985, most of whom have been named among ''George Allen's Best'' in the preceding chapters. The second area is potential special teams hall-of-famers who have been playing and/or coaching from 1986 to the present.

Before the nominations begin, it is important to say just a few words about the type of people who achieve the degree of success required to be nominated to this hall of fame. The one common denominator running through these individuals is the belief that *nothing is impossible!* These men usually make the team in the first place because they have developed this attitude, and they have had to work hard for almost everything. For that reason they understand, value, respect, and cherish their accomplishments.

St. Francis of Assisi, who is unquestionably the patron saint of special teams players, once wrote: ''To accomplish the impossible you must start with what is necessary; then you accomplish what is possible and, before long, the impossible has been done.'' I believe that to be the basic credo of these ''special'' men.

I think you can now understand just how I feel about all the people who have been a part of this important phase of the great game of football, and these are the best of them.

Former NFL Players

Kickoff Returners

Travis Williams
Green Bay Packers

Gale Sayers
Chicago Bears

Ron Smith
Los Angeles Rams

Hugh McElhenny
San Francisco Forty Niners

Punt Returners

Eddie Brown
Washington Redskins

Terry Metcalf
St. Louis Cardinals

Jon Arnett
Los Angeles Rams

Leslie "Speedy" Duncan
San Diego Chargers

Kickoff and Punt Coverage Men

Rusty Tillman
Washington Redskins

Alex Hawkins
Baltimore Colts

Rocky Bleir
Pittsburgh Steelers

Jeff Barnes
Oakland Raiders

Centers

Ted Fritsch
Washington Redskins

Charlie Ane
Detroit Lions

Tom Catlin
Cleveland Browns

Chuck Bednarik
Philadelphia Eagles

Punt Blockers

Bill Malinchak
Washington Redskins

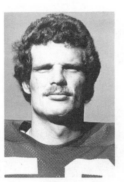

Ted Hendricks
Green Bay Packers

Punters

Ray Guy
Oakland Raiders

Bobby Joe Green
Chicago Bears

Yale Lary
Detroit Lions

Dave Jennings
New York Giants

Field Goal Kickers

George Blanda
Oakland Raiders

Lou Groza
Cleveland Browns

Mark Moseley
Washington Redskins

Jan Stenerud
Kansas City Chiefs

Holders

Paul Krause
Minnesota Vikings

Sonny Jurgensen
Washington Redskins

Richie Petitbon
Chicago Bears

Kick Blockers

Alan Page
Minnesota Vikings

Ron McDole
Washington Redskins

Combined Kick Returners

Alvin Haymond
Washington Redskins/Los Angeles Rams

Bruce Harper
New York Jets

The Best AFC Active Special Teamers

BUFFALO
Mark Pike, Butch Rolle, Steve Tasker, Leonard Smith, Robb Riddick, Bruce Bethoven, Carlton Bailey

CINCINNATI
Ed Brady**, Leo Barker, Barney Bussey

CLEVELAND
Mike Oliphant, Frank Minnifield, Steve Braggs

DENVER
Ken Bell, Bruce Klostermann, Bobby Humphrey

HOUSTON
Kenny Johnson*, Tracy Eaton, Scott Kozak

INDIANAPOLIS
Michael Ball, Jeff Herrod, Orlando Lowry, Fredd Young, Anthony Henton

KANSAS CITY
Angelo Snipes, Albert Lewis, Lewis Cooper, Deron Cherry, Walker Lee Ashley

LOS ANGELES RAIDERS
Stefon Adams, Eddie Anderson, Trey Junkin, Steve Strachan, Tim Ware, Ethan Horton

MIAMI
Jim Jensen, Greg Clark, Neuu Faaola, Bob Brudzinski, Liffort Hobley

NEW ENGLAND
Vincent Brown, Darryl Holmes, Mosi Tatupu

NEW YORK JETS
Marion Barber, Joe Mott, Ken Rose

PITTSBURGH
Dwight Stone, David Johnson, Rod Woodson

SAN DIEGO
Gary Plummer, Tim Spencer, Elvis Patterson, Ken Woodward, Cedric Figaro

SEATTLE
M.L. Johnson, Nesby Glasgow, Darin Miller

*injured reserve—physically able to play in pro bowl; **long snapper.

The Best NFC Active Special Teamers

ATLANTA
Tim Gordon, Elbert Shelley, Jessie Tuggle, Gary Wilkens, Keith Jones

CHICAGO
Dennis Gentry, Glen Kozlowski, Troy Johnson, Maurice Douglass, Lemuel Stinson, Lorenzo Lynch

DALLAS
Bill Bates, Vince Albritton, Scott Ankrom, Mannie Hendrix, Daryl Johnston, Jessie Solomon

DETROIT
George Jamison, Toby Caston, Tony Paige, Mel Gray

GREEN BAY
Chuck Cecil, John Dorsey, Tiger Greene, Jeff Query, Mike Weddington

LOS ANGELES RAMS
James Washington, Bob Delpino, Anthony Neuman, Richard Brown, Darryl Henley, Mike McDonald**

MINNESOTA
Ray Berry, Wymon Henderson, Joey Browner, John Galvin

NEW ORLEANS
Gene Atkins, Buford Jordan, Dave Waymer, Alvin Toles

NEW YORK GIANTS
Lee Rouson, Adrian White, Steve De Ossie*, David Megett

PHILADELPHIA
Byron Evans, William Frizzell, Clyde Simmons, Terry Hoage, Ty Allert

PHOENIX
Ron Wolfley**, Garth Jax, Phil McConkey, Tony Baker, Randy Kirk**, Vai Sikahema

SAN FRANCISCO
Harry Sydney, Tom Rathman, Wesley Walls, Jim Fahnhorst, Spencer Tillman

TAMPA BAY
Donnie Elder, Jackie Walker, Sam Anno*

WASHINGTON
Ravin Caldwell, Reggie Branch, Dave Harbour, Greg Manusky, Kurt Gouveia

*longsnapper; **selected by the NFC

NFL *Best Active Specialists*

PUNT RETURNERS
John Taylor—*San Francisco Forty Niners*
Mel Gray—*Detroit Lions*
Jo Jo Townsell—*New York Jets*

PUNTERS
Jim Arnold—*Detroit Lions*
Harry Newsome—*Pittsburgh Steelers*
Mike Horan—*Denver Broncos*

KICKOFF RETURNERS
Tim Brown—*Los Angeles Raiders*
Donnie Elder—*Tampa Bay Buccaneers*
Anthony Miller—*San Diego Chargers*

FIELD GOAL KICKERS
Mike Cofer—*San Francisco Forty Niners*
Scott Norwood—*Buffalo Bills*
Morton Anderson—*New Orleans Saints*

TWO THAT SCARE ME
(WHO AREN'T USED ON A REGULAR BASIS)
Anthony Carter—*Minnesota Vikings*
Darrell Green—*Washington Redskins*

In my opinion, an underrated field goal kicker is Eddie Murray of the Detroit Lions. Murray's superb season went unnoticed because of the Lions' poor season and his lack of attempts. Murray converted 22 of 23 P-A-Ts and was 20 out of 21 in field goals. His field goal percentage of 95.24% tied the all-time season percentage record set by Mark Moseley of the Redskins who was 20 of 21 in 1982.

Note. Due to Plan B (free agency), players may now have changed teams.

APPENDIX A

What Coaches Say About the Kicking Game

The following comments from some of the best college and professional coaches in the game today further illustrate how important commitment to the kicking game has become.

All of these football coaches hold deep and strong commitments to special teams. Most of them have these views because of their own background and experiences, on a highly personal level, with the kicking game. Marv Levy, for example, was the second special teams coordinator in the NFL, whom I hired while with the Los Angeles Rams, and he went with me to the Washington Redskins. Later, when he became head coach of the Kansas City Chiefs, he brought in a special teams coordinator, Frank Gansz (who eventually became the Kansas City head coach). In 1986, the Chiefs made the playoffs for the first time in 15 years. I believe,

as does Coach Levy, that what got them to the playoffs that year was the outstanding play of their special teams—blocking kicks, returning kicks, blocking punts, and a tough, aggressive, well-organized, and well-planned kicking game effort all season, under the coordination of Frank Gansz.

The special teams of the 1986 Kansas City Chiefs were responsible for scoring 28 points in a game against the Pittsburgh Steelers. This single game caused Pittsburgh Steeler head coach Chuck Noll to reevaluate his special teams play and, as a result, to finally bring a special teams coach to the Steelers in 1987.

Mike Ditka, with a similar background, as Tom Landry's special teams coordinator for the Dallas Cowboys and now as head coach of the Chicago Bears, consistently has highly ranked special teams. Jim Mora brought his New Orleans Saints to their first playoffs in history largely due to the excellent kicking game he developed there. These fine coaches have all been through the "special teams wars," and because of their personal successes and failures, they have become believers. As my longtime friend and coaching adversary Tom Landry wrote in a recent letter to me, "I believe that any successful head coach would place great emphasis on the importance of special teams. We find that when we plan our practice schedule, we start off with special teams." That is a great tribute to the importance of the kicking game from one of the game's all-time great coaches.

There is no question that without quality special teams performance the opportunity to win is minimized. We have always said that special teams is a third of the game, however, the difference between 1966 and today is that we no longer just give it lip service; it is much more sophisticated and the utilization of personnel is more specialized. In both of our Super Bowl years our special teams made significant contributions to our efforts to become World Champions. Being sound and consistent is the key to quality special teams.

Bill Walsh, Former Head Coach, San Francisco Forty Niners

The kicking game has become more than just a play designed to exchange possession of the ball. The punt, the kickoff, and the punt return and kickoff return have become specific plays designed to gain field position, to create a turnover, or to initiate a change in the momentum of the game.

Very few teams in the National Football League can afford to go into combat one coach short. That coach, of course, being the special teams coach. In today's football, the game has become so sophisticated that that part of the game can win or lose not only one outing, it can cost you an opportunity to make the playoffs. Since Dick Vermeil took the title of special teams coach back in 1966 under George Allen in Los Angeles, the rest of the National Football League has slowly but surely found this to be a necessity in the journey for success.

In 1987, the Bengals suffered through a strike year that left them with a 4-11 record. In two of the games, we suffered blocked field goals that turned out to be the difference in the outcome. One game in particular (against the New York Jets in New York) came down to the final two minutes of the game in which our field goal team attempted what would have been the winning field goal, only

to have it blocked, picked up by the New York Jets and run all the way back for a touchdown, giving them control of the game and the ultimate victory. This is a classic example of the special teams deciding the outcome of a game.

Sam Wynche, Head Coach, Cincinnati Bengals

You can be successful in this area only if you treat the kicking game as being exactly equal in importance to the other two departments—defense and offense. This means allowing sufficient practice time to the kicking game, including daily segments for technique work in small groups just as fundamental time is allotted daily for offense and defense.

In my mind the special teams coach must be viewed in the same light as an offensive or defensive coordinator. The special teams coaching role should not be assigned to an inexperienced coaching candidate.

Marv Levy, Head Coach, Buffalo Bills

I believe that any successful coach would place great emphasis on the importance of special teams in the pro game today. We see too much evidence of games being won and lost because of the contribution that special teams make. You have made a tremendous contribution to the importance of special teams through your early efforts in this area.

Now we find that when we plan our practice schedule, we start off with a special team period and then break into the middle of practice to work with our special teams, since there is such a tremendous emphasis on their importance today.

Tom Landry, Former Head Coach, Dallas Cowboys

Special teams are still a very important part of winning or losing a football game. [The] difference now is that most all coaches and teams realize it. [You] can't steal a game anymore the way we could in the early 60s.

Don F. Shula, Head Coach, Miami Dolphins

There is a tendency now to expand the special teams staff. This has only just begun. Both the Redskins and the New York Giants now have two people coaching this area as their primary concern.

I am proud of our special teams' performance.

In the last 6 years, the Jets special teams have provided a margin of victory play on an average of 4-1/2 games a year. Two of the most dramatic games were: (a) On Monday night versus the Saints in 1983. My first year as head coach, Kirk Springs returned a punt with 2 minutes left to go for 76 yards and a touchdown to win the game. (b) In 1985 versus the Patriots (the 12th game of the year) the game went into overtime. Kurt Sohn returned a punt to the Patriot 23 yardline and Pat Leahy kicked the winning fieldgoal to go into sole possession of first place. And perhaps one of the most spectacular games ever played in 1986, the Jets and Dolphins played to a 45-45 tie in regulation. Wesley Walker caught his 4th touchdown pass in overtime to win, but in the game our special teams contributed to 10 points.

(a) A recovered punt fumble led to a T.D.

(b) A punt returned to the Dolphin 18 yardline resulted in a fieldgoal.

Joseph F. Walton, Head Coach, New York Jets

Special teams plays are consistently the most meaningful plays of any football game. Number one, there is either a score involved with every kicking play or a big chunk of yardage (40 yds. plus) so the outcome of many games is decided by the 25 to 35 kicking plays. The proficiency of the special teams depends somewhat on the ability of the kicker or punter but the plays still involve the ten other players on protection and coverage. The return men are also important but the blocking scheme will be the difference in having a consistent productive return team versus an occasional good play or bad play.

Several years ago most football teams would work on the special teams for a few minutes the day before the game as opposed to now most teams that do a good job on special teams have special team meetings every day covering a different kicking situation plus most teams have a special teams segment as part of their regular practice schedule every day. In conclusion, the kicking game or returns have become more a part of an extension of the offense or defense using the situational players that have improved the overall play of the team.

With the time and talent we devote to special teams we have benefited through wins and league leading performers to greatly contribute to our team and make the special teams players have pride in their unit.

Jack Pardee, Head Coach, University of Houston

The area of special teams is one of the most difficult yet one of the most overlooked areas in football. It's amazing how many plays throughout the course of a contest are comprised of some aspect of special teams play. We presently have two coaches on our staff who are directly responsible for the implementation and success of our entire kicking game. I think that is a real statement to the importance we place upon this vital, interesting part of the game of football.

As I look back over my career and try to evaluate the games that we lost, it becomes increasingly more and more apparent to me that we generally broke down at some facet of our special teams play. It has been a very hard but important lesson for me to learn throughout my coaching career—the true significance of quality special teams play.

Terry Donahue, Head Coach, UCLA

General Comments:

1. Place your best players on all special teams units.
2. Study film of your opponents; film study is different than film breakdown! Study their personnel, i.e., punter, kicker, coverage personnel, return people.
3. Know your opponent's punter and kicker! Chart them and present the charts to your units and return personnel.
4. Involve your football team with your special teams; show the entire squad the weekly special teams reel; they place peer pressure on one another.
5. Don't miss a day during the week going over some phase of special teams.
6. Repetition is the key! Work in practice on what you will actually see on game day.
7. Teams that take a lot of "pride" in their kicking game do not become victims of "bad breaks."
8. A deficient kicking game handicaps a team by 33%.

The key to successful special teams play is emphasis on the little things in one or two phases of special teams, i.e., punt and punt return one day, and then one or two other phases the next day in practice. Too many teams hurry through too many, or all, phases of special teams during a short time period in practice. The key, as we see it, is to insure that we understand our assignments, rather than running a wave of bodies down the field daily.

Pat Jones, Head Coach, Oklahoma State University

I believe very strongly in the importance of the kicking game and we spend a great deal of meeting time and practice time in special teams' preparation. Our players really believe that the kicking game has and will win games for us and they play and practice special teams with an intensity that indicates this.

Jim Mora, Head Coach, New Orleans Saints

I really believe that the Head Coach's emphasis on special teams today is much greater to that of twenty years ago. That has been a major reason why we have experienced success with the Stars in the U.S.F.L. and in our two years with the N.F.L. . . . Coach Mora believes in the kicking game and sells it to our players . . . that makes my job a little easier.

Joe Marciano, Special Teams Coach, New Orleans Saints

Special teams play is very important to me. I've always stressed and believed it to be just as important as offense or defense. Actually, you can establish the tempo at which the game is going to be played by your kickoff coverage and your kickoff returns. This year we are thinking about establishing a roster position just for a special teams player (not a return man).

I believe if anything is important it must be done right and in order to do it right it must be emphasized and practiced. As long as I'm coach of the Bears we will always place our special teams on the same level of importance as offense and defense.

Mike Ditka, Head Coach, Chicago Bears

I was an assistant coach in Dallas for ten years before becoming the Head Coach of the Denver Broncos. The most important year of those years of being an assistant was in 1974 when I was the coach of the special teams. I always felt that special teams plays were at least one-third of the game.

When I became the Head Coach at Denver it was easy for me to allow adequate time for special teams practice. I also developed a knowledge and philosophy that helped mold our special teams. I think it is important to have your team feel that 1 to 2 games a year can be won because of special teams play.

We feel that the special teams are so important that we meet with our special teams first each day and start each practice with special teams.

Dan Reeves, Head Coach, Denver Broncos

I believe the special teams is probably the second most important item in winning, with the first being defense. I don't know of anybody who has brought out the importance of special teams more than George Allen did when he was with the Washington Redskins. I think Tim Brown won the Heisman not only because of his outstanding talents and abilities as a runner and a receiver, but specifically because he was the most explosive punt return and kickoff return man in the country the last couple years. We spend a great deal of time on our special teams, prepare scouting reports specifically for them, test our athletes on their assignments, and generally have objectives and goals for every phase of our kicking game. If there is one area that has improved me as a coach more than any other, it is the fact that you illustrated the importance of special teams, and the results have been very helpful to us.

Lou Holtz, Head Coach, University of Notre Dame

The kicking game is one of the three phases of play. Players and coaches must believe and give attention to the kicking game. I have always developed my teams in this order: (1) defense, (2) special teams, and (3) offense. It is our belief that most close games are won by the team with the best kicking game. I believe that we will win (or lose) one or two games a year as a result of our kicking game.

I believe special teams today are certainly being handled with much more precision than in 1966. Coaches and players are now realizing that more hidden yards are gained in the kicking game than most coaches thought of in the late 1960s. They know that every yard counts toward better field position and coaches are now willing to take the extra practice and meeting time to get those yards through the kicking game. It is becoming a more dangerous weapon to have great special teams in your overall football attack.

I believe that in order to have an excellent kicking game you must be prepared. Kicking situations must be practiced daily and at a high intensity. Your team must be knowledgeable in regards to the rules of the kicking game so they can make breaks occur for them. Finally, a great kicking team will be proficient in all kicking areas, both in offensive and defensive special teams play.

Joseph V. Paterno, Head Coach, Penn State

Special teams has become an integral segment of our philosophy of coaching football at USC. In the days of General Neyland at Tennessee the kicking game was used to win games and championships. Gradually, however, football coaches became more interested in the intricacies of offense and defense. But faced with the pressures of "finding ways to win" coaches are turning their attention to the kicking game. Coaches are beginning to realize that games are usually won or lost because of soundness in the kicking game, a big play, or a mistake on the part of the special teams. It isn't just offense or defense anymore.

Currently, at USC we designate 35% of our practice time on the kicking game. We use our best and most talented players on the "special teams." Our coaches, individually and collectively, coach the kicking game the same as we do our offense and defense. The kicking game has truly become the most important phase of our coaching. We feel that is a weapon we use to win games and championships.

Larry Smith, Head Coach, University of Southern California

Statistical data and past experience tell us that the play of special teams will make up over 1/5 of the total game. It's a means to gain an edge on the opponent. We at the University of Georgia continue to divide our responsibilities. Each unit is graded on every play, goals and standards have been developed, and a reward system established.

Vincent J. Dooley, Head Coach, University of Georgia

Most coaches say they really believe in the kicking game but do not give enough practice time to this most important aspect of football. When we came to Washington in 1975, we wanted to use this phase as an "edge" so we probably spent twice the amount of time on kicking as did most teams. We would not have won enough games to win a PAC 10 Championship if it had not been for our kicking game. We work it into our practices at different times and every coach on my staff is assigned a kicking responsibility.

Don James, Head Coach, University of Washington

We try to devote a great deal of time to special teams play. We feel that special teams constitute fully one third of the game of football and usually are the biggest plays in the game. We spend approximately 20 minutes a day on our kicking game.

Tom Osborne, Head Coach, University of Nebraska

Field position is probably the most important situation in offensive and defensive football. Field position is created many times by the special teams with offense or defense. The emphasis on special teams seems to have increased over the years. Back years ago special teams had to be made up of players who were regulars on offense and defense. The emphasis was not as great and the coach would hope none of the regular team members would be injured while working on a special team assignment. In the middle 60's the emphasis became greater on the use of special teams. It has graduated to the point today that special teams and players are receiving much more credit for their valuable contribution to the game.

Bob Devaney, Athletic Director and Former Head Coach, University of Nebraska

Without question, the single most important reason for our success is emphasis. For years we had a cautious approach to special teams play, meaning "let's not get beat in this area." With the arrival of Coach Johnson, however, we exercised a philosophy of "let's win and be aggressive on special teams."

On Sunday, when our players come over to watch film, our entire staff and every player get together in the large meeting room and analyze and evaluate our special teams reel for the game we just played. Believe me, a loaf or less than 100% effort in any aspect of our special teams can cause a very embarrassing moment for that particular player. Great effort and play-making performance, on the other hand, will receive an award and special mention.

We used to emphasize punt and field goal protection during practice and cover the rest of the special teams on the Thursday before each game. Now we set aside practice time all week long to cover, in detail, and film, every aspect of the kicking game and then review in-depth on Thursday.

With the added emphasis we have placed on special teams, we have enjoyed great success in every area of the kicking game. Whether it's blocking kicks, protecting kicks, returning kicks, covering kicks or just kicking, we feel our teams have dominated the special teams over the last 4 years and as a result of this, we have played in New Year's Day bowls all 4 years and won a national title.

We also have special team meetings the night before and day of the game and you can witness the pride and intensity that our players take in dominating the kicking game and making ''big'' plays.

Art Kehoe, Assistant Coach, University of Miami

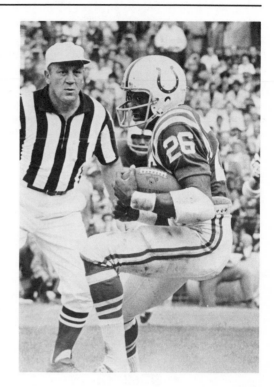

Players' Handouts

PLAYERS PUNT PROTECTION AND COVERAGE "QUICK" SHEET

CALLS

PROTECTIONS:
BASE
TURN R-NUMBER
TURN L-NUMBER
GREEN
RED
MIDDLE
"IN"

TYPE OF PUNTS:
DOWN-IT
DANGER
PRESSURE
TAKE SAFETY
KILL CLOCK

POSITION TECHNIQUES

C
1. Snap
2. Release
3. Ball Man
4. Brake
5. Force
6. Tackle

G/T
1. Hop-Slam
2. Long Block
3. Green
4. Stack Block
5. Release
6. Shoulder Ball
7. Brake
8. Tackle
9. Down Punt

END
1. Split Release
2. "In" Call
   Hop-Slam
   Green
   Stack
   Release
3. Ball Man
4. Tackle
5. Down Punt

WING
1. Double Bump
2. Single Block
3. Release
4. Force
5. Sure Tackle

PP
1. Make Calls
2. Solid Block
3. Safety
4. Adjustment
5. Brake
6. Sure Tackle

PUNTER
1. Field Snap
2. Punt
3. Down-it Punt
4. Take Safety
5. Pass Fake
6. Safety Angles
7. Sure Tackle

REMINDERS

1. Net punt is the only statistic that is of great importance to us.
2. Listen to the call. Are you an offside or onside blocker?
3. Count and point out the man you will block. Communicate with each other.
4. Initial alignment splits should be 2 feet.
5. Snapper—only be concerned with the snap.
6. Use technique when you release from the L.O.S. hands and technique.
7. Against any abnormal shifting fronts we will audible to "Green." This is our zone protection.
8. Ends, always look inside when split for an "In" call.
9. When executing a long block, adjust your alignment.
10. "Red" means hurry and get set.
11. On down-it punts be alert to the football taking abnormal bounces.
12. If the returner signals for a fair catch on a down-it punt, tackles and ends run past him to the 5 yard line, turn and look to field the ball.

PUNT RULES

1. Report to the official if your position number is incorrect.
2. Only the ends may release prior to the ball being punted.
3. If the punt does not cross the L.O.S., you may advance it.
4. You must be completely "Set" in your stance a second prior to the snap.
5. You cannot interfere with the returner's right-of-way to catch the punt.
6. If the returner gives a fair catch signal and bobbles the ball, he cannot be touched until the ball hits the ground.
7. To down a punt, you must have possession with both feet in the field of play prior to the ball crossing the goal line.
8. The punter is no longer protected from roughness penalty if the ball touches the ground on the snap or he begins to run.

Punt team thought process

Read from bottom of page. Steps you will go through in covering a punt—based on a 40 yard punt.

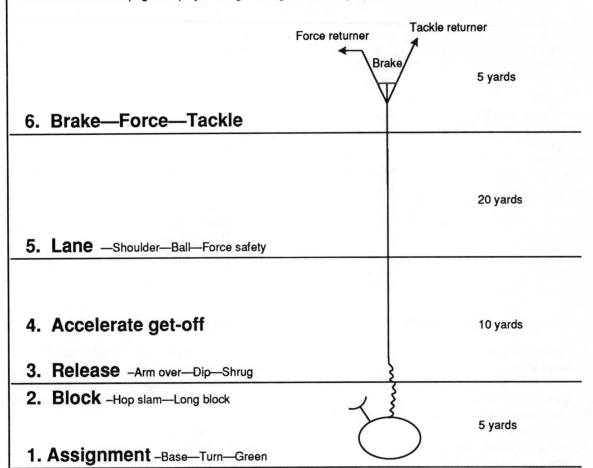

Force returner   Tackle returner

Brake

5 yards

6. Brake—Force—Tackle

20 yards

5. Lane —Shoulder—Ball—Force safety

4. Accelerate get-off   10 yards

3. Release –Arm over—Dip—Shrug

2. Block –Hop slam—Long block

5 yards

1. Assignment –Base—Turn—Green

PLAYERS PUNT RETURN AND PUNT BLOCK "QUICK" SHEET

CALLS

BLOCKS
   FLOP
   SPEED
RETURNS
   LEFT
   RIGHT
SAFE (DEFENSE)
SAFE PETER
TWINS
ALERT
CHECK "BLUE"
FAIR CATCH

POSITION TECHNIQUES

A/B/C/D
1. Shoulder
2. Gap
3. Slip
4. Block Punt
5. Scoop-up Ball
6. Pin
7. Double Team
8. Wall

R/L
1. Shoulder
2. Gap
3. Slip
4. Block Punt
5. Scoop-up Ball
6. Pin
7. Force Punt
8. Wall
9. Alert

HALFBACK
1. Shoulder
2. Gap
3. Slip
4. Block Punt
5. Scoop-up Ball
6. Double Team
7. Alert

CORNER
1. Shoulder
2. Block Punt
3. Scoop-up Ball
4. Double Team
5. Single End

RETURNER
1. Field Ball
2. Fair Catch
3. Ball to Wall

REMINDERS

1. Opponent net punt is our most important statistic.
2. Stem intelligently and with confidence. No one is better at this aspect than we are.
3. If we do not block the punt, locate the ball and set the wall.
4. Expect to block the punt. No one is the designated blocker.
5. Halfbacks must stem intelligently.
6. Be alert to fakes. Positions dictate eligibility, not numbers.
7. In blocking the punt, do not lay out. Take the ball off the punter's foot.
8. In setting our wall, the returner will bring the covermen to you. Wait, be patient.
9. In safe, play for the fake.
10. Blue is our formation check.
11. Returners must attempt to field and return all punts. Be smart.
12. Study protections and the snapper. Your knowledge makes game day adjustments simpler.
13. Do not be drawn offsides by a nonrhythmic cadence.

PUNT RETURN RULES

1. We can not block below the waist.
2. Inadvertent roughing the punter is a 5-yard penalty, not an automatic first down.
3. The punter has no roughing penalty protection if:
   - The ball touches the ground.
   - The punter begins to run.
   - The punt is partially blocked.
4. The returner has the right of way in catching the punt.
5. The corner and halfback do *not* adhere to the 5-yard "chuck" rule vs. the ends.
6. A partially blocked punt crossing the line of scrimmage is treated as if it had not been blocked.
7. A punt not crossing the line of scrimmage can be advanced by either team.
8. You can use your hands to rush the punter.
9. A fair catch signal must be above the helmet and very clear as to the intention.
10. Any eligible receiver can go in motion.
11. The end man in the formation is the ball man. If it is a TE/WING formation the end is still the ball man.

Punt blocking team thought process

The mental thoughts you should have as you proceed to the punter.

15 yards deep	**Punter**	
9 yards deep	**Step 3**	

Block point
1. Take ball off foot
2. Block with hands
3. Stay on feet
4. Volleyball block
5. Don't blink eyes

6 yards deep   **Step 2**

Prep. Point
1. See ball
2. Elongate body
3. Do not slow up
4. Upper body mechanics

Step 1

Line of Scrimmage
1. Stance
2. Get off
3. Technique
   — Shoulder
   — Gap
   — Slip

PLAYERS KICKOFF COVERAGE "QUICK" SHEET

CALLS

LEFT HASH
RIGHT HASH
  UNDER
    CROSSFIELD
    OVER
MIDDLE
  MOM
  MEL
  MARS
ENDER
ONSIDE KICK
K.O. PUNT FOLLOWING
  SAFETY

POSITION TECHNIQUES

COVERMEN NUMBER 1-9

1. Get-Off
2. Adjustment
3. Beat Blocker Techniques
4. Close
5. Force Ball or Tackle
6. Shoulder Technique
7. Ball Technique
8. Knife Technique
9. Fielding Onside Kicks

NO. 10

1. Safety
2. Sure Tackle
3. Fielding Onside Kicks

KICKER

1. Ball Placement
2. Ender
3. Onside Kick
4. Safety
5. Sure Tackle

REMINDERS

1. Yardline average of where the opponent returns the ball to is of great importance statistically to us.
2. See the kicker as he approaches the ball. This will eliminate ignorant offside penalties.
3. As you sprint downfield—adjust.
4. Have a "Plan" to beat the blocker as you approach him.
5. If you feel yourself being double teamed DO NOT stop gaining ground.
6. If the ball is on the ground, recover it. It's live!
7. Know your leverage and assignment. Shoulder or ball.
8. Kicker—kick the ball high (4.0+) and to the designated spot.
9. Safeties must make sure, high tackles.
10. During an onside kick, *everyone* is responsible for recovering the ball.
11. If we kick a game ender, DO NOT slow down. Bigger people (wedge) that field enders are at times very difficult to tackle.
12. Good coverage will result if we are crossing the 30-yard line when the returner catches the ball.

KICKOFF RULES

1. If the ball travels 10 yards, it is a free ball.
2. If the ball travels less than 10 yards and hits an opponent, it is a free ball.
3. The receiving team cannot block you below the waist.
4. We cannot "Attack" (take out) blockers below the waist.
5. If we kick the ball (untouched by the opponent) out of bounds, the receiving team will assume possessions on the 35-yard line.
6. The receiving team *CAN* fair catch a kickoff. (Punt receiving rules apply.)
7. If a fair catch is muffed, fumbled, or allowed to hit the ground, it is a free ball.
8. Following a safety against us, we must kickoff (punt) from the 20-yard line.
9. If the returner downs a kickoff in the end zone, you cannot touch him.

Kickoff coverage team thought process

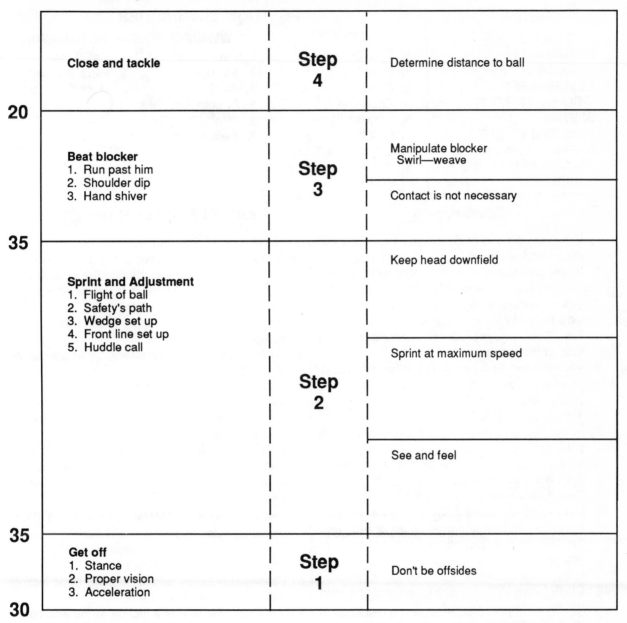

Note: The above is the process you should go through in covering kickoffs. This is a reminder chart of important coaching points in that process.

PLAYERS KICK-OFF RETURN "QUICK" SHEET

CALLS

RETURN
  CONVERT LEFT
RETURN LEFT
  CONVERT RIGHT
SPECIAL
POSSIBLE ONSIDE
DEFINITE ONSIDE (SUB)
RETURN FOLLOWING A
  SAFETY

POSITION TECHNIQUES

C/G/T

1. Turn-Drop
2. Plant-Drive
3. Block
4. Zone Call
5. Convert Block
6. C-Soft
7. G/T-Double Team
8. Recover Onside

WEDGE

1. Turn-Drop
2. Set-Up
3. Block
4. Double Team
5. "Go" Call
6. Field Kicks

RETURNERS

1. Catch Ball
2. Field Squibs
3. Backside Blocker

REMINDERS

1. If the ball goes outside the hash opposite the return call—convert.
2. In any possible or definite onside situation see the ball kicked. Note: When we are ahead.
3. Front line must always be alert to a surprise onside kick. Note: When we are ahead.
4. Front line—always block with the shoulder to the side of the return.
5. Wedge—Set up 10 yards in front of the returner who is fielding the ball. Accelerate on the "Go" call.
6. Always be alert to a stunt.
7. In identifying covermen count 1-10 to the return side.
8. When in doubt if your block is a clip or below the waist, do not attempt it.
9. Returnmen field every ball. It's "live."
10. Returnmen must use discretion on balls kicked near the sideline. Our offense takes over with the ball on the 35-yard line if it goes out of bounds.
11. Returnmen must know all touchback rules.
12. Off-Returner: You have the critical block. Find the most dangerous man.
13. Stay on your feet.
14. Return yardline is more important than what the return average is.

KICKOFF RETURN RULES

1. No blocking below the waist.
2. If the ball travels 10 yards, it is a free ball.
3. Our front line must align behind the 45-yard line.
4. You can fair catch a kickoff, however *if* it touches the ground, it is a free ball.
5. All run blocking rules apply in regards to hand usage.
6. A coverage man cannot attack our wedge below the waist.
7. If the ball is kicked out of bounds it is our ball on the 35-yard line.
8. If the ball is kicked into the end zone, we must down the ball.
9. If the momentum of your catch takes you into the end zone or you muff (not fumble) the ball and it goes into the end zone, you do not have to return the ball. Down it.

Kickoff return team thought process sheet

Front line —Process covers 45 yardline to approximately the opposite 35 yardline.

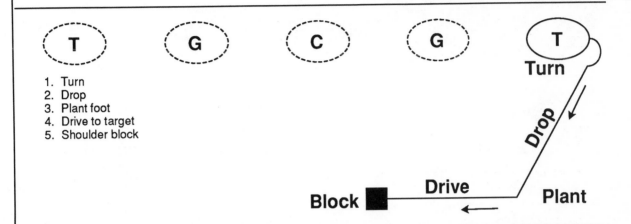

1. Turn
2. Drop
3. Plant foot
4. Drive to target
5. Shoulder block

Wedge —Process covers 25 yardline to the 10 yardline. Approximately 15 years, depending on kick.

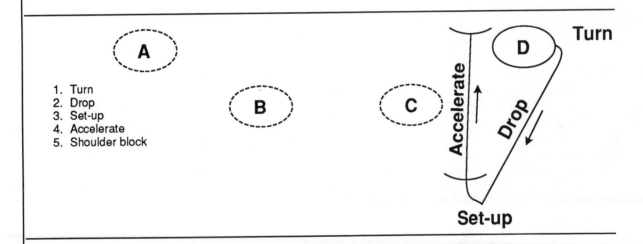

1. Turn
2. Drop
3. Set-up
4. Accelerate
5. Shoulder block

APPENDIX C

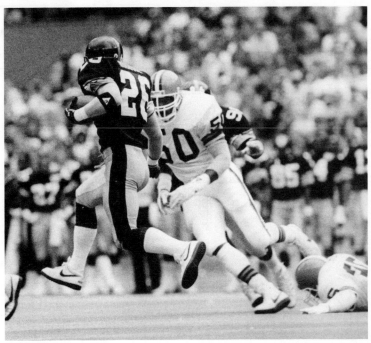

Scouting Charts

Stats

Punt

Punts	Average	Returns	Average return

Punt returns

Returns	Average return	F.C.	Other	Blocks	Long	TD

KO cover

Returns	Average return

KO return

Returns	Average return	Long	TD

Punt team

Punter	No.	Punts	Average	Net	H. T.	Drop	Foot	

Comments:

Down it punt:

React to pressure:

Snapper	Accuracy	Velocity	Snap time

Comments:

Punt team

General comments:

Punt distance/Hang time/Direction

30		
35		
40		
45		
50		
55		
60		

Accuracy Chart
Center Snap
(Mark with "X" or dot for each snap.)

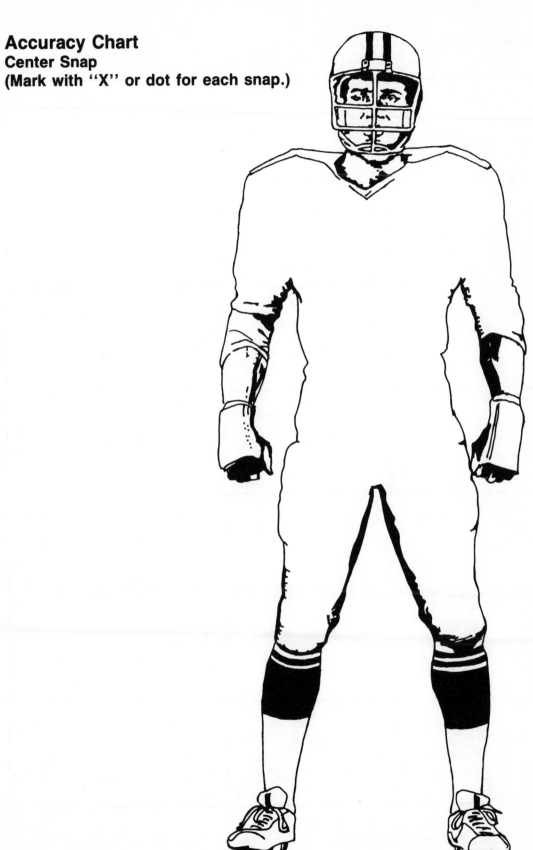

Coverage lanes

Best coverman:

Punt formations

Punt protection charts

Fakes

Down it punt

Punt return/block team

Returner	No.	Returns	F. C.	Average	Long	Fumbles	

Comments:

System

Returns

Blocks

Shifting

Overall

Personnel

Comments:

Blocks

Kickoff team

System:

Coverage:

Best covermen: Safeties

Kicker:

   Direction:
   Hang time:
   Distance:
   Onside:

Personnel

Kickoff hit chart

Kickoff coverage (lanes)

Kickoff coverage onside

Kickoff return team

Returner	No.	Returns	Average	Long	Fumbles		

Comments:

System

Personnel

Kickoff return

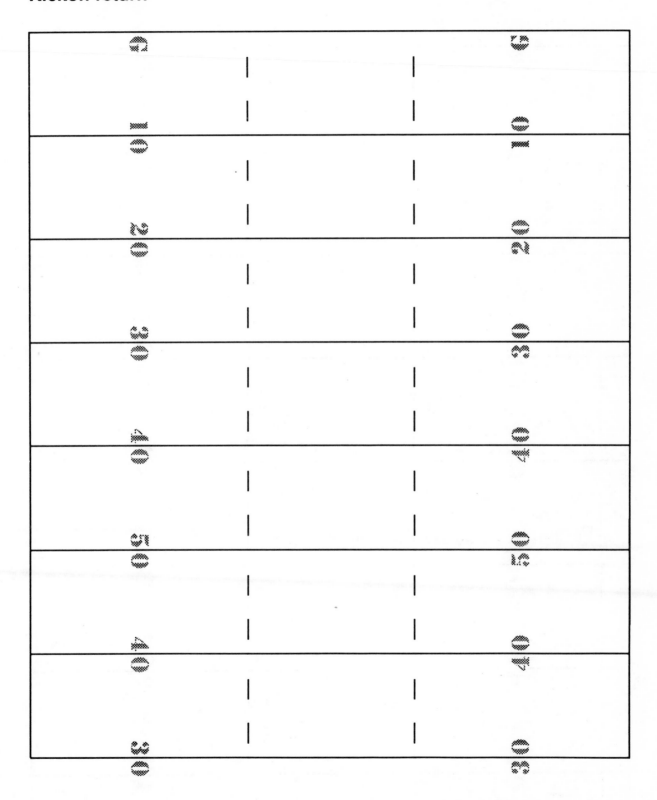

Kickoff coverage onside

PAT/FG

Kicker	No.	PAT%	FG%	0–19	20–29	30–39	40–49	50+	Foot

Comments:

Holder	No.	Position	Comment

Snapper	No.	Position–size	Comment

Kick time (snap to kick):

Personnel

H —

Vulnerability:

Fakes

Field goal protection charts

APPENDIX D

Special Teams Rules

GENERAL RULES

1. Once a kickoff travels 10 yards, it is a free ball and belongs to the recovering team.
2. A kickoff that does not travel 10 yards is treated as follows:
   a. If it rolls dead, it is kicked again after the kicking team is penalized 5 yards.
   b. If the receiving team recovers it, the ball belongs to them at the place where the receiver is tackled.
   c. If the receiving team touches it but does not control it, the ball is free and belongs to whichever team recovers it.
3. A kickoff recovered in the end zone by the kicking team is a touchdown whether or not the receiving team touched it. (Does not apply to high school football.)
4. To down a punt, the covering man must *stay with the ball until the whistle*.
5. If the covering team on a punt touches the ball but fails to officially down it, the receiv-

ing team can try to advance it—at *no risk to themselves*. If they gain, they can take the gain. If they *fumble* or *lose yardage, they can elect to take the ball where it was first touched by the covering team.*
6. A blocked punt can be advanced by either team.
7. A partially blocked punt is treated exactly the same as a regular punt. It should be "Poison!" to the men on the receiving team.
8. On a punt rush it is the responsibility of the rushers to avoid touching or roughing the kicker. Penalty is 5 yards for touching and 15 yards for roughing. The latter is an automatic first down.
9. Coverers on a punt cannot interfere with the free movement of a receiver in his effort to catch any punt.
10. A fair catch cannot be advanced by either team, nor may the fair-catcher be bumped or tackled.
11. A muffed fair catch that hits the ground is a free ball and belongs to the team that

recovers it. The exception is when the ball is muffed *into* the end zone.

12. A man signaling a fair catch cannot subsequently block.

13. After making a fair catch, the receiving team has the option of utilizing a free kick on the next play. If it is a placekick (from a hold) and it goes between the uprights, a field goal is scored.

14. A missed field goal:

   a. The ball is returned to the line of scrimmage or the 20-yard line, whichever is farther from the goal line.

   b. Or the ball can be returned from the end zone.

15. If there is a foul

   a. from time of snap until a kick from behind line or beyond line of scrimmage ends, or

   b. before the kick has been returned,

   enforcement is from

   a. the previous spot, or

   b. the spot of the kick.

16. During a kick from scrimmage, only the end men, as eligible receivers on the line of scrimmage at the time of the snap, are permitted to go beyond the line before the ball is kicked.

Exception: An eligible receiver who, at the snap, is aligned or in motion behind the line and more than 1 yard outside the end man on his side of the line, clearly making him the outside receiver, *replaces* that end man as the player eligible to go downfield after the snap. All other members of the kicking team must remain at the line of scrimmage until the ball has been kicked.

IMPORTANT PUNT RULES

1. If you do not have the proper (offensive) number for your position in the punt alignment, you must report to the referee as you take the field.

   Example: The right tackle is #36. He must report to referee.

2. Only the end men on the line of scrimmage are permitted to go beyond the line before the ball is punted.

3. Once the ball is punted and you cross the line of scrimmage, you may use your hands to ward off, push, or pull aside an opponent trying to block or obstruct your release and coverage.

4. The return team must block you above the waist and in front of you, except for high blocks. A block from the side is up to the judgment of the official.

5. Punter: You may not be roughed after a punt. However, contact by the rushers is legal if

   a. the punt has been blocked,

   b. *you* start running toward the line of scrimmage with the ball, or

   c. the ball touches the ground (even though you field it perfectly).

6. If a punt does not cross the line of scrimmage, either team may advance it (even if the punt is blocked). The punt team can run or pass for first down. The return team can pick it up and score.

7. A partially blocked punt that *crosses* the line of scrimmage is treated as a normal punt. The punt team cannot recover it and regain possession. If you do, you are *downing* the punt.

8. You cannot go out of bounds voluntarily to avoid a potential blocker. If you do, you cannot return. (This is important for our ends in split formation.)

9. If you are *forced* out of bounds, you can continue in the play. However, you cannot touch, down, or recover a punt until it has been touched by the return team. Alert to this on "down-it" punts.

10. If the punt goes out of bounds between the goal lines, or comes to a stop inbounds and no player attempts to secure it, the ball becomes dead and belongs to the return team at the dead-ball spot.

11. You may catch a punt in flight if no one on the return team attempts to catch it. The ball becomes dead at the spot (down-it punt situation).

12. To down a punt, you must stay with the ball until the whistle blows. If you touch the ball, but fail to down it, the return team can try to advance it. (If they then fumble and we recover, it is their ball where we first touched it.)

13. To down a punt inside the 5-yard line, you must have possession before the ball crosses the goal line. If your momentum carries the ball to the end zone, it is a touchback. Both of your feet must be in the field of play while you have possession of the ball.

14. A punt that touches the end zone before it touches a player on the return team is immediately dead and a touchback.

15. Punts into the end zone are touchbacks unless

    a. we (the punt team) touch the ball outside the 20-yard line,
    b. they field and run back the ball, or
    c. we recover the ball in the end zone after the returner touches the ball in the field of play.
       Ruling: It is our ball at the spot of touch in the field of play.

16. A muff cannot be advanced. (A *muff* is the touching of the ball by a return-team member in an effort to secure possession.) We must recover all muffs. Do not attempt to pick them up.

17. A fumble may be advanced. (A *fumble* is an act resulting in loss of player possession of the ball.)

18. A muffed fair catch that hits the ground is a free ball—recover it!

19. Once any member of the return team has muffed or fumbled the ball, we can catch it or recover it.

20. A returner who signals for a fair catch is not obligated to catch the ball. If he does not catch it, he cannot block you.

21. A *fair catch signal* is a hand extended clearly overhead, waved from side to side. The ball once caught, cannot be advanced. We cannot bump or tackle him.

22. If the returner shades his eyes from the sun, the ball is live and may be advanced.

23. No player on the return team who is in a position to catch a punt may be interfered with, by any of *us* (covering the punt), while the ball is in flight. The protection terminates the moment he or a teammate touches the ball.

24. If a return man signals a fair catch and bobbles it, he cannot be touched until the ball touches the ground.

25. We must not "flinch" at false starts on the line of scrimmage. If we are moving at the snap, it is illegal motion.

26. If a rusher is blocked into our punter or "inadvertently" roughs the punter, it is now a 5-yard penalty (not an automatic first down).

IMPORTANT PUNT RETURN AND BLOCK RULES

1. There is no roughing the punter if

   a. the snap skips off ground,
   b. the punter begins to run,
   c. the punter drops ball, or
   d. you block or partially block the punt.

2. We have the right to catch the ball with or without a fair catch.

3. The punt team must report eligibility to a referee if their numbers do not coincide with their eligibility. They may change alignment during the course of the game to make a previously ineligible player eligible. Play the position eligibility, not the number.

4. We may not block below the waist or make contact with the back of an opponent. Never touch a coverman if you can read his name.

5. Corners and halfbacks must adhere to the 5-yard-chuck rule. You may use your hands to make contact in the first 5 yards. But you may not contact ends after that zone until the ball is punted.

6. The fair catch signal is one arm extended full length above the head, waving from side to side. You are protected until the ball touches the ground. If you signal but do not attempt to field the ball, you may *not* block anyone on the cover team (15-yard penalty).

7. The punt team must cover and possess the ball to down it. If they should incidentally touch it and walk away, you may advance it. An official will blow the whistle to down it.

8. If the catch momentum carries our return man into the end zone, you do not have to bring the ball out. However, if you take the ball into the end zone, you must bring it out or it will be ruled a safety.

9. The ball cannot be advanced after a fair catch signal unless

   a. the ball touches the ground, or
   b. the ball strikes one of the covermen in flight.

10. If the returner muffs a kick, the ball may not be advanced by the punt team if recovered. If the returner has gained possession and fumbles, the ball may be advanced by the punt team.

11. A partially blocked punt crossing the line of scrimmage is as if it had not been blocked. Get away from it. Call "Peter."

12. A fourth-down punt not crossing the line of scrimmage will be our ball, so you may try to advance it. A third-down punt is a free ball.

13. The punt team can snatch the ball in flight if we do not attempt to catch it.

14. Once a member of the return team touches, muffs, or fumbles the ball after it has crossed

the neutral zone, any player may catch or recover the ball.

15. A punt that touches our end zone before it touches a player on our team is immediately dead and a touchback.

16. If the punt fails to cross the line of scrimmage, *any* player on either team may recover and advance the ball. The punt team may pick it up and run for a first down, or the return team may pick it up and score.

17. If the punt goes out of bounds or comes to rest inbounds and no player attempts to secure it, the ball becomes dead and belongs to the return team at the dead-ball spot.

18. We may use our hands to rush the punter (to avoid blockers).

19. It is our responsibility to avoid the punter. He can run into you, but we cannot run into him! Only incidental contact is permitted. Be an actor, because he will!

IMPORTANT KICKOFF COVERAGE RULES

1. We must align behind the restraining line before the ball is kicked off.
   Normal kickoff: 35-yard line
   Kickoff following safety: 20-yard line
   On penalty: Restraining line will adjust (usually to the 30- or 50-yard line, depending on the foul).

2. A holder (if needed) can align in front of the restraining line.

3. The receiving team must align at least 10 yards from our restraining line.

4. We can recover a kickoff after
   a. it touches an opponent (anywhere);
   b. the ball travels 10 yards (beyond the receiver's restraining lane);
   c. the ball touches an opponent, the ground, or an official after traveling 10 yards; or
   d. a receiver muffs or fumbles a fair catch.
   Note: Do not think in this circumstance. Recover the ball.

5. If we catch the kickoff or recover it, the ball is dead (and our ball).

6. You cannot voluntarily go out of bounds during the kickoff and then reenter the field and take part in the play.

7. If the ball goes into the end zone without being touched, the returner must *down* it. If he does not down the ball, *recover* it! It is a touchdown for us! Make sure he downs it and the whistle blows.

8. If the returner touches the ball in the end zone, recover it for a touchdown!

9. If the ball is kicked high and has not touched the ground, the returner has the right to field the ball before it touches the ground (as with a punt). We cannot interfere with this opportunity until the ball touches the ground.

10. A receiver *can* fair-catch a kickoff. If he fumbles, muffs, or fakes a fair catch, the ball is live.

11. If a kick strikes the goalpost, it is an automatic touchback.

12. The receiving team cannot block you below the waist.

13. You *cannot* "bust the wedge" by attacking a blocker or blockers below the waist.

14. A kick is never blown dead in the field of play. It is a free ball.

15. Following a safety, the ball must be kicked within 1 yard of the restraining line (20-yard line).

16. A free kick may be employed following a fair catch. Do not get caught off guard. It counts as a field goal if it goes through the uprights. People will use this in half-ending situations or overtime.

17. During an onside kick attempt, we cannot block a return team player before the ball passes the return team's restraining line (10 yards).

18. During an onside kick attempt, the ball must travel 10 yards to be live. If we touch the ball before it goes 10 yards or before it touches an opponent within the 10-yard area, an illegal touch is called and the ball must be rekicked.

19. If we kick the ball out of bounds, the return team will get the ball on the 35-yard line. There will not be a rekick!

20. An opponent can fair-catch a kickoff (provided it travels 10 yards). If a fair catch is signaled and the ball is fumbled or not caught, it is a free ball.

21. You are permitted to push or pull a receiving team member away from a loose ball in an effort to recover a free ball. However, you are not permitted to do so in an effort to allow a teammate to recover the ball.

IMPORTANT KICKOFF RETURN RULES

1. We may not block below the waist or to the back of an opponent player. If you see his name, do not block him.

2. Once a kickoff travels 10 yards, it is a free ball.

   a. If it does not travel 10 yards or is touched by kicking team member before it travels 10 yards, the kicking team is penalized and must rekick.

   b. We may step into the 10-yard zone to field a short kick, but once we touch the ball it is a free ball.

3. A coverman cannot low-block the wedge; he must attack you above the waist.

4. If a kickoff travels out of bounds, we have the option of taking the ball at the spot or at the 35-yard line.

5. No member of the receiving team may cross the 45-yard line until the ball is kicked. This is considered offsides.

6. Run-blocking rules apply regarding use of hands on a block.

7. Anyone may fair catch a kickoff. *Never fake a fair catch*. The ball is live when it hits the ground.

8. Rules for receivers:

   a. If the catch momentum carries you into the end zone, you do *not* have to bring the ball out.

   b. If you muff a catch in the field of play and it goes into the end zone, you do *not* have to bring it out.

   c. If you muff a catch in the end zone and recover in the end zone, you do *not* have to bring it out.

   d. If you catch the ball in the field of play and retreat into the end zone, you *must* bring it out.

   e. If you catch the ball in the end zone and *any* part of your body touches the field of play (crosses the goal line), you *must* bring the ball out.

   f. A ball muffed in the end zone that rolls into the field of play *must* be recovered.

   g. A ball fumbled from the field of play into the end zone *must* be run out.

9. A normal kickoff comes from the 35. A kickoff after a safety comes from the 20. The same rules apply to the live ball after 10 yards as apply to a regular kickoff. (Remember the fair catch option.) Always check with coach.

10. If the ball goes into the end zone, it is *not* dead. You must down the ball to ensure a touchback.

11. In forming our wedge, we cannot join hands in our setup. We must get close to one another, but do not hold out your arms and grab hands. This is an illegal wedge.

George Allen's Professional Football Coaching Record

CHICAGO BEARS

1963 (11-1-2, First place)
Coach: George S. Halas
Assistant Coach: George Allen

Regular Season	Chicago	Opponent
Green Bay	10	3*
Minnesota	28	7
Detroit	37	21
Baltimore	10	3*
Los Angeles	52	14
San Francisco	14	20
Philadelphia	16	7*
Baltimore	17	7
Los Angeles	6	0*
Green Bay	26	7
Pittsburgh	17	17*
Minnesota	17	17*
San Francisco	27	7
Detroit	24	14*
	301	144***

NFL Championship
New York Giants	14	10*

LOS ANGELES RAMS

1966 (8-6-0, Third Place)

Regular Season	Los Angeles	Opponent
Atlanta	19	14*
Chicago	31	17*
Green Bay	13	24
San Francisco	34	3*
Detroit	14	7
Minnesota	7	35
Chicago	10	17
Baltimore	3	17
San Francisco	13	21
New York	55	14
Minnesota	21	6
Baltimore	23	7*
Detroit	23	3*
Green Bay	23	27
	269	212

1967 (11-1-2, First Place)

Regular Season	Los Angeles	Opponent
New Orleans	27	13
Minnesota	39	3
Dallas	35	13
San Francisco	24	27*
Baltimore	24	24*
Washington	28	28*
Chicago	28	17
San Francisco	17	7*
Philadelphia	33	17*
Atlanta	31	3
Detroit	31	7
Atlanta	20	3

Green Bay	27	24*
Baltimore	34	10
	398***	196***

Playoffs
Green Bay	7	28

Playoff Bowl
Cleveland	30	6*

1968 (10-3-1, Second Place)

Regular Season	Los Angeles	Opponent
St. Louis	24	13
Pittsburgh	45	10
Cleveland	24	6
San Francisco	24	10
Green Bay	16	14*
Atlanta	27	14*
Baltimore	10	27
Detroit	10	7*
Atlanta	17	10*
San Francisco	20	20*
New York	24	21*
Minnesota	31	3
Chicago	16	17
Baltimore	24	28
	312	200

1969 (11-3-0, First Place)

Regular Season	Los Angeles	Opponent
Baltimore	27	20*
Atlanta	17	7
New Orleans	36	17
San Francisco	27	21*
Green Bay	34	21
Chicago	9	7*
Atlanta	38	6
San Francisco	41	30*
Philadelphia	23	17*
Dallas	24	23*
Washington	24	13*
Minnesota	13	20
Detroit	0	28
Baltimore	7	13*
	320	243**

Playoffs
Minnesota	20	23*

Playoff Bowl
Dallas	31	0*

1970 (9-4-1, Second Place)

Regular Season	Los Angeles	Opponent
St. Louis	34	13
Buffalo	19	0*
San Diego	37	10
San Francisco	6	20
Green Bay	31	21*
Minnesota	3	13
New Orleans	30	17

*Special teams played a prominent role. **Division leader. ***NFL leader.

Atlanta	10	10*
New York Jets	20	31
Atlanta	17	7*
San Francisco	30	13
New Orleans	34	16
Detroit	23	28
New York Giants	31	3*
	325	202**

WASHINGTON REDSKINS

1971 (9-4-1, Second Place)

Regular Season	Washington	Opponent
Saint Louis	24	17
New York Giants	30	3
Dallas	20	16*
Houston	22	13*
Saint Louis	20	0
Kansas City	20	27
New Orleans	24	14*
Philadelphia	7	7
Chicago	15	16*
Dallas	0	13
Philadelphia	20	13*
New York	23	7
Los Angeles	38	24*
Cleveland	13	20
	276	190**

Playoffs
San Francisco	20	24*

1972 (11-3, First Place)

Regular Season	Washington	Opponent
Minnesota	24	21*
Saint Louis	24	10*
Boston	23	24*
Philadelphia	14	0
Saint Louis	33	3
Dallas	24	20*
New York Giants	23	16*
New York Jets	35	17*
New York Giants	27	13
Atlanta	24	13
Green Bay	21	16
Philadelphia	23	7
Dallas	24	34
Buffalo	17	24
	336	218**

Playoffs
Green Bay	16	3*
Dallas	26	3*
Playoff Bowl		
Dolphins	7	14

1973 (10-4, First Place)

Regular Season	Washington	Opponent
San Diego	38	0
Saint Louis	27	34
Philadelphia	28	7
Dallas	14	7
New York Giants	21	3
Saint Louis	31	13*
New Orleans	3	19
Pittsburgh	16	21
San Francisco	33	9
Baltimore	22	14*
Detroit	20	0
New York Giants	27	24*
Dallas	7	27
Philadelphia	38	20*
	325	198**

Playoffs
Vikings	20	27

1974 (10-4, First Place)

Regular Season	Washington	Opponent
New York Giants	13	10*
Saint Louis	10	17
Denver	30	3
Cincinnati	17	28
Miami	20	17*
New York Giants	24	3
Saint Louis	20	23*
Green Bay	17	6*
Philadelphia	27	20*
Dallas	28	21
Philadelphia	26	7
Dallas	23	24*
Los Angeles	23	17*
Chicago	42	0
	320	196**

Playoffs
Rams	10	19

1975 (8-6, Third Place)

Regular Season	Washington	Opponent
New Orleans	41	3
New York Giants	49	13
Philadelphia	10	26
Saint Louis	27	17*
Houston	10	13*
Cleveland	23	7
Dallas	30	24*
New York Giants	21	13*
Saint Louis	17	20*
Oakland	23	26*
Minnesota	31	30*
Atlanta	30	27*
Dallas	10	31
Philadelphia	3	26
	325	276**

1976 (10-4, Second Place)

Regular Season	Washington	Opponent
New York Giants	19	17*
Seattle	31	7
Philadelphia	20	17*
Chicago	7	33
Kansas City	30	33*
Detroit	20	7
Saint Louis	20	10*
Dallas	7	20
San Francisco	24	21*
New York Giants	9	12*
Saint Louis	16	10*
Philadelphia	24	0
New York Jets	37	16
Dallas	27	14*
	291	217

Playoffs

Vikings	20	35

1977 (9-5, Second Place)

Regular Season	Washington	Opponent
New York Giants	17	20*
Atlanta	10	6*
Saint Louis	24	14*
Tampa Bay	10	0*
Dallas	16	34
New York Giants	6	17
Philadelphia	23	17*
Baltimore	3	10
Philadelphia	17	14*
Green Bay	10	9*
Dallas	7	14*
Buffalo	10	0*
Saint Louis	26	20*
Los Angeles	17	14*
	196	189*

THE CHICAGO BLITZ (USFL)

1983 (12-6, First place)

Regular Season	Chicago	Opponent
Washington	28	17
Arizona	29	30*
Denver	13	16
Los Angeles	20	14*
Tampa Bay	42	0
Birmingham	22	11*
Michigan	12	17
New Jersey	17	14*

Los Angeles	38	17
Washington	31	3
Philadelphia	24	31
New Jersey	19	13*
Arizona	36	11
Boston	15	21
Tampa Bay	31	8
Birmingham	29	14
Michigan	19	34
Oakland	31	7
	456***	281***

Playoffs

Philadelphia	38	44

ARIZONA WRANGLERS (USFL)

1984 (10-8, First Place Tie, Western Conference Champions)

Regular Season	Arizona	Opponent
Oakland	35	7
Tampa	17	20
Washington	37	7
Michigan	26	31
Oklahoma	49	7
Denver	7	17
Philadelphia	21	22*
New Jersey	20	3*
Houston	24	37*
San Antonio	23	24*
New Orleans	28	13*
Oakland	3	14
Denver	41	6
Los Angeles	17	24
Birmingham	38	28*
Jacksonville	45	14
Chicago	36	0
Los Angeles	35	10
	402	282***

Playoffs

Houston	17	16*
Los Angeles	35	23*
Philadelphia	3	23

CAREER SUMMARY

7 conference first places

5 conference second places

2 conference third places

Winning percentage: 70.5

Index

About the Authors

George Allen was a head coach in the NFL and the USFL for 14 years. In both leagues he took unsuccessful teams and turned them around. During his pro football career his teams never placed lower than third in their divisions. He is the only coach to take four different teams to the playoffs, including one to the Super Bowl and one to the Championship Game. He won 70.5% of his games—the highest percentage of anyone who has coached more than 10 years in the pros.

A leading football innovator, Allen hired the first special teams coach, was the first to develop situation subsitution, and introduced weight training for football in 1948 while at Morningside College. Allen has also been an innovator off the field—he wrote the best-selling *Encyclopedia of Football Drills* in 1951 and initiated the first drug education program for athletes in 1966.

In addition, he chaired the President's Council on Physical Fitness and Sports from 1981 to 1988, developed the Soviet Youth Fitness Test Exchange Program, and is now chairman of the National Fitness Foundation.

Allen and his wife of 28 years, Etty, have four grown children—George, Greg, Bruce, and Jennifer. He enjoys 5- and 10K races, mini-triathlons, marathons, bikeathons, swimming, and weightlifting in his leisure time.

Joseph G. Pacelli is the author of *Building Your High School Football Program: In Pursuit of Excellence*. He was a head coach and special teams coach for 12 years at the junior high, high school, and college levels. Joe, who recently retired from full-time coaching, lives in Big Bear Lake, California, with his wife Alesta. Although he spends most of his time writing, he still works with the football coaching staff at Big Bear High School and lectures at football clinics.